THE FABER BOOK
OF RELIGIOUS VERSE

THE FABER BOOK
OF RELIGIOUS VERSE

edited by
HELEN GARDNER

FABER AND FABER LIMITED
London & Boston

First published in 1972
by Faber and Faber Limited
3 Queen Square London WC1
First published in Faber Paperbacks 1979
Printed in Great Britain by
Whitstable Litho Ltd Whitstable Kent
All rights reserved

British Library Cataloguing in Publication Data

Faber book of religious verse
1. Christian poetry, English
I. Gardner, Dame Helen, b. 1908
II. Book of religious verse
821'.05   PR1195.C48

ISBN 0-571-11452-0

PREFACE

The editor of any specialized anthology is confronted at the outset
with a problem of definition, and I had to decide what, apart
from its merits as a poem, qualified a poem for inclusion as a
'religious' poem. I attempted to work with a fairly strict and
objective definition of the word 'religious', which I found allowed
me to include a certain number of poems whose presence may at
first sight seem odd and be unexpected in an anthology with
this title.

I started from the general definition in the Oxford Dictionary,
which accepts the etymology of 'religion' as deriving from
religare, 'to bind' and defines it as 'recognition on the part of man
of some higher unseen power as having control of his destiny, and
as being entitled to obedience, reverence, and worship; the
general mental and moral attitude resulting from this belief, with
reference to its effect upon the individual or the community;
personal or general acceptance of this feeling as a standard of
spiritual and practical life.'

The concept of commitment or obligation seemed to me the
distinguishing mark separating the religious poem from the
poem of metaphysical speculation, religious musing, or the poem
of incidental apprehension of the divine. Since religious commit-
ment is, or appears to be to those who accept it, the response to
something given, or handed down from those to whom it was
given, and not something made up or deduced from experience,
I arrived at the criterion that a religious poem was a poem con-
cerned in some way with revelation and with man's response to
it. This does not equate religious poetry with Christian poetry,
although the majority of the poems in this book are Christian
poems. The religious sense of commitment to 'the awful shadow
of some unseen Power' in Shelley, the sense of dedication in the
passages from *The Prelude*, and Emily Brontë's devotion to her
'God of Visions' owe nothing to the specific Christian revelation.
And since a response may be negative or uncertain, my definition

allows me to include poems that refuse commitment, or express doubt more powerfully than affirmation. The test here is the recognition of the nature of the claim that is unacceptable and the strength with which doubt is expressed. I have also been able to include satire on religious hypocrisy and on the corruption of religion, as a mask for self-interest.

The arrangement of the poems is strictly chronological, by date of birth of the author and, when more than one poem by an author is included, by date of composition if this is known. This allows readers to make their own connexions and comparisons and to see the interaction through the centuries of changes in religious sensibility and in poetic ideals. Religion is a historic phenomenon and the substance of what is held to be eternal truth is mediated through accidents of place and time. A chronological arrangement makes clear how religious poetry adapts the secular myths of its age and exercises itself in the dominant poetical forms.[1]

Spelling and punctuation have been modernized throughout. For many readers old spelling and punctuation are a hindrance to understanding and pleasure, and few persons even among students of literature, find old spelling a reliable guide to phonetic values. It as often misleads as informs. I have gone further than most modernizers in attempting to present even medieval texts in modern spelling, and in standardizing their verbal and other forms. It is impossible to do this completely, or even with complete consistency; but I hope the gain will outweigh any loss. Modern spelling greatly reduces the tiresome necessity of glossing; but I think also that the force and directness of the medieval poems are more apparent when a spelling that inevitably suggests quaintness is as far as possible modified. An exception had to be made for the two poems by Dunbar, which stand out as does the poem by Burns later in the volume. So many forms and words

[1] For extended discussion of religious poetry as a *genre*, of the relations between divine and secular poetry in England throughout the centuries, and of reasons for the pre-eminence of the seventeenth century in religious poetry, see my lectures on 'Religious Poetry' in *Religion and Literature* (Faber and Faber, 1971).

had to be left that there was no advantage here in tampering with the manuscript spelling.

More important for modern readers than the uncertain guidance of spelling is editorial guidance as to when a syllable which is now suppressed should be pronounced, or when the stress on a word differs from the modern stress. I have employed a dot above a vowel to indicate that it has syllabic value. It is not always certain, particularly at the ends of lines or when scansion is doubtful, whether an 'e' was pronounced or not, and an editor has to exercise judgement here. When the stress on a word differs from the modern stress the stressed syllable is marked with a grave accent. A difficult problem is presented by words ending in terminations such as '–ience', '–ious', or '–ion', which today are pronounced as monosyllables and take no accent. In medieval poetry, and often as late as the seventeenth century, these termin-ations were dissyllabic and the second syllable carried a stress. Thus a word such as 'confèssiòn' (No. 17, line 11) has four syllables and carries two stresses, allowing it to rhyme with 'town'. I have not marked this, thinking that readers of sixteenth and seventeenth-century poetry are fairly well accustomed to giving syllabic value to both vowels in such endings and have often met with rhymes on the final syllable.

Where titles have been supplied, either to short poems without original or established titles, or to extracts from long poems, they are given within square brackets, unless the title is the first line of the poem or the extract, in which case it is given in quotation marks. Any omissions within a poem, or within an extract from a poem, are signalized in the usual way by dots. Where the omis-sion is substantial asterisks dividing the poem into sections have been employed.

In the medieval section, where much glossing is required, line references are given in the right-hand margin. After this, when glossing is only occasional, an index number in the text calls attention to a gloss.

The sources from which the texts have been edited are given on pp. 338–41. Standard modern editions of collected works are given under the author's name in the biographical notes on pp. 352–71.

I have to thank Professor Norman Davis for advice and help in modernising medieval texts and Mr. Roger Holdsworth and Mrs. Bridget Bertram for their help in preparing this book for the press.

HELEN GARDNER

ACKNOWLEDGEMENTS

For permission to reprint copyright material I have to thank the following:

For use of the text of 'Quia Amore Langueo' established by Celia and Kenneth Sisam in *The Oxford Book of Medieval English Verse*, the Clarendon Press, Oxford.

For 'The Darkling Thrush', by Thomas Hardy, the Trustees of the Hardy Estate, and Macmillan and Co. Ltd.

For 'Johannes Milton, Senex', by Robert Bridges, from *Poetical Works*, the Clarendon Press, Oxford.

For 'Christ in the Universe' and 'Easter Night', by Alice Meynell, Sir Francis Meynell.

For 'Easter Hymn' and 'For my Funeral', by A. E. Housman, from *Collected Poems*, The Society of Authors as the literary representative of the Estate of A. E. Housman, and Jonathan Cape Ltd.

For 'Vacillation', 'Supernatural Songs', and 'The Black Tower', by W. B. Yeats, from *Collected Poems*, M. B. Yeats, Macmillan and Co. Ltd., London, and The Macmillan Co. of Canada.

For 'Pax' and 'Shadows', by D. H. Lawrence, from *The Complete Poems*, Laurence Pollinger Ltd., and the Estate of the late Mrs. Frieda Lawrence.

For 'Faith Unfaithful', by Siegfried Sassoon, G. T. Sassoon.

For 'The Border', 'Annunciation', and 'One Foot in Eden', by Edwin Muir, from *Collected Poems 1921-1958*, Faber and Faber Ltd.

For 'Still Falls the Rain', by Edith Sitwell, David Higham Associates Ltd., and Macmillan and Co. Ltd.

For 'The Hippopotamus', 'Journey of the Magi', 'Ash Wednesday', I and VI, 'Marina', and 'Little Gidding', by T. S. Eliot, from *Collected Poems 1909-1962*, Faber and Faber Ltd.

For 'In Westminster Abbey' and 'Christmas', by John Betjeman, John Murray (Publishers) Ltd.

For 'New Year Letter' (lines 1651-1684), and 'At the Manger', from *For the Time Being*, by W. H. Auden, from *Collected Longer Poems*, Faber and Faber Ltd.

For 'Prayer in Mid-Passage', by Louis MacNiece, from *Collected Poems*, Faber and Faber Ltd.

For '*Ecce Homo*', by David Gascoyne, from *Collected Poems*, the Oxford University Press.

For 'Country Clergy' and 'The Musician', by R. S. Thomas, Granada Publishing Ltd.

CONTENTS

13

Contents

Contents

Contents

Contents

Contents

Contents

Contents

Contents

Contents

Contents

Contents

ANONYMOUS

I   The Dream of the Rood*

(Translated from the Anglo-Saxon)

Rod is min nama,   geo ic ricne cyning
Bær byfigynde,   blode bestemed.[1]

Listen! I will tell the most treasured of dreams,
A dream that I dreamt the deep middle of the night,
After the race of men had gone to their rest.
It seemed to me I saw the strangest of Trees,
Lifted aloft in the air, with light all around it,
Of all Beams the brightest. It stood as a beacon,
Drenched in gold; gleaming gems were set
Fair around its foot; five such flamed
High upon its cross-branch. Hosts of angels gazed on it
In world-without-end glory. This was no felon's gallows.
Holy souls in heaven hailed it with wonder
And mortal men on earth and all the Maker wrought.
Strange was that Tree of Triumph – and I a transgressor,
Stained by my sins. I saw the Tree of Glory
Bright with streaming banners, brilliantly shining,
Gilded all with gold. Glittering jewels
Worthily adorned the Tree of the World's Ruler.
Yet beneath the gold I glimpsed the signs
Of some ancient agony when again as of old
Its right side sweated blood. Sorrow seized me;
I was full of fear. I saw the beacon flicker,
Now dazzling, now darkened; at times drenched and dripping
Running red with blood, at times a royal treasure.

---

* For notes, see p. 342.
[1] 'Rood is my name, once a mighty king I bore, trembling and soaked in blood.'
These verses are inscribed on a reliquary containing a fragment of the True
Cross at Brussels.

Yet even so I lay there for a long while,
Sorrowing at the sight of my Saviour's Tree;
When on a sudden I heard it speak;
The precious wood uttered these words:

   'Many years ago – the memory abides –
I was felled to the ground at the forest's edge,
Severed from my roots. Enemies seized me,
Made of me a mark of scorn for criminals to mount on;
Shoulder-high they carried me and set me on a hill.
Many foes made me fast there. Far off then I saw
The King of all mankind coming in great haste,
With courage keen, eager to climb me.
I did not dare, against my Lord's dictate,
To bow down or break, though I beheld tremble
The earth's four corners. I could easily
Have felled his foes; yet fixed and firm I stood.
Then the young Hero – it was God Almighty –
Strong and steadfast, stripped himself for battle;
He climbed up on the high gallows, constant in his purpose,
Mounted it in sight of many, mankind to ransom.
Horror seized me when the Hero clasped me,
But I dared not bow or bend down to earth,
Nor falter, nor fall; firm I needs must stand.
I was raised up a Rood, a royal King I bore,
The High King of Heaven: hold firm I must.
They drove dark nails through me, the dire wounds still show,
Cruel gaping gashes, yet I dared not give as good.
They taunted the two of us; I was wet with teeming blood,
Streaming from the warrior's side when he sent forth his spirit.
High upon that hill helpless I suffered
Long hours of torment; I saw the Lord of Hosts
Outstretched in agony; all embracing darkness
Covered with thick clouds the corpse of the World's Ruler;
The bright day was darkened by a deep shadow,
All its colours clouded; the whole creation wept,
Keened for its King's fall; Christ was on the Rood.

Yet warriors from afar eagerly came speeding
To where he hung alone. All this I beheld.
Sore sorrow seized me, yet I stooped to men's hands
Humbly, but with courage keen. They clasped Almighty God,
Raised him from the rack; me they let remain,
Standing soaked in blood, wounded by sharp arrows.
They laid his wearied limbs on earth; the watchers at his head
Looked down on the Lord of Heaven, lying there at rest
Forspent from his great fight. Then they framed for him a tomb,
Shaped it of bright stone in the sight of me who slew him.
They laid in it the Lord of Victories, then raised the loud lament,
Sang at the sunsetting, then sadly turned away,
Left their glorious Lord. Alone he lay and rested there.
But we three weeping for a long while yet
Stood at our stations as there sank into silence
The cry of the warriors. The corpse grew cold,
The soul's sweet dwelling-place. Us they then struck down,
Felled us all to earth, awful was our fate.
They dug a deep pit, deep down they buried us;
Yet even there the Lord's friends, his faithful thanes found me.
With gleaming gold and silver they made me glorious.

   Now you have heard – beloved hero –
How I endured the evil men did to me,
Suffered great sorrow. Now the season is come
When all things honour me, here and everywhere,
Mortal men on earth and all the Maker wrought;
They bow before this beacon. On me the only Begotten,
The Son of God suffered; and so in splendour now
I tower high under heaven; and I have power to heal
Each and all who honour me and hold me in awe.
I was deemed in former days the direst of torments,
I was hated and abhorred until I made a highway,
The right Way of Life, for the race of men.
Lo, the King of Glory, the Keeper of the Gates of Heaven,
Favoured me above all the trees of the forest,
Even as his maiden-mother, Mary herself,

27

Almighty God favoured above all womankind.

Now, therefore, I bid you – beloved hero –
Say what you have seen to the sons of men,
Make manifest in words the mystery of the Beam of Glory
On which Almighty God endured bitter throes,
For all mankind and for their many sins,
And for Adam's deed done ages since.
Death he drank there; yet from death the Lord arose
With might and power to be man's helper.
He ascended into heaven, yet hither again
To this middle world he will come, once more to seek mankind.
At the Last Day, the Lord Himself,
Almighty God, attended by angels,
Will descend to give doom – who has power to give doom –
To each and every man as erewhile here
In this earthly life he earned evil or good.
Nor may any man there be unafraid
When he hears the words the World's Ruler will utter.
He will ask in sight of many where is the man
Who for the Lord's sake would give up life,
Drink bitter death as he did on the Beam;
And all then shall fear and few of them will know
How justly they may answer Christ the Judge of all.
But none need be afraid to abide his appearing
Who has borne in his bosom this brightest of beacons.
For through this Cross shall come to the Kingdom,
From this earthly life, each and every soul
Who longs with his Lord to live in life everlasting.'

Then I prayed to that blessed Beam, blithe in spirit,
With courage keen; no comrade was by me,
I lay there alone. There was longing in my heart,
I was fain to fare forth; and since then I have felt
Many hours of longing. I live my life in hope
That I may trust in and seek that Tree of Triumph,
Alone honour and serve it above all others.

This is my heart's desire; in this is my delight;
My refuge is the Rood. Rich friends and mighty
I have none to help me, for they have gone hence,
Left this world's glories to seek the King of Glory,
They live now in Heaven with the High Father,
They abide in bliss; and here below I wait
For the coming of the day when the Cross of my Lord
Which here on this earth my own eyes have looked on,
From this fleeting life will fetch my soul away
And will bring me then where there is much bliss,
Great gladness in Heaven, where the people of God
Are seated at his Feast in fullness of joy,
And me there will set down where I hereafter may
Abide in bliss and among the blessed
Take my fill of joy. May the Lord be my friend,
Who erstwhile on earth endured bitter throes,
Suffered on the gallows-tree for the sins of men.
He loosed us from bondage and life he gave to us
And a home in Heaven. Hope sprang up again
Bright with blessing to those burning in pain.
Christ the Son of God journeyed as a Conqueror,
Mighty and Victorious, when with many in his train,
A great company of souls, he came to God's Kingdom –
The one Almighty to the bliss of the angels
And of all the holy ones who in heavenly places
Abode in glory – when Almighty God,
The King of Kings, came home to his own country.

2   'White was his naked breast'

            White was his naked breast
                And red of blood his side,
            Blaik was his fair andlèd,
                His woundès deep and wide;

2. 3 *Blaik*: pale *andlèd*: face

And his armès y-streight 5
    High upon the rood;
On five stedès on his body
    The streamès ran of blood.

3   'Now goeth sun under wood'

Now goeth sun under wood –
Me rueth, Mary, thy fairè rode.
Now goeth sun under tree –
Me rueth, Mary, thy son and thee.

4   [In Praise of Mary]

Of one that is so fair and bright,
    Velut maris stella,
Brighter than the dayès light,
    Parens et puella,
I cry to thee; thou see to me! 5
Lady, pray thy son for me,
    Tam pia,
That I motè come to thee
    Maria.

Lady, flower of allè thing, 10
    Rosa sine spina,
Thou borè Jesu, heavenès king,
    Gratia divina.
Of allè thou bearst the prize,
Lady, queen of Paradise 15
    Electa.

5. *y-streight*: stretched 7 *stedès*: places
3. 2 *Me rueth*: I grieve for *rode*: face
4. 5 *see to*: look upon 8 *motè*: may 14 You are best of all

Maidè mildè mother is
    Effecta.

Of carè conseil thou art best,
    Felix fecundata,   20
Of allè weary thou art rest,
    Mater honorata.
Beseech him with mildè mood
That for us allè shed his blood
    In cruce   25
That we moten come to him
    In luce.

All this worèld were forlore
    Eva peccatrice,
Till our Loverd was y-bore   30
    De te genetrice.
With '*Ave*' it went away
Thuster night, and com'th the day
    Salutis.
The wellè springeth out of thee   35
    Virtutis.

Well he wot he is thy son
    Ventre quem portasti;
He will not wernè thee thy boon,
    Parvum quem lactasti.   40
So hendè and so good he is,
He haveth brought us to bliss
    Superni,
That hath y-dit the foulè pit
    Inferni.

19 In distress you are the best counsellor 23 *mildè mood* gentle heart 28 *were forlore*: would have been lost 30 *Loverd*: Lord 33 *Thuster*: dark 39 *wernè*: deny 41 *hendè*: gracious 44 *y-dit*: shut

31

5   ['Wait a little!']

Loverd, thou clepedest me,
And I nought ne answered thee
But wordės slow and sleepy:
'Tholė yet! Thole a litel!'
But 'yet' and 'yet' was endėless   5
And 'thole a litel' a long way is.

6   ['Undo!']

Alas, alas, well evil I sped!
For sin Jesu from me is fled,
    That lively fere.
At my door he stands alone
And calls 'Undo!' with rueful moan   5
    On this manère:

'Undo, my lief, my dovė dear,
Undo! Why stand I steken out here?
    I am thy make.
Lo, my head and minė locks   10
Are all biweved with bloody drops
    For thinė sake.'

5. 1 *Lord, you called me* 3 *But*: except 4 *Tholė*: wait
6. 1 . . . *I have fared very ill* 3 *That eager friend* 7 *lief*: beloved 8 *steken*: shut
9 *make*: spouse 11. *biweved*: covered

FRIAR WILLIAM HEREBERT
(died 1333)

7   [Who is This that Cometh from Edom?]

What is he, this lordling, that cometh from the fight
With blood-red weed so grisliche y-dight,
So fair y-cointìsèd, so seemly in sight,
So stiflichè gangeth, so doughty a knight?

'I it am, I it am, that ne speak butè right,   5
Champion to healen mankind in fight.'

'Why then is thy shroud red, with blood all y-ment,
As treaderès in wring with must all besprent?'

'The wring I have y-trodden all myself one,
And of all mankind ne was none other wone.   10
I them have y-trodden in wrath and in grame
And all my weed is besprent with their blood y-same,
And all my robe y-foulèd to their greatè shame.
The day of th'ilkè wrechè liveth in my thought;
The year of meedès yielding ne forget I nought.   15

I looked all aboutè some helping man;
I sought all the routè, but help n'as there none.
It was mine ownè strengthè that this botè wrought,
Myn ownè doughtinessè that help there me brought.'

'On Godès milsfulness I will bethinkè me,   20
And herien him in allè thing that he yieldeth me.'

7. A paraphrase of Isaiah 63 : 1–7 2 *grisliche* . . . : terribly arrayed 3 *y-cointìsèd*:
apparelled *seemly* . . . : fair to see 4 *So* . . . *gangeth*: who goes so bravely 6
healen: save 7 *shroud*: clothing *y-ment*: mingled 8 *wring*: wine-press *besprent*:
spattered 9 *one*: alone 10 *of*: for *wone*: hope 11 *grame*: anger 12 *y-same*:
together 14 *wrechè*: vengeance 15 *meedès yielding*: reward-giving 16 *some* . . . :
for some man to help 17 *sought*: searched 18 *botè*: salvation 20 *milsfulness*:
mercy 21 *herien*: praise

'I have y-trodden the folk in wrath and in grame,
Adreint all with shenness, y-drawn down with shame.'

8   An Orison to the Blessed Virgin

Thou woman butè fere
Thine own father bere,
Great wonder this was,
That one woman was mother
To father and her brother,   5
So never other n'as.

Thou my sister and mother,
And thy son my brother:
Who shouldè then dread?
Whoso hath the king to brother,   10
And eek the queen to mother,
Well oughtè for to speed.

Damè! – sister and mother –
Say thy son, my brother,
That is Doomèsman,   15
That for thee that him bere
To me be debonair –
My robe he hath upon.

Sith he my robe took
Also I find in Book,   20
He is to me y-bound;
And help he will, I wot,
For Love the charter wrote
And the ink ran of his wound.

I take to witnessing   25
The spear and the crowning,

23 *Adreint*: drowned *shenness*: ignominy
8. 1 *butè fere*: without a companion, i.e. matchless 2 *bere*: bore 18 *my robe*: i.e.
my human nature 20 *Also*: As

34

The nailės and the Rood:
That he that is so kind
This ever hath in mind,
That bought us with his blood.   30

When thou yeve him my weed,
Dame, help at the need –
I wot thou might full well:
That for no wretched guilt
I be to hell y-pult,   35
To thee I make appeal.

Now, Dame, I thee beseech
At th'ilkė day of wreech
Be by thy sonnės throne,
When sinnė shall be sought   40
In work, in word, in thought,
And speak for me, thou one.

When I mot need appear
For minė guiltės here
Tofore the Doomėsman,   45
Sister, be there my fere,
And make him debonair
That my robe hath upon.

For have I thee and him,
That marks beareth with him,   50
That charity him took,
The woundės all bloody,
The tokens of his mercy,
As teacheth Holy Book,
Tharf me nothing dread: 55
Satan shall not speed,
With wrenches ne with crook. Amen.

31 i.e. Since thou gave him my nature   35 *y-pult*: thrust   38 *wreech*: vengeance
42 *thou one*: thou only   43 *mot*: must   46 *fere*: friend   55 *Tharf me*: I need
57 *wrenches . . . crook*: tricks . . . guile

9 [Advent]

I saw him with flesh all be-spread: He came from East.
I saw him with blood all be-shed: He came from West.
I saw that many he with him brought: He came from South.
I saw that the world of him ne rought: He came from North.

'I come from the wedlock as a sweet spouse that have my wife
    with me y-nome.   5
I come from fight as a stalwart knight that my foe have
    overcome.
I come from the cheaping as a rich chapman that mankind have
    y-bought.
I come from an uncouth land as a silly pilgrim that far have
    y-sought.'

10 [The Virgin's Song]

    Jesu, sweetė sonė dear,
    On poorful bed liest thou here,
      And that me grieveth sore;
    For thy cradle is as a bere,
    Ox and assė be thy fere: 5
      Weep I may therefòre.

    Jesu, sweetė, be not wroth,
    Though I n'avė clout ne cloth
      Thee on for to fold,

9. 1 I saw him with his body all spread out 2 *be-shed*: drenched 4 *rought of*:
cared for 5 *have y-nome*: have taken 7 *cheaping*: market *chapman*: merchant
8 *uncouth*: unknown *silly*: innocent *far . . .* : have travelled far
10. 2 *poorful*: wretchedly poor 4 *bere*: byre 5 *fere*: companions 9 To fold
thee in

Thee on to foldè ne to wrap,   10
For I n'avè clout ne lap;
But lay thou thy feet to my pap
    And wite thee from the cold.

11   'Lullay, lullay, little child'*

Lullay, lullay, little child,
Thou that were so stern and wild,
Now art becomen meek and mild,
    To save that was forlore.

But for my sin I wot it is   5
That Goddès son suffered this;
Mercy, Lord! I have done miss,
    I-wis I will no more.

Against my Father's will I ches
An apple with a rueful res;   10
Wherefore mine heritage I les,
    And now thou weepest therefore.

An apple I took of a tree
God it had forbidden me:
Wherefore I should damnèd be,   15
    If thy weeping ne wore.

Lullay for woe, thou little thing,
Thou little baron, thou little king;
Mankind is cause of thy mourning,
    That thou hast lovèd so yore.   20

11 *lap*: fold of a garment   13 *wite*: keep
* See note, p. 342
11. 8 *I-wis*: certainly   9 *ches*: chose   10 *res*: rashness   11 *les*: lost   16 If it were not
for thy weeping   20 *so yore*: so long

For man that thou hast ay loved so
Yet shalt thou suffer painès mo,
In head, in feet, in handès too,
   And yet weepen well more.

That pain us make of sinnè free,   25
That pain us bring, Jesu, to thee,
That pain us help ay to flee,
   The wicked fiendès lore. Amen.

12   [Christ's Love-Song]

Love me brought,
And love me wrought,
   Man, to be thy fere.
Love me fed,
And love me led   5
   And love me lettet here.

Love me slew,
And love me drew,
   And love me laid on bier.
Love is my peace;   10
For love I chese,
   Man to buyen dear.

Ne dread thee nought,
I have thee sought,
   Bothen day and night,   15
To haven thee
Well is me,
   I have thee won in fight.

12. 3 *fere*: mate 6 *lettet*: allows 11 *chese*: chose

WILLIAM LANGLAND*
(?1330–?1400)

13   *[Et Incarnatus Est]*

Love is the plant of peace and most precious of virtues;
For heaven hold it ne might so heavy it seemed,
Till it had on earth yoten himself.
Was never leaf upon linden lighter thereafter,
As when it had of the fold flesh and blood taken;   5
Then was it portative and piercing as the point of a needle.
May no armour it let, neither high walls.
For-thy is love leader of our Lord's folk of heaven.

14   *[The Jousting of Jesus]*†

Woolward and wet-shod went I forth after,
As a reckless renk that of no woe recketh,
And went forth like a lorel all my life-time,
Till I waxed weary of the world, and willed eft to sleep,
And leaned me till Lent-time, and long time I slept,   5
Rested me there and routed fast till *ramis palmarum.*
Of girls and *gloria laus* greatly me dreamed,
And how *osanna* to the organs old folk sang.
One semblable to the Samaritan and somedeal to Piers Plowman
Barefoot on an ass-back bootless came pricking,   10
Without spurs or spear sprightly he looked,
As is the kind of a knight that cometh to be dubbed,

* For notes, see p. 343

13. 3 *yoten*: poured out 5 *fold*: earth 6 *portative*: light to carry 7 *let*: hinder
8 Therefore is love leader of the people of our Lord of Heaven

† For translations and comments on the liturgical Latin phrases, see notes, p. 343
14. 1 *Woolward*: wearing wool near the skin, for penance (or poverty) 2 *renk*:
man 3 *lorel*: vagrant 4 *eft*: again 5 *leaned me*: idled 6 *routed*: snored 7 *girls*:
young of both sexes

To get him gilt spurs or cut galoshes.
Then was Faith in a fenester, and cried '*A! fili David!*'
As doth an herald of arms when adventurers come to joust.   15
Old Jews of Jerusalem for joy they sang,
  Benedictus qui venit in nomine domini.

Then I frayned at Faith what all that fare bemeant,
And who should joust in Jerusalem. 'Jesus', he said,
'And fetch what the fiend claimeth, the fruit of Piers the   20
  Plowman.'
'Is Piers in this place?' quod I, and he prinked at me:
'This Jesus of his gentry will joust in Piers' arms,
In his helm and habergoun *humana natura*;
That Christ be not beknown here for *consummatus deus*,
In Piers the Plowman's plate-armour this pricker shall ride;   25
For no dint shall him dere, as *in deitate patris.*'

'Who shall joust with Jesus?', quod I, 'Jews or scribes?'
'Nay', quod he, 'the foul fiend and Falsehood and Death.
Death saith he shall fordo and adown bring
All that liveth or looketh on land or in water.   30
Life saith that he lieth, and layeth his life to wed,
That for all that Death can do within three days
To walk and fetch from the fiend the fruit of Piers the Plowman,
And lay it where him liketh, and Lucifer bind,
And forbeat and adown bring bale and death forever: 35
  O mors, ero mors tua!'

Then came Pilate with much people *sedens pro tribulani*,
To see how doughtily Death should do, and deem of them both
  rightly.
The Jews and the Justices against Jesus they were,
And all their court on him cried '*Crucifige*' sharply.   40
Then put him forth a piller before Pilate, and said,

14 *fenester*: window 18 *frayned at*: enquired of 21 *prinked*: nodded 22 *gentry*:
noble nature 26 *dere*: hurt 31 . . . and stakes his life as pledge 41 *piller*: pillager,
robber

'This Jesus of our Jews' temple japed and despised,
To fordo it in one day, and in three days after
Edify it eft new (here he stands that said it),
And yet make it as much in all manner points   45
Both as long and as large by loft and by ground.'

'*Crucifige*', quod a catch-poll, 'I warrant him a witch!'
'*Tolle, tolle!*', quod another, and took of keen thorns,
And began of keen thorn a garland to make,
And set it sore on his head, and said in envy,   50
'*Ave Rabbi!*' quod that ribald and threw reeds at him,
Nailed him with three nails naked on the rood,
And poison on a pole they put up to his lips,
And bade him drink his death-evil; his days were done.
'And if that thou subtle be, help now thyself,   55
If thou be Christ, and king's son, come down from the rood;
Then shall we leve that Life thee loveth, and will not let thee die!'
'*Consummatum est*', quod Christ, and commenced for to swoon,
Piteously and pale as a prisoner that dieth;
The Lord of Life and of Light then laid his eyes together.   60
The day for dread withdrew, and dark became the sun,
The wall wagged and clove, and all the world quavered.
Dead men for that din came out of deep graves
And told why that tempest so long time dured.
'For a bitter battle', the dead body said;   65
'Life and Death in this darkness the one fordoeth the other;
Shall no wight weet witterly who shall have the mastery,
Ere Sunday about sun-rising' and sank with that to earth.
Some said that he was God's son that so fairly died,
          Vere filius Dei erat iste, etc.   70

*   *   *

What for fear of this ferly, and of the false Jews,
I drew me in that darkness to *descendit ad inferna*.

46 *by loft and by ground*: above and below 47 *catch-poll*: sergeant *witch*: sorcerer
65 *For*: because of 67 *witterly*: truly 71 *ferly*: marvel

And there I saw soothly *secundum scripturas*,
Out of the west coast a wench, as me thought,
Came walking in the way, to hell-ward she looked.   75
Mercy hight that maid, a meek thing withal,
A full benign burd, and buxom of speech.
Her sister, as it seemed, came softly walking
Even out of the east, and westward she looked.
A full comely creature, Truth she hight.   80
When these maidens met, Mercy and Truth,
Either asked other of this great wonder,
Of the din and of the darkness, and how the day rowed,
And what a light and a leam lay before Hell.
'I have ferly of this fare in faith', said Truth,   85
'And am wending to weet what this wonder meaneth.'
'Have no marvel', quod Mercy, 'mirth it betokneth.
A maiden that hight Mary, and mother, without feeling
Of any kind of creature, conceived through speech
And grace of the Holy Ghost; waxed great with child;   90
Withouten wem into this world she brought him;
And that my tale be true I take God to witness.
Since this bairn was born been thirty winters passed;
And he died and death tholed this day about midday.
And that is cause of this eclipse that closeth now the sun,   95
In meaning that man shall from mirkness be drawn,
The while this light and this leam shall Lucifer blind.
For patriarchs and prophets have preached hereof often,
That man shall man save through a maiden's help,
And what was tint through a tree a tree shall it win,   100
And what death down brought death shall releve.'

'That thou tellest', quod Truth, 'is but a tale of Waltrot!
For Adam and Eve, and Abraham with others,
Patriarchs and prophets that in pain lie,
Believe thou never that yon light them aloft will bring,   105

77 *burd*: maiden 83 *rowed*: dawned 84 *leam*: gleam 85 *I have ferly of*: I marvel
at 91 *wem*: stain of sin 94 *tholed*: suffered 100 *tint*: lost 101 *releve*: lift up 102
tale of Waltrot: trifling story

Nor have them out of hell. Hold thy tongue, Mercy!
It is but a trifle that thou tellest; I, Truth, wot the sooth,
For what is once in hell out cometh it never;
Job the prophet, patriarch, reproveth thy saws,
  Quia in inferno nulla est redemptio.'   110

Then Mercy full mildly mouthed these words,
'Through experience', quod she, 'I hope they shall be saved.
For venom fordoth venom, and that I prove by reason.
For of all venoms foulest is the scorpion's,
May no medicine help the place where he stingeth,   115
Till he be dead and put thereto, and then it destroyeth
The first venom through venom of himself.
So shall this death fordo, I dare my life lay,
All that Death fordid first through the devil's enticing;
And right as through guile man was beguiled,   120
So shall grace that began make a good sleight.
  Ars ut artem falleret.'

'Now suffer we', said Truth, 'I see as me thinketh,
Out of the nip of the north, not full far hence,
Righteousness come running; rest we the while;   125
For she wot more than we, she was ere we both.'
'That is sooth', said Mercy, 'and I see here by south,
Where Peace cometh playing, in patience y-clothed;
Love hath coveted her long, believe I none other
But he sent her some letter what this light bemeaneth   130
That overhoveth hell thus; she us shall tell.'

When Peace, in patience y-clothed, approached near them twain,
Righteousness her reverenced for her rich clothing,
And prayed Peace to tell her to what place she would,
And in her gay garments whom she thought to greet?   135
'My will is to wend', quod she, 'and welcome them all
That many day might I not see for murkiness of sin.

121 *sleight*: trick or device 131 *overhoveth*: hovers over

Adam and Eve and other more in hell,
Moses and many more mercy shall have;
And I shall dance thereto, do thou so, sister!   140
For Jesus jousted well, Joy beginneth to dawn;
      Ad vesperum demorabitur fletus, et ad matutinum laetitia.'

     *   *   *

'Suffer we', said Truth, 'I hear and see both
How a spirit speaketh to hell, and bids unspar the gates':
      '*Attollite portas, principes, vestras; et elevamini, portae*   145
        eternales.'
A voice loud in that light to Lucifer crieth,
'Princes of this palace, unpin and unlock!
For here cometh with crown the king of all glory.'
Then sighed Satan, and said to them all,
'Such a light against our leave Lazarus it fetched;   150
Care and cumbrance is come to us all.
If this king come in, mankind will he fetch,
And lead them where he liketh, and lightly me bind.
Patriarchs and prophets have parled hereof long,
That such a lord and a light should lead them all hence.'   155

'But rise up, Ragamuffin, and reach me all the bars
That Belial, thy Belsire, beat with thy dam,
And I shall let this lord and his light stop;
Ere we through brightness be blinded, bar we the gates.
Check we and chain we, and each chink stop,   160
That no light leap in at louver nor at loophole.
And thou, Ashtoroth, hot out and have out our knaves,
Colting and all his kin, our chattels to save.
Brimstone boiling, burning, outcast it
All hot on their heads that enter nigh the walls.   165
Set bows of brake and brazen guns,

141 *For*: Because 154 *parled*: spoken 157 *Belsire*: grandfather 158 *let*: hinder
161 *louver*: a hole in the roof of a hall to let out smoke 162 *hot out*: call out 166
bows of brake: bows with cranks, i.e. cross-bows

And shoot out shot enough his shildtrum to blind.
Set Mahound at the mangonel, and mill-stones throw,
With crooks and with caltrops accloy we them each one.'

*　　*　　*

Eft the light bade unlock and Lucifer answered,　　170
'What lord art thou?' quod Lucifer, '*quis est iste?*'
'*Rex Gloriae*', the light soon said,
'And lord of might and of main and all manner virtues;
　　Dominus Virtutum;
Dukes of this dim place, anon undo these gates,　　175
That Christ may come in, the king's son of heaven.'

And with that breath hell broke with Belial's bars;
For any wight or ward, wide open the gates.
Patriarchs and prophets, *populus in tenebris,*
Sang saint John's song, '*Ecce Agnus Dei*'.　　180
Lucifer look ne might so light him blinded;
And those that our lord loved into his light he lifted.

Then he said to Satan, 'Lo! here my soul to amends
For all sinful souls, to save those that be worthy.
Mine they be, and of me I may the better them claim.　　185
Although reason record, and rightly of myself,
That if they ate the apple all should die,
I behight them not here hell forever.
For the deed that they did thy deceit it made;
With guile thou them got, against all reason.　　190
For in my palace, paradise, in person of an adder
Falsely thou fetchest thence thing that I loved.
Thus like a lizard, with a lady's visage,
Thievely thou me robbedst; the old law granteth

---

167 *shildtrum*: squadron 168 *mangonel*: engine to cast stones 169 *crooks*: hooks
fastened on a long pole, for use as grappling irons *caltrops*: balls with spikes to
injure horses' feet *accloy*: encumber 178 *For*: In spite of 183 *to amends*: as
satisfaction 188 *behight*: promised

That guilers be beguiled, and that is good reason;   195
    Dentem pro dente, et oculum pro oculo.

✳   ✳   ✳

Now beginneth thy guile against thee to turn,
And my grace to grow ay greater and wider.
The bitterness that thou hast brewed, brook it thy self,
That art doctor of death, drink what thou madest.   200
For I, that am lord of life, love is my drink,
And for that drink today I died upon earth.
I fought so, me thirsteth yet for man's soul's sake;
May no drink me moisten nor my thirst slake
Till the vintage fall in the vale of Jehoshaphat,   205
That I drink right ripe must, *resurrectio mortuorum.*
And then I shall come as a king, crowned with angels,
And have out of hell all men's souls.

Fiends and fiendkins before me shall stand,
And be at my bidding wheresoever me liketh.   210
But to be merciable to man then my kind it asketh;
For we be brethren of blood but not in baptism all.
But all that be my whole brethren in blood and in baptism
Shall not be damned to the death that is withouten end. . . .
And my mercy shall be shewed to many of my brethren.   215
For blood may suffer blood both hungry and a-cold,
But blood may not see blood bleed, but him rueth.' –
    Audivi arcana verba, quae non licet homini loqui. –
'But my righteousness and right shall rule all hell,
And mercy all mankind before me in heaven.   220
For I were an unkind king but I my kind helped,
And namely at such a need where needs help behoveth.'
    Non intres in judicium cum servo tuo, Domine.
'Thus by law', quod our Lord, 'lead I will from hence
Those that me loved and believed in my coming.   225

199 *brook*: enjoy 211 *my kind*: my nature 216 *blood*: the tie of blood 221 *my kind*: my fellows

And for thy leasing, Lucifer, that thou lied to Eve,
Thou shalt buy it bitterly', and he bound him with chains.
Ashtoroth and all the rout hid them in herns;
They durst not look on our Lord, the boldest of them all,
But let him lead forth what him liked, and let what him list.   230

Many hundreds of angels harped and sang
            '*Culpat caro, purgat caro; regnat Deus Dei caro.*'
Then piped Peace of poesy a note,
'*Clarior est solito post maxima nebula Phoebus,
Post inimicitias clarior est et amor.*'   235

'After sharp showers', quod Peace, 'most sheen is the sun;
Is no weather warmer than after watery clouds,
Nor no love liefer nor liefer friends
Than after war and woe, when Love and Peace be masters.
Was never war in this world nor wickedness so keen,   240
That ne Love, and him list, to laughing it brought,
And Peace through patience all perils stopped.'
'True', quod Truth, 'thou tellest us sooth, by Jesus!
Clip we in covenant, and each of us kiss other!'
'And let no people', quod Peace, 'perceive that we chid!   245
For impossible is nothing to him that is almighty.'
'Thou sayest sooth', said Righteousness, and reverently she kissed
Peace, and Peace her, *per saecula saeculorum.*
            *Misericordia et veritas obviaverunt sibi; justitia et pax
                osculatae sunt.*
Truth trumpeted then, and sang '*Te Deum laudamus*';   250
And then to her lute Love in a loud note
            '*Ecce quam bonum et quam jocundum est habitare fratres
                in unum.*'
Till the day dawned these damsels danced,
That men rang to the resurrection, and right with that I waked,
And called Kit my wife and Calote my daughter –   255
'Arise and reverence God's resurrection,

226 *leasing*: falsehood   228 *herns*: corners   241 *and*: if   244 *Clip*: Embrace

47

And creep to the cross on knees, and kiss it for a jewel!
For God's blessed body it bore for our boot,
And it affrighteth the fiend, for such is the might,
May no grisly ghost glide where it shadoweth!'   260

GEOFFREY CHAUCER
(?1343–1400)

Truth
Balade de Bon Conseil

Flee from the press, and dwell with soothfastness,
Suffice unto thy good, though it be small;
For hoard hath hate, and climbing tickleness,
Press hath envỳ, and weal blent overall;
Savour no more than thee behovè shall;   5
Rule well thyself, that other folk canst rede;
And Truth thee shall deliver, it is no dread.

Tempest thee nought all crooked to redress,
In trust of her that turneth as a ball:
Great restè stant in little busyness;   10
Be ware also to spurn against an awl;
Strive not, as doth the crockè with the wall.
Dauntè thyself, that dauntest others' deed;
And Truth thee shall deliver, it is no dread.

That thee is sent, receive in buxomness,   15
The wrestling for this world asketh a fall.
Here is no home, here n'is but wilderness:
Forth, pilgrim, forth! Forth, beast, out of thy stall!
Know thy countrỳ, look up, thank God of all;
Hold the highway, and let thy ghost thee lead;   20
And Truth thee shall deliver, it is no dread.

Envoy

Therefore, thou Vache, leave thine old wretchedness

15. 2 *Suffice unto*: be satisfied with 3 *tickleness*: precariousness 4 *weal blent overall*: prosperity blinds one completely 6 *rede*: advise 9 *her*: Fortune 11 *to spurn against an awl*: to kick against the pricks 13 *Dauntè*: overcome 15 *buxomness*: submissiveness 20 *ghost*: spirit 22 *Vache*: probably the name of the person addressed, perhaps Sir Philip Vache, who married a daughter of one of Chaucer's close friends. He seems to have been in disfavour from 1386–89 and in need of this 'good counsel'. But there is some doubt of the authenticity of the Envoy.

Unto the world; leave now to be thrall;
Cry him mercỳ, that of his high goodnèss
Made thee of nought, and in especial   25
Draw unto him, and pray in general
For thee, and eek for other, heavenly meed;
And Truth thee shall deliver, it is no dread.

16   [Love Unfeigned]

O youngè freshè folkès, he or she,
In which that love upgroweth with your age,
Repaireth home from worldly vanity,
And of your heart upcasteth the visàge,
To thilkè God that after his imàge   5
You made, and thinketh all n'is but a fair
This world, and passeth soon as flowers fair.

And loveth him, the which that right for love
Upon a cross, our soulès for to buy,
First starf, and rose, and sit in heaven above;   10
For he n'ill falsen no wight, dare I say,
That will his heart all wholly on him lay.
And since he best to love is, and most meek,
What needeth feignèd lovès for to seek?

17   [A Wanton Merry Friar]

A Friar there was, a wanton and a merry,
A limiter, a full solèmpnè man.
In all the orders four is none that can

---

16. 10 *starf*: died *sit*: sits 11 *n'ill*: ne will
17. 2 *limiter*: a friar licensed to beg in a certain district *full solèmpnè*: very
impressive 3 *can*: knows

So much of dalliance and fair languàge.
He haddè made full many a marriàge 5
Of youngè women at his ownè cost.
Unto his order he was a noble post.
Full well beloved and fàmiliar was he
With franklins overall in his countrỳ,
And eke with worthy women of the town; 10
For he had power of confession,
As said himself, more than a curàte,
For of his order he was licenciate.
Full sweetly heardè he confession
And pleasant was his absolution: 15
He was an easy man to give penànce,
There as he wist to have a good pittànce.
For unto a poor order for to give
Is signè that a man is well y-shrive;
For if he gave, he durstè make avaunt, 20
He wistè that a man was repentànt;
For many a man so hard is of his heart,
He may not weep, although him sorè smart.
Therefore, instead of weeping and prayèrs
Men mote give silver to the poorè friars. 25
His tippet was ay farcèd full of knives
And pinnès, for to given fairè wives.
And certainly he had a merry note:
Well could he sing and playen on a rote,
At yeddings he bore utterly the prize. 30
His neckè white was as the fleur-de-lys;
Thereto, he strong was as a champiòn.
He knew the taverns well in every town,
And every hosteler and tappester
Bet than a lazar or a beggester; 35
For unto such a worthy man as he
Accorded not, as by his faculty,

7 *post*: pillar 9 *overall*: everywhere 25 *mote*: must 26 *farcèd*: stuffed 29 *rote*:
a primitive violin 30 *yeddings*: songs or ballads 34 ostler and tapster, the latter
can be either male or female 35 *beggester*: beggar, again male or female

To have with sickė lazars acquaintànce.
It is not honest, it may not advance,
For to dealen with no such poraille   40
But all with rich and sellers of vitaille.
And overall, there as profit should arise,
Courteous he was and lowly of servìce.
There nas no man nowhere so virtuous.
He was the bestė beggar in his house;   45
For though a widow haddė nought a shoe,
So pleasant was his 'In principio',
Yet would he have a farthing, ere he went.
His purchase was well better than his rent.
And rage he could, as it were right a whelp.   50
In lovė-days there could he muchė help,
For there he was not like a cloisterer
With a threadbare cope, as is a poor scholàr,
But he was like a master or a pope.
Of double-worsted was his semi-cope,   55
That rounded as a bell out of the press.
Somewhat he lispėd, for his wantonness,
To make his English sweet upon his tongue;
And in his harping, when that he had sung,
His eyen twinkled in his head aright,   60
As do the starrės in the frosty night.

18   [A Poor Parson]

A good man was there of religion,
And was a poorė parson of a town,
But rich he was of holy thought and work.

40 *poraille*: paupers   41 *vitaille*: victuals   47 '*In principio*': the opening words of
St. John's Gospel, held to have magical power   49 he picked up a good deal on
the side   51 *lovė-days*: days for settling disputes by arbitration   52 *cloisterer*: a
cloistered monk   56 *press*: the mould for casting a bell
18. 2 *town*: village

He was alsò a learned man, a clerk,
That Christès gospel truly wouldè preach;   5
His parishens devoutly would he teach.
Benign he was, and wonder diligent,
And in adversity full patient,
And such he was y-provèd oftè sithes.
Full loath were him to cursen for his tithes,   10
But rather would he given, out of doubt
Unto his poorè parishens about
Of his offering and eke of his substànce.
He could in little thing have suffisànce.
Wide was his parish, and houses far asunder,   15
But he ne leftè not, for rain ne thunder,
In sickness nor in mischief to visìte
The farthest in his parish much and lite,
Upon his feet, and in his hand a stave.
This noble ensample to his sheep he gave   20
That first he wrought and afterward he taught. . . .

He settè not his benefice to hire
And left his sheep encumbered in the mire
And ran to London unto Saintè Paulès
To seeken him a chantèry for soulès,   25
Or with a brotherhood to be withhold;
But dwelt at home, and keptè well his fold,
So that the wolf ne made it not miscarry;
He was a shepherd and nought a mercenary.
And though he holy were and virtuous,   30
He was to sinful men not despitous,
Ne of his speechè dangerous ne digne,
But in his teaching discreet and benign.
To drawen folk to heaven by fairnèss,
By good ensample, this was his businèss.   35

6 *parishens*: parishioners   9 *oftè sithes*: oftentimes   10 to excommunicate for
non-payment of tithes   17 *mischief*: misfortune   18 *much and lite*: great and small
31 *despitous*: scornful   32 *dangerous ne digne*: arrogant or haughty   34 *fairnèss*:
gentleness

But it were any person obstinate,
What so he were, of high or low estate,
Him would he snibben sharply for the nonès.
A better priest I trow that nowhere none is.
He waited after no pomp and reverence,   40
Ne makèd him a spicèd conscience,
But Christès lore and his apostles' twelve
He taught, but first he followed it himself.

38 Him he would rebuke especially sharply   41 *a spicèd conscience*: a finicky
conscience, concerning itself with trifles

19 ['Come out, Lazarus!']

'Come out, Lazar, what-so befall!'
Then might not the fiend of hell
Longer make that soul to dwell,
So dreadful was that ilkè cry
To that feloùn, our enemy.   5
The Kingès trumpet blew a blast:
'Come out!', it said, 'be not aghast'.
With that voice the fiend gan quake
As doth the leaf when windès wake.
    'Come out' is now a wonder soun: 10
It hath overcome that foul feloùn;
And all his careful company
For dread thereof they gunnè cry.
Yet is 'Come out' a wonder song;
For it has broken the prison strong,   15
Fetters, chains and bondès mo,
That wroughten wretched soulès woe.
'Come out!': that Kingès voice so free
It maketh the devil and death to flee.
Say me now, thou serpent sly,   20
Is not 'Come out' an asper cry?
'Come out' is word of battàil:
For it gan hellè soon t'assail.
Why stoppest thou not, fiend, thine ear,
That this word enter not there?   25
He that said that word of might
Shop him felly to the fight;
For with that word he won the field,
Withouten spear, withouten shield,
And brought them out of prison strong   30

19. 5 *feloùn*: traitor   8 *gan quake*: quaked   10 *wonder*: wonderful   12 *careful* wretched   13 *gunnè cry*: cried   16 *mo*: besides   18 *free*: noble   21 *asper*: harsh   23 *soon*: at once   27 advanced valiantly to battle

That weren holden there with wrong.
Tell now, tyrant, where is thy might?
'Come out' hath felled it all with fight.

20   ['Quia Amore Langueo']*

In the vale of restless mind
   I sought in mountain and in mead,
Trusting a true love for to find.
    Upon an hill then took I heed;
    A voice I heard – and near I yede –   5
      In huge doloùr complaining tho:
    'See, dear soul, my sidès bleed,
      Quia amore langueo.'

Upon this mount I found a tree;
   Under this tree a man sitting;   10
From head to foot wounded was he,
    His heartè-blood I saw bleeding;
    A seemly man to be a king
      A gracious face to look unto.
    I asked him how he had paining.   15
      He said: '*Quia amore langueo.*

'I am true love that false was never:
   My sister, man's soul, I loved her thus;
Because I would on no wise dissever,
    I left my kingdom glorious;   20
    I purveyed her a place full precious;
      She flit, I followed; I loved her so
    That I suffered these painès piteous,
      Quia amore langueo.

* For note, see p. 345
20. 5 *near*: nearer *yede*: went 6 *tho*: then 8 Song of Songs, 2.5 15 *how*: why
19 *dissever*: be separated 22 *flit*: fled

'My fair love and my spousė bright,   25
   I saved her fro beating and she hath me bet;
I clothed her in grace and heavenly light,
   This bloody surcote she hath on me set.
   For longing love I will not let;
     Sweetė strokės be these, lo!   30
   I have loved her ever as I het,
     Quia amore langueo.

'I crowned her with bliss, and she me with thorn;
   I led her to chamber, and she me to die;
I brought her to worship, and she me to scorn;   35
   I did her reverence, and she me villainy.
   To love that loveth is no maistrỳ;
     Her hate made never my love her foe;
   Ask then no mo questions why,
     Quia amore langueo.   40

'Look unto mine handės, man!
   These gloves were given me when I her sought;
They be not white, but red and wan,
   Embroidered with blood, my spouse them bought;
   They will not off, I leave them nought,   45
     I woo her with them wherever she go;
   These hands full friendly for her fought,
     Quia amore langueo.

'Marvel not, man, though I sit still;
   My love hath shod me wonder strait;   50
She buckled my feet, as was her will,
   With sharpė nails – well thou maist wait!
   In my love was never deceit,
     For all my members I have opened her to;
   My body I made her heartės bait,   55
     Quia amore langueo.

26 *bet*: beaten 29 *For*: Because of *let*: cease 31 *het*: promised 35 *worship*: honour 36 *villainy*: indignity 39 To love one that loves is no hard task 43 *wan*: discoloured 45 *leave . . .*: am never without them 52 *wait*: see 54 *her to*: to her

'In my side I have made her nest;
   Look in me how wide a wound is here!
This is her chamber, here shall she rest,
   That she and I may sleep in fere.   60
   Here may she wash, if any filth were,
      Here is succour for all her woe;
   Come if she will, she shall have cheer,
      Quia amore langueo.

'I will abide till she be ready,   65
   I will her sue if she say nay;
If she be reckèless, I will be ready,
   If she be dangerous, I will her pray.
   If she do weep, then bid I nay;
      Mine arms be spread to clip her me to;
   Cry onès: I come. Now, soul, assay!   70
      Quia amore langueo.

'I sit on an hill for to see far,
   I look to the vale; my spouse I see:
Now runs she awayward, now comes she nearer,   75
   Yet fro my eye-sight she may not be.
   Some wait their prey to make her flee;
      I run tofore to chastise her foe.
   Recover, my soul, again to me,
      Quia amore langueo.   80

'My sweetè spouse, will we go play?
   Apples be ripe in my gardène;
I shall clothe thee in new array,
   Thy meat shall be milk, honey, and wine.
   Now, dear soul, let us go dine,   85
      Thy sustenance is in my scrippè, lo!
   Tarry not now, fair spousè mine,
      Quia amore langueo.

60 *in fere*: together 63 *cheer*: welcome 66 *sue*: follow 67 *reckèless*; thoughtless
ready: prudent 68 *dangerous*: haughty 69 *bid . . .*: I shall beg her not to 71 *onès*:
once *assay*: try 77 *wait*: lie in wait for 79 *Recover*: Return 86 *scrippè*: bag

'If thou be foul, I shall make thee clean;
  If thou be sick, I shall thee heal,   90
If thou ought mourn, I shall bemene.
    Spouse, why wilt thou nought with me deal?
    Thou foundest never love so leal;
      What wilt thou, soul, that I shall do?
    I may of unkindness thee appeal,   95
      Quia amore langueo.

'What shall I do now with my spouse?
    Abide I will her gentleness.
Would she look onės out of her house
    Of fleshly affections and uncleanness,   100
    Her bed is made, her bolster is bliss,
      Her chamber is chosen, such are no mo.
    Look out at the windows of kindness,
      Quia amore langueo.

'Long and love thou never so high,   105
    Yet is my love more than thine may be;
Thou gladdest, thou weepest, I sit thee by;
    Yet might thou, spouse, look onės at me!
    Spouse, should I alway feedė thee
      With childės meat? Nay, love, not so!   110
    I prove thy love with adversity,
      Quia amore langueo.

'My spouse is in chamber, hold your peace;
    Make no noise, but let her sleep.
My babe shall suffer no disease,   115
    I may not hear my dear child weep;
    For with my pap I shall her keep.
      No wonder though I tend her to:
    This hole in my side had never been so deep,
      But *quia amore langueo.*   120

91 *ought*: at all *bemene*: condole 95 I may accuse thee of ingratitude 115 *disease*:
discomfort 117 *with*: close to 118 *tend*: attend

'Wax not weary, mine own dear wife:
   What meed is aye to live in comfòrt?
For in tribulation I run more rife
   Oftentimes than in disport;
   In wealth, in woe, ever I support,   125
     Then, dear soul, go never me fro!
   Thy meed is markèd, when thou art mort,
    Quia amore langueo.'

122 What reward is there in living always in comfort 123 *run more rife*: run (to help) more quickly 127 *markèd*: assigned *mort*: dead

JOHN AUDELAY
(fl. 1426)

21   ['Passion of Christ Strengthen Me']

Lady, help! Jesu, mercỳ!
Timor mortis conturbat me.

Dread of death, sorrow of sin
   Troubles my heart full grievously;
My soul it noyeth with my lust then –   5
   Passio Christi conforta me.

For blindness is a heavy thing,
   And to be deaf therewith only,
To lose my light and my hearing –
   Passio Christi conforta me;   10

And to lose my taste and my smelling,
   And to be sick in my body;
Here I have lost all my liking –
   Passio Christi conforta me.

Thus God he gives and takes away,   15
   And, as he will, so mote it be.
His name be blest both night and day –
   Passio Christi conforta me.

Here is a cause of great mourning:
   Of myself nothing I see   20
Save filth, uncleanness, vile stinking –
   Passio Christi conforta me.

Into this world no more I brought;
   No more I get with me truly
Save good deed, word, will, and thought –   25
   Passio Christi conforta me.

21. 5 My soul is distressed by my sinful desires then 8 *only*: especially 16
mote: must 24 *get*: acquire to take

The fivè wounds of Jesu Christ
   My medicine now mote they be,
The fiendès power doun to cast –
   Passio Christi conforta me.   30

As I lay sick in my langòur,
   With sorrow of heart and tear of eye,
This carol I made with great dolòur –
   Passio Christi conforta me.

Oft with this prayer I me blest: 35
   '*In manus tuas, Domine;*
Thou take my soul into thy rest –
   Passio Christi conforta me.

Mary, mother, merciful may,
   For the joys thou hadst, ladỳ,   40
To thy Son for me thou pray –
   Passio Christi conforta me.'

Learn this lesson of blind Awdlay:
   When bale is highest, then bote may be.
If thou be noyèd night or day,   45
   Say '*Passio Christi conforta me.*'

39 *may*: maiden 44 When trouble is at its height, the remedy may come
45 *noyèd*: troubled

22   'I sing of a maiden'

I sing of a maiden
   That is makèless:
King of all kingès
   To her son she ches.

He came all so stillè   5
   There his mother was,
As dew in Aprìllè
   That falleth on the grass.

He came all so stillè
   To his mother's bower,   10
As dew in Aprìllè
   That falleth on the flower.

He came all so stillè
   There his mother lay,
As dew in Aprìllè   15
   That falleth on the spray.

Mother and maiden
   Was never none but she;
Well may such a lady
   Goddès mother be.   20

23   *[O Felix Culpa!]*

Adam lay y-bounden
   Bounden in a bond;

22. 2 *makèless*: matchless, without a mate 4 *ches*: chose 5 *all so stillè*: as silently
6 *There*: Where

Four thousand winter
  Thought he not too long:
And all was for an apple,   5
  An apple that he took,
As clerkės finden written
  In theirė book.
Ne had the apple taken been,
  The apple taken been,   10
Ne haddė never our Lady
  A been heaven's queen.
Blessed be the time
  That apple taken was!
Therefore we may singen   15
  '*Deo Gracias!*'

24   'Woefully arrayed'*

Woefully arrayed,
My blood, man,
For thee ran,
It may not be nayed:
My body blue and wan,   5
Woefully arrayed.

Behold me, I pray thee, with all thine whole reason,
And be not hard-hearted for this encheason,
That I for thy soul's sake was slain in good season,
Beguiled and betrayed by Judas' false treason,   10
  Unkindly entreated,
  With sharp cords sore fretted,
  The Jewės me threated,
They mowėd, they spitted and despised me
Condemnėd to death, as thou maist see.   15

23. 7 *clerkės*: learned men
* For note, see p. 345
24. 5 *wan*: discoloured 8 *encheason*: cause 14 *mowėd*: grimaced

Thus naked am I nailèd, O man, for thy sake.
I love thee, then love me. Why sleepest thou? Awake!
Remember my tender heart-root for thee brake,
With painès my veinès constrainèd to crack.
   Thus was I defacèd,   20
   Thus was my flesh rasèd,
   And I to death chasèd,
  Like a lamb led unto sacrifice,
  Slain I was in most cruel wise.

Of sharp thorn I have worn a crown on my head,   25
So rubbèd, so bobbèd, so rueful, so red;
Sore painèd, sore strainèd, and for thy love dead,
Unfeignèd, not deemèd, my blood for thee shed;
   My feet and hands sore
   With sturdy nails bore.   30
   What might I suffer more
  Than I have suffered, man, for thee.
  Come when thou wilt and welcome to me!

Dear brother, none other thing I desire
But give me thy heart free, to reward mine hire.   35
I am he that made the earth, water and fire.
Sathanas, that sloven, and right loathly sire,
   Him have I overcast
   In hell-prison bound fast,
   Where aye his woe shall last.   40
I have purveyèd a place full clear
For mankind, whom I have bought dear.

25   ['Wit wonders']

    A God and yet a man,
    A maid and yet a mother:

21 *rasèd*: scratched 26 *bobbèd*: beaten, or insulted 28 In reality and not in mere
deeming 35 *hire*: service done expecting payment

Wit wonders what wit can
Conceive this or the other.

A God and can he die?   5
A dead man, can he live?
What wit can well reply?
What reason reason give?

God, Truth itself, doth teach it.
Man's wit sinks too far under   10
By reason's power to reach it:
Believe and leave to wonder.

26   'O, my heart is woe!'

'O, *my heart is woe!*' *Mary she said so,*
'*For to see my dear son die, and sons I have no mo.*'

'When that my sweet son was thirty winter old,
Then the traitor Judas waxèd very bold:
For thirty plates of money his master he had sold.   5
But when I it wistè, Lord, my heart was cold!

'Upon Sherè Thursday then truly it was
On my sonnès death that Judas did compàss.
Many were the false Jews that followed him by trace;
And there before them all he kissed my sonnès face.   10

'My son before Pilate brought was he,
And Peter said three times he knew him not, pardee.
Pilate said unto the Jews: 'What say ye?'
Then they cried with one voice: '*Crucifige*!'

25. 12 *leave*: cease
26. 5 *plates*: pieces 7 *Sherè Thursday*: Maundy Thursday 8 *compàss (on)*: plot
9 *him . . .* : in his path

66

'On Good Friday, at the mount of Calvary,   15
My son was done on the cross, nailed with nailès three.
Of all the friends that he had, never one could he see
But gentle John the Evangelist, that still stood him by.

'Though I were sorrowful, no man have at it wonder;
For huge was the earthquake, horrìble was the thunder.   20
I looked on my sweet son on the cross that I stood under;
Then came Longeus with a spear and cleft his heart in sunder.'

27   Corpus Christi Carol*

Lully, lullay, lully, lullay,
The falcon hath borne my make away.

He bore him up, he bore him down;
He bore him into an orchard brown.

In that orchard there was an hall,   5
That was hanged with purple and pall.

And in that hall there was a bed
It was hanged with gold so red.

And in that bed there lieth a knight,
His woundès bleeding day and night.   10

By that bed's side there kneeleth a may,
And she weepeth both night and day.

And by that bed's side there standeth a stone,
Corpus Christi written thereon.

18 *still*: always 22 *Longeus*: Longinus, the name given in the apocryphal *Acta Pilati* to the soldier who pierced Christ's side
* For note, see p. 346
27. 2 *make*: mate 6 *pall*: rich cloth 11 *may*: maiden

WILLIAM DUNBAR
(?1460–?1520)

['Unto us a Child is Born']

Rorate coeli desuper.
Hevins distill your balmy schouris,
For now is rissin the bricht day ster
Fro the ros Mary, flour of flouris;
The cleir sone quhome no clud devouris,   5
Surmunting Phebus in the est,
Is cummin of his hevinly touris
Et nobis Puer natus est.

Archangellis, angellis, and dompnationis,
Tronis, potestatis, and marteiris seir,   10
And all ye hevinly operationis,
Ster, planeit, firmament, and speir,
Fyre, erd, air, and watter cleir,
To him gife loving, most and lest,
That come in to so meik maneir   15
Et nobis Puer natus est.

Synnaris, be glaid and pennance do
And thank your makar hairtfully,
For he that ye mycht nocht cum to
To yow is cummin full humly;   20
Your saulis with his blud to by
And lous yow of the feindis arrest,
And only of his awin mercy
Pro nobis Puer natus est.

All clergy do to him inclyne   25

28. 1 and 8 From the services for Christmas Eve and Christmas Day: Isa.
45.8 and 9.6 9–10 The martyrs are joined to some of the hierarchy of heaven:
seraphim, cherubim and thrones; dominations, virtues and powers; princi-
palities, archangels and angels 10 *seir*: various 12 *speir*: sphere 14 *lest*: least

And bow unto that barne benyng,
And do your observance devyne
To him that is of kingis king;
Ensence his altar, reid and sing
In haly kirk, with mynd degest,   30
Him honouring attour all thing
Qui nobis Puer est.

Celestiall fowlis in the aire,
Sing with your nottis upoun hicht,
In firthis and in forrestis fair   35
Be myrthfull now, at all your mycht;
For passit is your dully nycht,
Aurora hes the cluddis perst,
The son is rissin with glaidsum lycht,
Et nobis Puer natus est.   40

Now spring up, flouris, fra the rute,
Revert yow upwart naturaly,
In honour of the blissit frute
That rais up fro the rose Marỳ;
Lay out your levis lustely,   45
Fro deid tak lyfe now at the lest
In wirschip of that Prince wirthỳ
Qui nobis Puer natus est.

Syng hevin imperiall most of hicht,
Regions of air mak armony;   50
All fishe in flud and foull of flicht
Be myrthfull and mak melody;
All *Gloria in excelsis* cry,
Hevin, erd, se, man, bird, and best:
He that is crownit abone the sky   55
Pro nobis Puer natus est.

26 *barne*: bairn, babe 30 *degest*: calm 31 *attour*: above 49 *hevin imperiall*: the highest heaven, the empyrean, seat of God and the angels

29   ['The Lord is Risen']

Done is a battell on the dragon blak,
Our campioun Chryst confountet hes his force;
The yettis of hell ar brokin with a crak,
The signe triumphall rasit is of the croce,
The divillis trymmillis with hiddous voce,   5
The saulis ar borrowit and to the blis can go,
Chryst with his blud our ransonis dois indoce:
Surrexit dominus de sepulchro.

Dungin is the deidly dragon Lucifer,
The crewall serpent with the mortall stang,   10
The auld kene tegir with his teith on char
Quhilk in a wait hes lyne for us so lang,
Thinking to grip us in his clowis strang:
The mercifull lord wald nocht that it wer so,
He maid him for to felye of that fang: 15
Surrexit dominus de sepulchro.

He for our saik that sufferit to be slane
And lyk a lamb in sacrifice wes dicht,
Is lyk a lyone rissin up agane,
And as a gyane raxit him on hicht: 20
Sprungin is Aurora radius and bricht,
On loft is gone the glorious Appollo,
The blissfull day depairtit fro the nycht:
Surrexit dominus de sepulchro.

29. 8 The first versicle for matins on Easter Sunday 2 *campioun*: champion
3 *yettis*: gates 6 *borrowit*: ransomed 7 *indoce*: endorse 9 *Dungin*: struck down
11 *on char*: ajar, open 15 *felye of that fang*: come short of his booty 18 *dicht*:
made ready 20 *raxit him*: raised himself up 22 *On loft*: on high

The grit victour agane is rissin on hicht 25
That for our querrell to the deth wes woundit;
The sone that wox all paill now schynis bricht,
And, dirknes clerit, our fayth is now refoundit:
The knell of mercy fra the hevin is soundit,
The Cristin ar deliverit of thair wo, 30
The Jowis and thair errour ar confoundit:
Surrexit dominus de sepulchro.

The fo is chasit, the battell is done ceis,
The presone brokin, the jevellouris fleit and flemit,
The weir is gon, confermit is the peis, 35
The fetteris lowsit and the dungeoun temit,
The ransoun maid, the presoneris redemit,
The feild is win, ourcummin is the fo,
Dispulit of the tresur that he yemit:
Surrexit dominus de sepulchro. 40

33 *done ceis*: made to stop   34 *jevellouris fleit and flemit*: jailers terrified and put to flight   36 *temit*: emptied   39 *yemit*: kept

SIR THOMAS MORE
(1478–1535)

[The Measure of Love]*

If love be strong, hot, mighty and fervènt,
There may no trouble, grief or sorrow fall,
But that the lover would be well content
All to endure and think it eke too small,
Though it were death, so he might therewithal
The joyful presence of that person get
On whom he hath his heart and love y-set.

Thus should of God the lover be content
Any distress or sorrow to endure,
Rather than to be from God absènt,
And glad to die, so that he may be sure
By his departing hence for to procure,
After this valley dark, the heavenly light,
And of his love the glorious blessed sight.

Not only a lover content is in his heart
But coveteth eke and longeth to sustain
Some labour, incommodity, or smart,
Loss, adversity, trouble, grief or pain:
And of his sorrow, joyful is and fain,
And happy thinketh himself that he may take
Some misadventure for his lover's sake.

Thus shouldest thou, that lovest God also,
In thine heart wish, covet, and be glad
For him to suffer trouble, pain and woe:
For whom if thou be never so woe bestead,
Yet thou ne shalt sustain (be not adread)
Half the dolour, grief and adversity
That he already suffered hath for thee.

* For note, see p. 346

31   [A Prayer]

Grant, I thee pray, such heat into mine heart
That to this love of thine may be equàl;
Grant me from Satan's service to astart,
With whom me rueth so long to have been thrall;
Grant me, good Lord and Creator of all,
The flame to quench of all sinful desire
And in thy love set all mine heart afire.

That when the journey of this deadly life
My silly ghost hath finished, and thence
Departen must without his fleshly wife,
Alone into his Lordès high presènce,
He may thee find, O well of indulgènce,
In thy lordship not as a lord, but rather
As a very tender, loving father.

EDMUND SPENSER
(1552–1599)

32

[Care in Heaven]

And is there care in heaven? and is there love?
In heavenly spirits to these creatures base,
That may compassion of their evils move?
There is: else much more wretched were the case
Of men than beasts. But O th'exceeding grace
Of highest God, that loves his creatures so,
And all his works with mercy doth embrace,
That blessed Angels he sends to and fro,
To serve to wicked man, to serve his wicked foe.

How oft do they their silver bowers leave,
To come to succour us that succour want!
How oft do they with golden pinions cleave
The flitting skies, like flying Pursuivant,
Against foul fiends to aid us militant!
They for us fight, they watch and duly ward,
And their bright squadrons round about us plant,
And all for love, and nothing for reward:
O why should heavenly God to men have such regard?

33

[Easter]

Most glorious Lord of life, that on this day
    Didst make thy triumph over death and sin;
    And having harrowed hell didst bring away
    Captivity thence captive, us to win:
This joyous day, dear Lord, with joy begin,
    And grant that we for whom thou didest die
    Being with thy dear blood clean washed from sin,
    May live forever in felicity.

And that thy love we weighing worthily,
 May likewise love thee for the same again;
 And for thy sake that all like dear didst buy,
 With love may one another entertain.
So let us love, dear love, like as we ought.
Love is the lesson which the Lord us taught.

SIR WALTER RALEGH
(*c.* 1552–1618)

34   The Passionate Man's Pilgrimage
Supposed to be written by one at the point of death[1]

Give me my scallop-shell of quiet,
My staff of faith to walk upon,
My scrip of joy, immortal diet,
My bottle of salvation,
My gown of glory, hope's true gage,
And thus I'll take my pilgrimage.

Blood must be my body's balmer,
No other balm will there be given,
Whilst my soul like a white palmer
Travels to the land of heaven,
Over the silver mountains,
Where spring the nectar fountains;
And there I'll kiss
The bowl of bliss,
And drink my eternal fill
On every milken hill.
My soul will be a-dry before,
But after it will ne'er thirst more.

And by the happy blissful way
More peaceful pilgrims I shall see,
That have shook off their gowns of clay
And go apparelled fresh like me.
I'll bring them first
To slake their thirst,
And then to taste those nectar suckets[2]
At the clear wells

[1] Ralegh was under sentence of death from 17 November to 3 December 1603
[2] *suckets*: sweetmeats, usually fruit candied in syrup

Where sweetness dwells,
Drawn up by saints in crystal buckets.

And when our bottles and all we
Are filled with immortality,
Then the holy paths we'll travel,
Strewed with rubies thick as gravel,
Ceilings of diamonds, sapphire floors,
High walls of coral and pearl bowers.

From thence to heaven's bribeless hall
Where no corrupted voices brawl,
No conscience molten into gold,
Nor forged accusers bought and sold,
No cause deferred, nor vain-spent journey,
For there Christ is the King's Attorney,
Who pleads for all without degrees,
And he hath angels, but no fees.

When the grand twelve million jury
Of our sins with sinful fury
'Gainst our souls black verdicts give,
Christ pleads his death, and then we live.
Be thou my speaker, taintless pleader,
Unblotted lawyer, true proceeder;
Thou mov'st salvation even for alms,
Not with a bribed lawyer's palms.

And this is my eternal plea
To him that made heaven, earth and sea:
Seeing my flesh must die so soon,
And want a head to dine next noon,
Just at the stroke when my veins start and spread,
Set on my soul an everlasting head.
Then am I ready, like a palmer fit,
To tread those blest paths which before I writ.

35   Epitaph*

    Even such is Time, which takes in trust
    Our youth, our joys, and all we have,
    And pays us but with age and dust;
    Who in the dark and silent grave,
    When we have wandered all our ways,
    Shuts up the story of our days:
    And from which earth, and grave, and dust,
    The Lord shall raise me up, I trust.

* For note, see p. 347

FULKE GREVILLE, LORD BROOKE
(1554–1628)

36

[Memento Mori]

When as man's life, the light of human lust,
In socket of his earthly lantern burns,
That all this glory unto ashes must,
And generation to corruption turns;
    Then fond desires that only fear their end
    Do vainly wish for life but to amend.

But when this life is from the body fled,
To see itself in that eternal glass
Where time doth end, and thoughts accuse the dead,
Where all to come is one with all that was;
    Then living men ask how he left his breath
    That while he livèd never thought of death.

37

[Vain Learning]

Man, dream no more of curious mysteries,
As what was here before the world was made,
The first man's life, the state of Paradise,
Where heaven is or hell's eternal shade;
  For God's works are like him all infinite,
  And curious search but crafty sin's delight.

The Flood that did, and dreadful Fire that shall,
Drown and burn up the malice of the earth,
The diverse tongues and Babylon's downfall,
Are nothing to the man's renewèd birth;
  First let the Law plough up thy wicked heart,
  That Christ may come and all these types depart.

When thou hast swept the house that all is clear,
When thou the dust hast shaken from thy feet,
When God's All-Might doth in thy flesh appear,
Then seas with streams above the sky do meet;[1]
    For goodness only doth God comprehend,
    Knows what was first and what shall be the end.

[1] Seas, the waters under the firmament, will no longer be divided from the waters above the firmament. What these last were is one of the 'curious mysteries' of the creation.

SIR PHILIP SIDNEY
(1554-1586)

38

[Splendidis Longum Valedico Nugis]

Leave me, O Love, which reachest but to dust;
   And thou, my mind, aspire to higher things;
Grow rich in that which never taketh rust;
   Whatever fades but fading pleasure brings.
Draw in thy beams, and humble all thy might
   To that sweet yoke where lasting freedoms be;
Which breaks the clouds and opens forth the light,
   That doth both shine and give us sight to see.
O take fast hold; let that light be thy guide
   In this small course which birth draws out to death,
And think how evil becometh him to slide,
   Who seeketh heaven, and comes of heavenly breath.
     Then farewell, world; thy uttermost I see;
     Eternal Love, maintain thy life in me.

ROBERT SOUTHWELL
(1561–1595)

39   The Nativity of Christ

Behold the father is his daughter's son,
The bird that built the nest is hatched therein,
The old of years an hour hath not outrun,
Eternal life to live doth now begin,
The Word is dumb, the mirth of heaven doth weep,
Might feeble is, and force doth faintly creep.

O dying souls, behold your living spring;
O dazzled eyes, behold your sun of grace;
Dull ears, attend what word this Word doth bring;
Up, heavy hearts, with joy your joy embrace.
From death, from dark, from deafness, from despairs,
This life, this light, this Word, this joy repairs.

Gift better than himself God doth not know;
Gift better than his God no man can see.
This gift doth here the giver given bestow;
Gift to this gift let each receiver be.
God is my gift, himself he freely gave me;
God's gift am I, and none but God shall have me.

Man altered was by sin from man to beast;
Beast's food is hay, hay is all mortal flesh.
Now God is flesh and lies in manger pressed
As hay, the brutest sinner to refresh.
O happy field wherein this fodder grew,
Whose taste doth us from beasts to men renew.

40   The Burning Babe

As I in hoary winter's night stood shivering in the snow,
Surprised I was with sudden heat which made my heart to glow;

And lifting up a fearful eye to view what fire was near,
A pretty Babe all burning bright did in the air appear;
Who scorchèd with excessive heat, such floods of tears did shed,
As though his floods should quench his flames which with his tears
    were fed.

'Alas!' quoth he, 'but newly born in fiery heats I fry,
Yet none approach to warm their hearts or feel my fire but I.
My faultless breast the furnace is, the fuel wounding thorns;
Love is the fire, and sighs the smoke, the ashes shame and scorns;
The fuel justice layeth on, and mercy blows the coals;
The metal in this furnace wrought are men's defilèd souls:
For which, as now on fire I am to work them to their good,
So will I melt into a bath to wash them in my blood.'
With this he vanished out of sight and swiftly shrunk away,
And straight I callèd unto mind that it was Christmas day.

41   New Heaven, New War

        Come to your heaven, you heavenly choirs!
        Earth hath the heaven of your desires;
        Remove your dwelling to your God,
        A stall is now his best abode,
        Sith men their homage do deny,
        Come, angels, all their fault supply.

        His chilling cold doth heat require,
        Come, seraphins, in lieu of fire;
        This little ark no cover hath,
        Let cherubs' wings his body swathe;
        Come, Raphaèl, this Babe must eat,
        Provide our little Toby meat.[1]

[1] Raphaèl, the 'sociable Archangel', accompanied the young Tobias and sup-
plied his needs.

Let Gabriel be now his groom,
That first took up his earthly room;
Let Michael stand in his defence,
Whom love hath linked to feeble sense;
Let graces rock when he doth cry,
And angels sing his lullaby.

The same you saw in heavenly seat,
Is he that now sucks Mary's teat;
Agnize[1] your King a mortal wight,
His borrowed weed lets not your sight;
Come kiss the manger where he lies,
That is your bliss above the skies.

This little Babe, so few days old,
Is come to rifle Satan's fold;
All hell doth at his presence quake,
Though he himself for cold do shake.
For in this weak unarmèd wise
The gates of hell he will surprise.

With tears he fights and wins the field,
His naked breast stands for a shield;
His battering shot are babish cries,
His arrows looks of weeping eyes,
His martial ensigns cold and need,
And feeble flesh his warrior's steed.

His camp is pitchèd in a stall,
His bulwark but a broken wall:
The crib his trench, hay-stalks his stakes,
Of shepherds he his muster makes;
And thus, as sure his foe to wound,
The angels' trumps alarum sound.

[1] *Agnize*: acknowledge

My soul, with Christ join thou in fight;
Stick to the tents that he hath pight;[1]
Within his crib is surest ward,
This little Babe will be thy guard;
If thou wilt foil thy foes with joy,
Then flit not from the heavenly boy.

42   Upon the Image of Death*

Before my face the picture hangs,
    That daily should put me in mind
Of those cold qualms and bitter pangs,
    That shortly I am like to find:
        But yet, alas, full little I
        Do think hereon, that I must die.

I often look upon a face
    Most ugly, grisly, bare and thin;
I often view the hollow place,
    Where eyes and nose had sometimes been;
        I see the bones across that lie,
        Yet little think that I must die.

I read the label underneath,
    That telleth me whereto I must;
I see the sentence eke that saith
    'Remember, man, that thou art dust!'
        But yet, alas, but seldom I
        Do think indeed that I must die.

Continually at my bed's head
    A hearse doth hang, which doth me tell,
That I ere morning may be dead,

[1] *pight*: pitched
* For note, see p. 347

Though now I feel myself full well:
  But yet, alas, for all this, I
  Have little mind that I must die.

The gown which I do use to wear,
  The knife wherewith I cut my meat,
And eke that old and ancient chair
  Which is my only usual seat;
    All these do tell me I must die,
    And yet my life amend not I.

My ancestors are turned to clay,
  And many of my mates are gone,
My youngers daily drop away,
  And can I think to 'scape alone?
    No, no, I know that I must die,
    And yet my life amend not I.

Not Solomon, for all his wit,
  Nor Samson, though he were so strong,
No king nor person ever yet
  Could 'scape, but death laid him along:
    Wherefore I know that I must die,
    And yet my life amend not I.

Though all the East did quake to hear
  Of Alexander's dreadful name,
And all the West likewise did fear
  To hear of Julius Caesar's fame,
    Yet both by death in dust now lie.
    Who then can 'scape, but he must die?

If none can 'scape death's dreadful dart,
  If rich and poor his beck obey,
If strong, if wise, if all do smart,
  Then I to 'scape shall have no way.
    Oh! grant me grace, O God, that I
    My life may mend, sith I must die.

43   'Hierusalem, my happy home'*

Hierusalem, my happy home,
    When shall I come to thee?
When shall my sorrows have an end,
    Thy joys when shall I see?

O happy harbour of the saints,
    O sweet and pleasant soil,
In thee no sorrow may be found
    No grief, no care, no toil. . . .

No dampish mist is seen in thee,
    Nor cold nor darksome night;
There every soul shines as the sun,
    There God himself gives light.

There lust and lucre cannot dwell,
    There envy bears no sway;
There is no hunger, heat, nor cold,
    But pleasure every way.

Hierusalem, Hierusalem,
    God grant I once may see
Thy endless joys, and of the same
    Partaker aye to be.

Thy walls are made of precious stones,
    Thy bulwarks diamonds square;
Thy gates are of right orient pearl,
    Exceeding rich and rare.

* For note, see p. 347

Thy turrets and thy pinnacles
   With carbuncles do shine;
Thy very streets are paved with gold
   Surpassing clear and fine.

Thy houses are of ivory,
   Thy windows crystal clear,
Thy tiles are made of beaten gold,
   O God, that I were there.

Within thy gates nothing doth come
   That is not passing clean;
No spider's web, no dirt, no dust,
   No filth may there be seen.

Ah, my sweet home, Hierusalem,
   Would God I were in thee!
Would God my woes were at an end,
   Thy joys that I might see! . . .

Thy gardens and thy gallant walks
   Continually are green;
There grows such sweet and pleasant flowers
   As nowhere else are seen. . . .

Quite through the streets with silver sound
   The flood of life doth flow;
Upon whose banks on every side
   The wood of life doth grow.

There trees for evermore bear fruit
   And evermore do spring;
There evermore the angels sit
   And evermore do sing.

There David stands with harp in hand
   As master of the Quire;

Ten thousand times that man were blest
   That might this music hear.

Our Lady sings *Magnificat*
   With tune surpassing sweet;
And all the virgins bear their parts
   Sitting about her feet.

Te Deum doth Saint Ambrose sing,
   Saint Austin doth the like;
Old Simeon and Zachary
   Have not their songs to seek.

There Magdalen hath left her moan
   And cheerfully doth sing,
With blessed saints whose harmony
   In every street doth ring.

Hierusalem, my happy home,
   Would God I were in thee!
Would God my woes were at an end,
   Thy joys that I might see!

WILLIAM ALABASTER
(1567–1640)

44   *Incarnatio est maximum Dei donum*

Like as the fountain of all light created
Doth pour out streams of brightness undefined
Through all the conduits of transparent kind
That heaven and air are both illuminated,
And yet his light is not thereby abated:
So God's eternal bounty ever shined
The beams of being, moving, life, sense, mind,
And to all things himself communicated.
But see the violent diffusive pleasure
Of goodness, that left not till God had spent
Himself by giving us himself, his treasure,
In making man a God omnipotent.
How might this goodness draw our souls above,
Which drew down God with such attractive love.

THOMAS CAMPION
(1567–1620)

45   [*De Profundis*]

Out of my soul's depth to thee my cries have sounded:
Let thine ears my plaints receive, on just fear grounded.
Lord, should'st thou weigh our faults, who's not confounded?

But with grace thou censur'st thine when they have errèd,
Therefore shall thy blessed name be loved and fearèd.
E'en to thy throne my thoughts and eyes are rearèd.

Thee alone my hopes attend, on thee relying;
In thy sacred word I'll trust, to thee fast flying,
Long ere the watch shall break, the morn descrying.

In the mercies of our God who live securèd,
May of full redemption rest in him assurèd,
Their sin-sick souls by him shall be recurèd.

46   ['O come quickly!']

Never weather-beaten sail more willing bent to shore,
Never tirèd pilgrim's limbs affected slumber more,
Than my wearied spright now longs to fly, out of my troubled
        breast:
    O come quickly, sweetest Lord, and take my soul to rest.

Ever-blooming are the joys of Heaven's high Paradise,
Cold age deafs not there our ears, nor vapour dims our eyes:
Glory there the sun outshines, whose beams the blessed only see:
    O come quickly, glorious Lord, and raise my spright to thee.

47   'Seek the Lord!'

Seek the Lord, and in his ways persever.
   O faint not, but as eagles fly;
   For his steep hill is high;
Then striving gain the top, and triumph ever.

When with glory there thy brows are crownèd,
   New joys so shall abound in thee,
   Such sights thy soul shall see,
That worldly thoughts shall by their beams be drownèd.

Farewell, World, thou mass of mere confusion,
   False light, with many shadows dimmed,
   Old Witch, with new foils trimmed,
Thou deadly sleep of soul, and charmed illusion.

I the King will seek, of kings adorèd;
   Spring of light, tree of grace and bliss,
   Whose fruit so sovereign is
That all who taste it are from death restorèd.

SIR HENRY WOTTON
(1568–1639)

48   A Hymn to my God in a night of
my late sickness

O thou great Power, in whom I move,
For whom I live, to whom I die,
Behold me through thy beams of love,
Whilst on this couch of tears I lie,
   And cleanse my sordid soul within
   By thy Christ's blood, the bath of sin.

No hallowed oils, no grains I need,
No rags of saints, no purging fire,
One rosy drop from David's seed
Was worlds of seas to quench thine ire.
   O precious ransom, which once paid
   That *Consummatum Est* was said:

And said by him that said no more,
But sealed it with his sacred breath.
Thou then, that hast dispunged my score,
And dying was the death of Death,
   Be to me now – on thee I call –
   My Life, my Strength, my Joy, my All.

JOHN DONNE
(1572–1631)

['Seek True Religion!']*

    Though Truth and Falsehood be
Near twins, yet Truth a little elder is.
Be busy to seek her; believe me this:
He's not of none, nor worst, that seeks the best.
To adore, or scorn an image, or protest,
May all be bad. Doubt wisely; in strange way
To stand inquiring right is not to stray;
To sleep or run wrong is. On a huge hill,
Cragged and steep, Truth stands, and he that will
Reach her, about must and about must go,
And what the hill's suddenness resists, win so.[1]
Yet strive so, that before age, death's twilight,
Thy soul rest, for none can work in that night.
To will implies delay; therefore now do.
Hard deeds the body's pains; hard knowledge too,
The mind's endeavours reach; and mysteries
Are like the sun, dazzling, yet plain to all eyes.
Keep the truth which thou hast found; men do not stand
In so ill case here that God hath with his hand
Signed kings blank charters to kill whom they hate,
Nor are they vicars, but hangmen to Fate.
Fool and wretch, wilt thou let thy soul be tied
To man's laws, by which she shall not be tried
At the last day? Will it then boot thee
To say a Philip or a Gregory,
A Harry, or a Martin[2] taught thee this?
Is not this excuse for mere[3] contraries
Equally strong? Cannot both sides say so?

* For note, see p. 347
[1] By contouring one may reach what a sudden towering crag prevents one
reaching [2] Philip II of Spain, Gregory XIII or XIV, Henry VIII, Martin Luther
[3] *mere*: absolute

That thou mayst rightly obey Power, her bounds know;
Those passed, her nature and name's changed; to be
Then humble to her is idolatry.
As streams are Power is; those blest flowers that dwell
At the rough stream's calm head thrive and prove well,
But having left their roots and themselves given
To the stream's tyrannous rage, alas, are driven
Through mills and rocks and woods, and at last, almost
Consumed in going, in the sea are lost.
So perish souls which more choose men's unjust
Power from God claimed than God himself to trust.

50   ['Good Lord, Deliver us!']

             From being anxious, or secure,[1]
        Dead clods of sadness, or light squibs of mirth,
             From thinking that great courts immure
        All, or no happiness, or that this earth
                    Is only for our prison framed,
                    Or that thou art covetous
        To them whom thou lov'st, or that they are maimed
        From reaching this world's sweet who seek thee thus
        With all their might, good Lord, deliver us.

             From needing danger to be good,
        From owing thee yesterday's tears today,
             From trusting so much to thy blood
        That in that hope we wound our souls away,
                    From bribing thee with alms to excuse
                    Some sin more burdenous,
        From light affecting, in religion, news,[2]
        From thinking us all soul, neglecting thus
        Our mutual duties, Lord, deliver us.

[1] *secure*: careless [2] From being frivolously attracted by novelty in religion

From tempting Satan to tempt us
By our connivance or slack company,
From measuring ill by vicious,
Neglecting to choke sin's spawn, vanity,
From indiscreet humility,
Which might be scandalous
And cast reproach on Christianity,
From being spies, or to spies pervious,[1]
From thirst, or scorn of fame, deliver us. . . .

When senses, which thy soldiers are,
We arm against thee, and they fight for sin,
When want, sent but to tame, doth war
And work despair a breach to enter in,
When plenty, God's image and seal,
Makes us idolatrous,
And love it, not him, whom it should reveal,
When we are moved to seem religious
Only to vent wit, Lord deliver us.

51   Holy Sonnets

(i)

Thou hast made me, and shall thy work decay?
Repair me now, for now mine end doth haste;
I run to death, and death meets me as fast,
And all my pleasures are like yesterday.
I dare not move my dim eyes any way;
Despair behind, and death before doth cast
Such terror, and my feebled flesh doth waste
By sin in it, which it towards hell doth weigh.
Only thou art above, and when towards thee
By thy leave I can look, I rise again;
But our old subtle foe so tempteth me

[1] *pervious*: open to the influence (of spies)

That not one hour I can myself sustain.
Thy grace may wing me to prevent his art,
And[1] thou like adamant draw mine iron heart.

(ii)

At the round earth's imagined corners blow
Your trumpets, angels, and arise, arise
From death, you numberless infinities
Of souls, and to your scattered bodies go:
All whom the flood did, and fire shall o'erthrow,
All whom war, dearth, age, agues, tyrannies,
Despair, law, chance hath slain, and you whose eyes
Shall behold God and never taste death's woe.
But let them sleep, Lord, and me mourn a space,
For if above all these my sins abound,
'Tis late to ask abundance of thy grace
When we are there. Here on this lowly ground
Teach me how to repent; for that's as good
As if thou hadst sealed my pardon with thy blood.

(iii)

Death, be not proud, though some have callèd thee
Mighty and dreadful, for thou art not so;
For those whom thou thinkst thou dost overthrow
Die not, poor Death, nor yet canst thou kill me.
From rest and sleep, which but thy pictures be,
Much pleasure — then, from thee much more must flow;
And soonest our best men with thee do go,
Rest of their bones and soul's delivery.
Thou'rt slave to fate, chance, kings, and desperate men,
And dost with poison, war, and sickness dwell;
And poppy or charms can make us sleep as well,
And better than thy stroke. Why swellst thou then?
One short sleep past, we wake eternally,
And death shall be no more. Death, thou shalt die.

[1] *And*: if

(iv)

What if this present were the world's last night?
Mark in my heart, O soul, where thou dost dwell,
The picture of Christ crucified, and tell
Whether that countenance can thee affright.
Tears in his eyes quench the amazing light,
Blood fills his frowns, which from his pierced head fell;
And can that tongue adjudge thee unto hell,
Which prayed forgiveness for his foe's fierce spite?
No, no; but as in my idolatry
I said to all my profane mistresses,
Beauty of pity, foulness only is
A sign of rigour, so I say to thee:
To wicked spirits are horrid shapes assigned;
This beauteous form assures a piteous mind.

(v)

Batter my heart, three-personed God, for you
As yet but knock, breathe, shine, and seek to mend;
That I may rise and stand, o'erthrow me and bend
Your force to break, blow, burn, and make me new.
I, like an usurped town to another due,
Labour to admit you, but O, to no end.
Reason, your viceroy in me, me should defend,
But is captived and proves weak or untrue.
Yet dearly I love you and would be loved fain,
But am betrothed unto your enemy.
Divorce me, untie, or break that knot again,
Take me to you, imprison me, for I,
Except you enthrall me, never shall be free,
Nor ever chaste except you ravish me.

(vi)

O, to vex me contraries meet in one;
Inconstancy unnaturally hath begot

A constant habit, that when I would not
I change in vows and in devotion.
As humorous[1] is my contrition
As my profane love, and as soon forgot,
As riddlingly distempered, cold and hot;
As praying as mute; as infinite as none.
I durst not view heaven yesterday, and today
In prayers and flattering speeches I court God;
Tomorrow I quake with true fear of his rod.
So my devout fits come and go away
Like a fantastic ague, save that here
Those are my best days when I shake with fear.

52   [The Progress of the Soul]*

    Think then, my soul, that Death is but a groom
Which brings a taper to the outward room,
Whence thou spiest first a little glimmering light,
And after brings it nearer to thy sight;
For such approaches doth heaven make in death.
Think thyself labouring now with broken breath,
And think those broken and soft notes to be
Division and thy happiest harmony.
Think thee laid on thy deathbed, loose and slack,
And think that but unbinding of a pack
To take one precious thing, thy soul, from thence.
Think thyself parched with fever's violence;
Anger thine ague more by calling it
Thy physic; chide the slackness of the fit.
Think that thou hear'st thy knell, and think no more
But that as bells called thee to church before,
So this to the Triumphant Church calls thee.

[1] *humorous*: subject to humours or moods
* For note, see p. 348

Think Satan's sergeants round about thee be,
And think that but for legacies they thrust;
Give one thy pride, to another give thy lust;
Give them those sins which they gave thee before,
And trust the immaculate blood to wash thy score.
Think thy friends weeping round, and think that they
Weep but because they go not yet thy way.
Think that they close thine eyes, and think in this,
That they confess much in the world amiss,
Who dare not trust a dead man's eye with that
Which they from God and angels cover not.
Think that they shroud thee up, and think from thence
They reinvest thee in white innocence.
Think that thy body rots, and (if so low,
Thy soul exalted so, thy thoughts can go)
Think thee a prince, who of themselves create
Worms which insensibly devour their state.
Think that they bury thee, and think that rite
Lays thee to sleep but a Saint Lucy's night.[1]

*   *   *

Think further on thyself, my soul, and think
How thou at first wast made but in a sink;
Think that it argued some infirmity
That those two souls which then thou found'st in me
Thou fed'st upon and drew'st into thee, both
My second soul of sense and first of growth.[2]
Think but how poor thou wast, how obnoxious,[3]
Whom a small lump of flesh could poison thus.
This curded milk, this poor unlittered whelp
My body, could, beyond escape or help,
Infect thee with original sin, and thou
Couldst neither then refuse nor leave it now.

[1] *Saint Lucy's night*: the longest night of the year by the old calendar [2] The rational soul, infused by God into the body, absorbs the 'vegetable soul' (the power to grow and reproduce) and the 'sensitive soul' (the power to move and apprehend) [3] *obnoxious*: liable to harm

Think that no stubborn, sullen anchorite
Which, fixed to a pillar or a grave, doth sit
Bedded and bathed in all his ordures, dwells
So foully as our souls in their first-built cells.
Think in how poor a prison thou didst lie
After, enabled but to suck and cry.
Think, when 'twas grown to most, 'twas a poor inn,
A province packed up in two yards of skin,
And that usurped or threatened with the rage
Of sicknesses or their true mother, age.
But think that death hath now enfranchised thee;
Thou hast thy expansion now, and liberty.
Think that a rusty piece, discharged, is flown
In pieces, and the bullet is his own
And freely flies. This to thy soul allow:
Think thy shell broke, think thy soul hatched but now,
And think this slow-paced soul, which late did cleave
To a body, and went but by the body's leave,
Twenty, perchance, or thirty mile a day,
Dispatches in a minute all the way
'Twixt heaven and earth. She stays not in the air
To look what meteors there themselves prepare;
She carries no desire to know, nor sense,
Whether the air's middle region be intense;
For the element of fire, she doth not know
Whether she passed by such a place or no;
She baits not at the moon, nor cares to try
Whether in that new world men live and die.
Venus retards her not to inquire how she
Can, being one star, Hesper and Vesper be.
He that charmed Argus' eyes, sweet Mercury,
Works not on her, who now is grown all eye,
Who, if she meet the body of the sun,
Goes through, not staying till his course be run,
Who finds in Mars his camp no corps of guard,
Nor is by Jove nor by his father barred,
But ere she can consider how she went,

At once is at, and through the firmament.
And as these stars were but so many beads
Strung on one string, speed undistinguished leads
Her through those spheres as through the beads a string
Whose quick succession makes it still one thing.
As doth the pith, which, lest our bodies slack,
Strings fast the little bones of neck and back,
So by the soul doth death string heaven and earth,
For when our soul enjoys this her third birth
(Creation gave her one, a second, grace),
Heaven is as near and present to her face
As colours are, and objects, in a room
Where darkness was before, when tapers come.
This must, my soul, thy long-short progress be.

*   *   *

But 'twere but little to have changed our room
If, as we were in this our living tomb
Oppressed with ignorance, we still were so.
Poor soul, in this thy flesh what dost thou know?
Thou know'st thyself so little, as thou know'st not
How thou didst die nor how thou wast begot.
Thou neither know'st how thou at first cam'st in
Nor how thou took'st the poison of man's sin.
Nor dost thou (though thou know'st that thou art so)
By what way thou art made immortal know.
Thou art too narrow, wretch, to comprehend
Even thyself, yea, though thou wouldst but bend
To know thy body. Have not all souls thought
For many ages that our body's wrought
Of air and fire and other elements?
And now they think of new ingredients,
And one soul thinks one, and another way
Another thinks, and 'tis an even lay.
Know'st thou but how the stone doth enter in
The bladder's cave and never break the skin?
Know'st thou how blood which to the heart doth flow

Doth from one ventricle to the other go?
And for the putrid stuff which thou dost spit,
Know'st thou how thy lungs have attracted it?
There are no passages; so that there is
(For ought thou know'st) piercing of substances.
And of those many opinions which men raise
Of nails and hairs, dost thou know which to praise?
What hope have we to know ourselves, when we
Know not the least things which for our use be?
We see in authors, too stiff to recant,
An hundred controversies of an ant,
And yet one watches, starves, freezes, and sweats
To know but catechisms and alphabets
Of unconcerning things, matters of fact:
How others on our stage their parts did act,
What Caesar did, yea, and what Cicero said.
Why grass is green, or why our blood is red
Are mysteries which none have reached unto.
In this low form, poor soul, what wilt thou do?
When wilt thou shake off this pedantery
Of being taught by sense and fantasy?
Thou look'st through spectacles; small things seem great
Below; but up unto the watch-tower get,
And see all things despoiled of fallacies.
Thou shalt not peep through lattices of eyes,
Nor hear through labyrinths of ears, nor learn
By circuit or collections to discern.
In heaven thou straight know'st all concerning it,
And what concerns it not, shall straight forget. . . .

53   A Hymn to Christ
At the Author's Last Going into Germany
1619

In what torn ship soever I embark,
That ship shall be my emblem of thy Ark;

What sea soever swallow me, that flood
Shall be to me an emblem of thy blood.
Though thou with clouds of anger do disguise
Thy face: yet through that mask I know those eyes,
　Which, though they turn away sometimes,
　They never will despise.

I sacrifice this island unto thee,
And all whom I loved there, and who loved me;
When I have put our seas 'twixt them and me,
Put thou thy sea betwixt my sins and thee.
As the tree's sap doth seek the root below
In winter, in my winter now I go
　Where none but thee, the eternal root
　Of true love, I may know.

Nor thou nor thy religion dost control[1]
The amorousness of an harmonious soul,
But thou wouldst have that love thyself. As thou
Art jealous, Lord, so I am jealous now.
Thou lov'st not, till from loving more thou free
My soul. Whoever gives, takes liberty.
　O, if thou car'st not whom I love,
　Alas, thou lov'st not me.

Seal then this bill of my divorce to all
On whom those fainter beams of love did fall;
Marry those loves which in youth scattered be
On Fame, Wit, Hopes (false mistresses), to thee.
Churches are best for prayer that have least light;
To see God only, I go out of sight,
　And to 'scape stormy days I choose
　An everlasting night.

[1] *control*: censure, or check

54   A Hymn to God the Father

Wilt thou forgive that sin where I begun,
　Which is my sin, though it were done before?
Wilt thou forgive those sins through which I run,
　And do them still, though still I do deplore?
　　When thou hast done, thou hast not done,
　　　For I have more.

Wilt thou forgive that sin by which I won
　Others to sin, and made my sin their door?
Wilt thou forgive that sin which I did shun
　A year or two, but wallowed in a score?
　　When thou hast done, thou hast not done,
　　　For I have more.

I have a sin of fear, that when I've spun
　My last thread, I shall perish on the shore;
Swear by thyself that at my death thy Sun
　Shall shine as it shines now, and heretofore;
　　And having done that, thou hast done,
　　　I have no more.

BEN JONSON
(1572–1637)

A Hymn to God the Father

Hear me, O God!
  A broken heart
  Is my best part:
Use still thy rod
  That I may prove
  Therein thy love.

If thou hadst not
  Been stern to me,
  But left me free,
I had forgot
  Myself and thee.

For sin's so sweet,
  As minds ill bent
  Rarely repent,
Until they meet
  Their punishment.

Who more can crave
  Than thou hast done,
  That gav'st a son
To free a slave,
  First made of nought,
  With all since bought?

Sin, Death, and Hell
  His glorious Name
  Quite overcame,
Yet I rebel,
  And slight the same.

But I'll come in,
    Before my loss
    Me farther toss,
As sure to win
    Under his cross.

PHINEAS FLETCHER
(1582–1650)

56   A Hymn

Drop, drop, slow tears
    and bathe those beauteous feet,
Which brought from heaven
    the news and Prince of peace:
Cease not, wet eyes,
    his mercies to entreat;
To cry for vengeance
    sin doth never cease:
In your deep floods
    drown all my faults and fears;
Nor let his eye
    see sin, but through my tears.

57   [The Divine Lover]

Me, Lord? Canst thou mispend
One word, misplace one look on me?
    Call'st me thy Love, thy Friend?
Can this poor soul the object be
Of these love-glances, those life-kindling eyes?
What? I the centre of thy arms' embraces?
    Of all thy labour I the prize?
Love never mocks, Truth never lies.
Oh how I quake: Hope fear, fear hope displaces:
I would, but cannot hope: such wondrous love amazes.

    See, I am black as night,
See, I am darkness: dark as hell.
    Lord, thou more fair than light;
Heaven's sun thy shadow: can suns dwell

With shades? 'twixt light and darkness what commerce?
True: thou art darkness, I thy Light: my ray
  Thy mists and hellish fogs shall pierce.
  With me, black soul, with me converse;
I make the foul December flowery May.
Turn thou thy night to me: I'll turn thy night to day.

    See, Lord, see, I am dead:
  Tombed in myself: myself my grave.
    A drudge: so born, so bred:
  Myself even to myself a slave.
Thou Freedom, Life: can Life and Liberty
Love bondage, death? *Thy Freedom I: I tied*
  To loose thy bonds: be bound to me:
  My yoke shall ease, my bonds shall free.
Dead soul, thy Spring of life, my dying side:
There die with me to live: to live in thee I died.

GILES FLETCHER
(1586–1623)

[He was made Man]

What hath man done that man shall not undo,
Since God to him is grown so near akin?
Did his foe slay him? He shall slay his foe.
Hath he lost all? He all again shall win.
Is sin his master? He shall master sin.
  Too hardy soul, with sin the field to try;
  The only way to conquer was to fly.
But thus long death hath lived, and now death's self shall die.

He is a path, if any be misled;
He is a robe, if any naked be;
If any chance to hunger, he is bread;
If any be a bondman, he is free;
If any be but weak, how strong is he!
  To dead men life he is, to sick men health;
  To blind men sight, and to the needy wealth,
A pleasure without loss, a treasure without stealth.

Who can forget, never to be forgot,
The time when all the world in slumber lies,
When, like the stars, the singing Angels shot
To earth, and heaven awakèd all his eyes
To see another Sun at midnight rise.
  On earth was never sight of pareil¹ fame:
  For God before man like himself did frame,
But God himself now like a mortal man became.

A child he was, and had not learnt to speak,
That with his word the world before did make;
His mother's arms him bore, he was so weak,

¹ *pareil*: equal

That with one hand the vaults of heaven could shake.
See how small room my infant Lord doth take,
 Whom all the world is not enough to hold.
 Who of his years or of his age hath told?
Never such age so young, never a child so old.

59   [Palm Sunday: Good Friday]

It was but now their sounding clamours sung,
'Blessed is he, that comes from the Most High',
And all the mountains with 'Hosanna' rung,
And now, 'Away with him, away', they cry,
And nothing can be heard but 'Crucify!'
 It was but now the crown itself they save,[1]
 And golden name of King unto him gave,
And now no King but only Caesar they will have.

It was but now they gathered blooming May,
And of his arms disrobed the branching tree,
To strew with boughs and blossoms all thy way,
And now, the branchless trunk a cross for thee,
And May, dismayed, thy coronet must be:
 It was but now they were so kind to throw
 Their own best garments where thy feet should go,
And now, thyself they strip, and bleeding wounds they show.

See where the author of all life is dying.
O fearful day! He dead, what hope of living?
See where the hopes of all our lives are buying.[2]
O cheerful day! They bought, what fear of grieving?
Love love for hate, and death for life is giving:
 Lo, how his arms are stretched abroad to grace thee,
 And, as they open stand, call to embrace thee.
Why stay'st thou then my soul; O fly, fly thither haste thee.

[1] *save*: keep for themselves (i.e. want a Jewish King)   [2] *are buying*: are being bought

[The Celestial City]

In midst of this City celestial
Where the eternal Temple should have rose,
Lightened the Idea Beatifical:
End and beginning of each thing that grows,
Whose self no end, nor yet beginning knows,
    That hath no eyes to see, nor ears to hear,
    Yet sees and hears, and is all-eye, all-ear,
That nowhere is contained, and yet is everywhere;

Changer of all things, yet immutable,
Before, and after all, the first, and last,
That moving all, is yet immoveable,
Great without quantity, in whose forecast,
Things past are present, things to come are past,
    Swift without motion, to whose open eye
    The hearts of wicked men unbreasted lie,
At once absent and present to them, far and nigh.

It is no flaming lustre made of light,
No sweet consent or well-timed harmony,
Ambrosia for to feast the appetite,
Or flowery odour mixed with spicery,
No soft embrace or pleasure bodily;
    And yet it is a kind of inward feast,
    A harmony that sounds within the breast,
An odour, light, embrace, in which the soul doth rest,

A heavenly feast no hunger can consume,
A light unseen, yet shines in every place,
A sound no time can steal, a sweet perfume
No winds can scatter, an entire embrace
That no satiety can e'er unlace.
    Ingraced into so high a favour there,
    The saints with their beau-peers whole worlds outwear,
And things unseen do see, and things unheard do hear.

ROBERT HERRICK
(1591–1674)

61   His Litany to the Holy Spirit

In the hour of my distress,
When temptations me oppress,
And when I my sins confess,
    Sweet Spirit comfort me!

When I lie within my bed,
Sick in heart and sick in head,
And with doubts discomforted,
    Sweet Spirit comfort me!

When the house doth sigh and weep,
And the world is drowned in sleep,
Yet mine eyes the watch do keep,
    Sweet Spirit comfort me!

When the artless Doctor sees
No one hope but of his fees,
And his skill runs on the lees,
    Sweet Spirit comfort me!

When his potion and his pill,
His, or none, or little skill,
Meet for nothing but to kill,
    Sweet Spirit comfort me!

When the passing-bell doth toll,
And the Furies in a shoal,
Come to fright a parting soul,
    Sweet Spirit comfort me!

When the tapers now burn blue,
And the comforters are few,

And that number more than true,
　　Sweet Spirit comfort me!

When the priest his last hath prayed,
And I nod to what is said,
'Cause my speech is now decayed,
　　Sweet Spirit comfort me!

When (God knows) I'm tossed about,
Either with despair or doubt,
Yet before the glass be out,
　　Sweet Spirit comfort me!

When the Tempter me pursu'th
With the sins of all my youth,
And half damns me with untruth,
　　Sweet Spirit comfort me!

When the flames and hellish cries
Fright mine ears and fright mine eyes,
And all terrors me surprise,
　　Sweet Spirit comfort me!

When the judgment is revealed,
And that opened which was sealed,
When to thee I have appealed,
　　Sweet Spirit comfort me!

62　　The White Island: Or the Place of the Blest

In this world (the Isle of Dreams)
While we sit by sorrow's streams,
Tears and terrors are our themes
　　　　　Reciting:

But when once from hence we fly,
More and more approaching nigh
Unto young Eternity
                Uniting:

In that whiter Island, where
Things are evermore sincere,
Candour here and lustre there
                Delighting:

There no monstrous fancies shall
Out of hell an horror call,
To create or cause at all
                Affrighting.

There in calm and cooling sleep
We our eyes shall never steep,
But eternal watch shall keep,
                Attending

Pleasures such as shall pursue
Me immortalized and you,
And fresh joys, as never to
                Have ending.

63   To Keep a True Lent

Is this a Fast, to keep
    The larder lean?
             And clean
From fat of veals and sheep?

Is it to quit the dish
    Of flesh, yet still
             To fill
The platter high with fish?

Is it to fast an hour,
　　Or ragg'd to go,
　　　　　Or show
A down-cast look and sour?

No: 'tis a Fast to dole
　　Thy sheaf of wheat
　　　　　And meat
Unto the hungry soul.

It is to fast from strife
　　And old debate,
　　　　　And hate;
To circumcise thy life.

To show a heart grief-rent;
　　To starve thy sin,
　　　　　Not bin;
And that's to keep thy Lent.

FRANCIS QUARLES
(1592–1644)

64   On Those that Deserve It[1]

O, when our clergy, at the dreadful Day,
Shall make their audit, when the Judge shall say
'Give your accounts. What have my lambs been fed?
Say, do they all stand sound? Is there none dead
By your defaults? Come, shepherds, bring them forth
That I may crown your labours in their worth.'
O, what an answer will be given by some!
'We have been silenced: Canons struck us dumb:
The great ones would not let us feed thy flock,
Unless we played the fools and wore a frock:
We were forbid unless we'ld yield to sign
And cross their brows – they say, a mark of thine.
To say the truth, great Judge, they were not fed,
Lord, here they be; but Lord, they be all dead.'
Ah, cruel shepherds! Could your conscience serve
Not to be fools, and yet to let them starve?
What if your fiery spirits had been bound
To antic habits, or your heads been crowned
With peacock's plumes; had ye been forced to feed
Your Saviour's dear-bought flock in a fool's weed?
He that was scorned, reviled, endured the curse
Of a base death in your behalf – nay worse,
Swallowed the cup of wrath charged up to th' brim –
Durst ye not stoop to play the fools for him?

---

[1] Many Puritan clergy preferred deprivation or suspension to obedience to the Canons of 1604 which enjoined the wearing of surplices and copes, and the use of the sign of the cross in baptism.

65   'Why dost thou shade thy lovely face?'

Wherefore hidest thou thy Face, and holdest me for thy enemy
(Job 13.24)

Why dost thou shade thy lovely face? O, why
Does that eclipsing hand so long deny
The sunshine of thy soul-enlivening eye?

Without that Light, what light remains in me?
Thou art my Life, my Way, my Light; in thee
I live, I move, and by thy beams I see.

Thou art my Life; if thou but turn away,
My life's a thousand deaths. Thou art my Way;
Without thee, Lord, I travel not but stray.

My Light thou art; without thy glorious sight
Mine eyes are darkened with perpetual night.
My God, thou art my Way, my Life, my Light.

Thou art my Way; I wander if thou fly:
Thou art my Light; if hid, how blind am I!
Thou art my Life; if thou withdraw, I die.

Mine eyes are blind and dark, I cannot see.
To whom, or whither, should my darkness flee
But to the Light? and who's that Light but thee?

My path is lost; my wandering steps do stray;
I cannot safely go, nor safely stay.
Whom should I seek but thee, my path, my Way?

O, I am dead: to whom shall I, poor I,
Repair? to whom shall my sad ashes fly
But Life? And where is life but in thine eye?

And yet thou turnst away thy face and fly'st me;
And yet I sue for grace and thou deny'st me;
Speak, art thou angry, Lord, or only try'st me?

Unscreen those heavenly lamps, or tell me why
Thou shad'st thy face. Perhaps, thou thinkest no eye
Can view those flames, and not drop down and die.

If that be all, shine forth and draw thee nigher;
Let me behold and die, for my desire
Is phoenix-like to perish in that fire.

Death-conquered Lazarus was redeemed by thee;
If I am dead, Lord, set death's prisoner free.
Am I more spent, or stink I worse than he?

If my puffed light be out, give leave to tine[1]
My flameless snuff at that bright Lamp of thine;
O what's thy Light the less for lighting mine?

If I have lost my path, great Shepherd, say,
Shall I still wander in a doubtful way?
Lord, shall a lamb of Israel's sheepfold stray?

Thou art the pilgrim's path, the blind man's Eye,
The dead man's Life; on thee my hopes rely.
If thou remove, I err, I grope, I die.

Disclose thy sunbeams; close thy wings and stay;
See, see, how I am blind, and dead, and stray,
O thou, that art my Light, my Life, my Way.

[1] *tine*: kindle

GEORGE HERBERT
(1593–1633)

66   Redemption

Having been tenant long to a rich Lord,
   Not thriving, I resolvèd to be bold,
   And make a suit unto him, to afford
A new small-rented lease, and cancel the old.
In heaven at his manor I him sought:
   They told me there that he was lately gone
   About some land, which he had dearly bought
Long since on earth, to take possession.
I straight returned, and knowing his great birth,
   Sought him accordingly in great resorts:
   In cities, theatres, gardens, parks, and courts.
At length I heard a ragged noise and mirth
   Of thieves and murderers: there I him espied,
   Who straight, *Your suit is granted*, said, and died.

67   Affliction

When first thou didst entice to thee my heart
               I thought the service brave:
So many joys I writ down for my part,
               Besides what I might have
Out of my stock of natural delights,
Augmented with thy gracious benefits.

I lookèd on thy furniture so fine,
               And made it fine to me:
Thy glorious household-stuff did me entwine
               And 'tice me unto thee.
Such stars I counted mine: both heaven and earth
Paid me my wages in a world of mirth.

What pleasures could I want, whose King I served,
                Where joys my fellows were?
Thus argued into hopes, my thoughts reserved
                No place for grief or fear.
Therefore my sudden soul caught at the place,
And made her youth and fierceness seek thy face.

At first thou gav'st me milk and sweetnesses;
                I had my wish and way:
My days were strewed with flowers and happiness;
                There was no month but May.
But with my years sorrow did twist and grow,
And made a party unawares for woe.

My flesh began[1] unto my soul in pain,
                'Sicknesses cleave my bones;
Consuming agues dwell in every vein,
                And tune my breath to groans.'
Sorrow was all my soul; I scarce believed,
Till grief did tell me roundly, that I lived.

When I got health, thou took'st away my life,
                And more, for my friends die:
My mirth and edge was lost; a blunted knife
                Was of more use than I.
Thus thin and lean, without a fence or friend,
I was blown through with every storm and wind.

Whereas my birth and spirit rather took
                The way that takes the town;
Thou didst betray me to a lingering book,
                And wrap me in a gown.
I was entangled in the world of strife,
Before I had the power to change my life.

---

[1] *began*: began to say

Yet, for I threatened oft the siege to raise,
                Not simpering all mine age,
Thou often didst with academic praise
                Melt and dissolve my rage.
I took thy sweetened pill, till I came where
I could not go away, nor persevere.

Yet lest perchance I should too happy be
                In my unhappiness,
Turning my purge to food, thou throwest me
                Into more sicknesses.
Thus doth thy power cross-bias me,[1] not making
Thine own gift good, yet me from my ways taking.

Now I am here, what thou wilt do with me
                None of my books will show:
I read, and sigh, and wish I were a tree;
                For sure then I should grow
To fruit or shade: at least some bird would trust
Her household to me, and I should be just.

Yet, though thou troublest me, I must be meek;
                In weakness must be stout.
Well, I will change the service, and go seek
                Some other master out.
Ah, my dear God! though I am clean forgot,
Let me not love thee, if I love thee not.

68   Prayer

Prayer, the Church's banquet, Angels' age,
    God's breath in man returning to his birth,
    The soul in paraphrase, heart in pilgrimage,

[1] *cross-bias me*: give me an inclination contrary to my own. The metaphor is from bowls

The Christian plummet, sounding heaven and earth;
Engine against the Almighty, sinner's tower,
   Reversèd thunder, Christ-side-piercing spear,
   The six-days' world transposing in an hour,
A kind of tune, which all things hear and fear;
Softness, and peace, and joy, and love, and bliss,
   Exalted manna, gladness of the best,
   Heaven in ordinary, man well drest,
The milky way, the bird of Paradise,
   Church-bells beyond the stars heard, the soul's blood,
   The land of spices; something understood.

69   The Temper

How should I praise thee, Lord! how should my rhymes
   Gladly engrave thy love in steel,
  If what my soul doth feel sometimes
   My soul might ever feel!

Although there were some forty heavens, or more,
   Sometimes I peer above them all;
  Sometimes I hardly reach a score,
   Sometimes to hell I fall.

O rack me not to such a vast extent;
   Those distances belong to thee:
  The world's too little for thy tent,
   A grave too big for me.

Wilt thou meet arms with man, that thou dost stretch
   A crumb of dust from heaven to hell?
  Will great God measure with a wretch?
   Shall he thy stature spell?

O let me, when thy roof my soul hath hid,
   O let me roost and nestle there;
    Then of a sinner thou art rid,
      And I of hope and fear.

Yet take thy way; for sure thy way is best:
   Stretch or contract me, thy poor debtor:
    This is but tuning of my breast,
      To make the music better.

Whether I fly with angels, fall with dust,
   Thy hands made both, and I am there:
   Thy power and love, my love and trust
    Make one place everywhere.

70   Denial

When my devotions could not pierce
          Thy silent ears;
Then was my heart broken, as was my verse;
   My breast was full of fears,
          And disorder.

My bent thoughts, like a brittle bow,
          Did fly asunder:
Each took his way; some would to pleasure go,
   Some to the wars and thunder
          Of alarms.

As good go anywhere, they say,
          As to benumb
Both knees and heart, in crying night and day,
   Come, come, my God, O come,
          But no hearing.

O that thou shouldst give dust a tongue
To cry to thee,
And then not hear it crying! all day long
My heart was in my knee,
But no hearing.

Therefore my soul lay out of sight,
Untuned, unstrung;
My feeble spirit, unable to look right,
Like a nipped blossom, hung
Discontented.

O cheer and tune my heartless breast,
Defer no time;
That so thy favours granting my request,
They and my mind may chime,
And mend my rhyme.

71   Dialogue

Sweetest Saviour, if my soul
Were but worth the having,
Quickly should I then control
Any thought of waving.
But when all my care and pains
Cannot give the name of gains
To thy wretch so full of stains,
What delight or hope remains?

What, Child, is the balance thine,
Thine the poise and measure?
If I say, Thou shalt be mine;
Finger not my treasure.
What the gains in having thee
Do amount to, only he,
Who for man was sold, can see;
That transferred the accounts to me.

But as I can see no merit,
 Leading to this favour,
So the way to fit me for it
 Is beyond my savour.[1]
As the reason then is thine,
So the way is none of mine;
I disclaim the whole design;
Sin disclaims and I resign.

That is all, if that I could
 Get without repining;
And my clay, my creature, would
 Follow my resigning:
That as I did freely part
With my glory and desert,
Left all joys to feel all smart —
 Ah! no more: thou break'st my heart.

72   The Collar

I struck the board, and cried, 'No more!
                I will abroad.
What? shall I ever sigh and pine?
My lines and life are free; free as the road,
 Loose as the wind, as large as store.
  Shall I be still in suit?
 Have I no harvest but a thorn
 To let me blood, and not restore
What I have lost with cordial fruit?
                Sure there was wine
Before my sighs did dry it: there was corn
 Before my tears did drown it.
 Is the year only lost to me?
 Have I no bays to crown it?

[1] *savour*: understanding

No flowers, no garlands gay? all blasted?
                    All wasted?
     Not so, my heart: but there is fruit,
                    And thou hast hands.
     Recover all thy sigh-blown age
On double pleasures; leave thy cold dispute
Of what is fit, and not. Forsake thy cage,
                    Thy rope of sands,
Which petty thoughts have made, and made to thee
     Good cable, to enforce and draw,
                    And be thy law,
     While thou didst wink and wouldst not see.
                    Away; take heed:
                    I will abroad.
Call in thy death's head there: tie up thy fears.
                    He that forbears
     To suit and serve his need,
                    Deserves his load.'
But as I raved and grew more fierce and wild
                    At every word,
     Methoughts I heard one calling, 'Child!'
     And I replied, 'My Lord'.

73   The Flower

     How fresh, O Lord, how sweet and clean
Are thy returns! even as the flowers in spring,
     To which, besides their own demean,[1]
The late-past frosts tributes of pleasure bring.
                    Grief melts away
                    Like snow in May,
     As if there were no such cold thing.

[1] *demean*: graceful bearing

Who would have thought my shrivelled heart
Could have recovered greenness? It was gone
   Quite underground; as flowers depart
To see their mother-root, when they have blown;
               Where they together
               All the hard weather,
   Dead to the world, keep house unknown.

These are thy wonders, Lord of power,
Killing and quickening, bringing down to hell
   And up to heaven in an hour;
Making a chiming of a passing-bell.[1]
               We say amiss,
               This or that is.[2]
   Thy word is all, if we could spell.

O that I once past changing were,
Fast in thy Paradise, where no flower can wither!
   Many a spring I shoot up fair,
Offering at heaven, growing and groaning thither:
               Nor doth my flower
               Want a spring shower,
   My sins and I joining together.

But while I grow in a straight line,
Still upwards bent, as if heaven were mine own,
   Thy anger comes and I decline:
What frost to that? what pole is not the zone,
               Where all things burn,
               When thou dost turn,
   And the least frown of thine is shown?

And now in age I bud again,
After so many deaths I live and write;

[1] *chiming-bell*: a bell that chimes pleasingly with others; *passing-bell*: a bell that tolls on a single tone [2] We say mistakenly that anything is in itself, and invariably: it is what it is by God's word.

I once more smell the dew and rain,
And relish versing: O my only light,
                 It cannot be
                 That I am he
On whom thy tempests fell all night.

These are thy wonders, Lord of love,
To make us see we are but flowers that glide;
  Which when we once can find and prove,
Thou hast a garden for us, where to bide.
                Who would be more,
                Swelling through store,
Forfeit their Paradise by their pride.

74   Bitter-Sweet

Ah my dear angry Lord,
Since thou dost love, yet strike;
Cast down, yet help afford;
Sure I will do the like.

I will complain, yet praise;
I will bewail, approve;
And all my sour-sweet days
I will lament, and love.

75   The Forerunners

The harbingers[1] are come. See, see their mark;
White is their colour, and behold my head.
But must they have my brain? Must they dispark

[1] Harbingers were sent ahead of a royal progress to purvey lodgings by chalking the doors.

Those sparkling notions, which therein were bred?
   Must dullness turn me to a clod?
Yet have they left me, *Thou art still my God*.

Good men ye be, to leave me my best room,
Even all my heart, and what is lodgèd there;
I pass not,[1] I, what of the rest become,
So *Thou art still my God* be out of fear.
   He will be pleasèd with that ditty;
And if I please him, I write fine and witty.

Farewell sweet phrases, lovely metaphors.
But will ye leave me thus? When ye before
Of stews and brothels only knew the doors,
Then did I wash you with my tears, and more,
   Brought you to Church well dressed and clad.
My God must have my best, even all I had.

Lovely enchanting language, sugar-cane,
Honey of roses, whither wilt thou fly?
Hath some fond lover 'ticed thee to thy bane?
And wilt thou leave the Church, and love a sty?
   Fie, thou wilt soil thy broidered coat,
And hurt thyself, and him that sings the note.

Let foolish lovers, if they will love dung,
With canvas, not with arras, clothe their shame:
Let folly speak in her own native tongue.
True beauty dwells on high: ours is a flame
   But borrowed thence to light us thither.
Beauty and beauteous words should go together.

Yet, if you go, I pass not; take your way.
For, *Thou art still my God*, is all that ye
Perhaps with more embellishment can say.
Go, birds of spring; let winter have his fee;

---

[1] *I pass not*: I care not

Let a bleak paleness chalk the door,
So all within be livelier than before.

76   Discipline

Throw away thy rod,
Throw away thy wrath:
        O my God,
Take the gentle path.

For my heart's desire
Unto thine is bent:
        I aspire
To a full consent.

Not a word or look
I affect to own,
        But by book,
And thy book alone.

Though I fail, I weep;
Though I halt in pace,
        Yet I creep
To the throne of grace.

Then let wrath remove;
Love will do the deed;
        For with love
Stony hearts will bleed.

Love is swift of foot,
Love's a man of war,
        And can shoot,
And can hit from far.

Who can 'scape his bow?
That which wrought on thee,
    Brought thee low,
Needs must work on me.

Throw away thy rod:
Though man frailties hath,
    Thou art God:
Throw away thy wrath.

77   Love

Love bade me welcome; yet my soul drew back,
    Guilty of dust and sin.
But quick-eyed Love, observing me grow slack
    From my first entrance in,
Drew nearer to me, sweetly questioning,
    If I lacked anything.

'A guest', I answered, 'worthy to be here.'
    Love said, 'You shall be he.'
'I, the unkind, ungrateful? Ah, my dear,
    I cannot look on thee.'
Love took my hand, and smiling did reply,
    'Who made the eyes but I?'

'Truth, Lord, but I have marred them; let my shame
    Go where it doth deserve.'
'And know you not', says Love, 'who bore the blame?'
    'My dear, then I will serve.'
'You must sit down', says Love, 'and taste my meat.'
    So I did sit and eat.

JOHN MILTON
(1608–1674)

78   Ode on the Morning of Christ's Nativity
Composed 1629

This is the month, and this the happy morn,
Wherein the Son of heaven's eternal King,
Of wedded Maid and Virgin Mother born,
Our great redemption from above did bring;
For so the holy sages[1] once did sing,
   That he our deadly forfeit should release,
And with his Father work us a perpetual peace.

That glorious form, that light unsufferable,
And that far-beaming blaze of majesty,
Wherewith he wont at heaven's high council-table
To sit the midst of Trinal Unity,
He laid aside; and here with us to be,
   Forsook the courts of everlasting day,
And chose with us a darksome house of mortal clay.

Say, Heavenly Muse, shall not thy sacred vein
Afford a present to the infant God?
Hast thou no verse, no hymn, or solemn strain,
To welcome him to this his new abode,
Now while the heaven, by the sun's team untrod,
   Hath took no print of the approaching light,
And all the spangled host keep watch in squadrons bright?

See how from far upon the eastern road
The star-led wizards[2] haste with odours sweet!
O run, prevent them with thy humble ode,
And lay it lowly at his blessed feet;

---

[1] *sages*: the prophets of the Old Testament   [2] *wizards*: the Magi, or three wise men

Have thou the honour first thy Lord to greet,
    And join thy voice unto the angel quire,
From out his secret altar touched with hallowed fire.

The Hymn

It was the winter wild
While the Heaven-born child
    All meanly wrapped in the rude manger lies;
Nature in awe to him
Had doffed her gaudy trim,
    With her great Master so to sympathize;
It was no season then for her
To wanton with the sun, her lusty paramour.

Only with speeches fair
She woos the gentle air
    To hide her guilty front with innocent snow,
And on her naked shame,
Pollute with sinful blame,
    The saintly veil of maiden white to throw,
Confounded that her Maker's eyes
Should look so near upon her foul deformities.

But he her fears to cease
Sent down the meek-eyed Peace;
    She, crowned with olive green, came softly sliding
Down through the turning sphere,
His ready harbinger,
    With turtle wing the amorous clouds dividing,
And waving wide her myrtle wand,
She strikes a universal peace through sea and land.

No war or battle's sound
Was heard the world around:
    The idle spear and shield were high uphung;

The hookèd[1] chariot stood
Unstained with hostile blood;
   The trumpet spake not to the armèd throng;
And kings sat still with awful eye,
As if they surely knew their sovran Lord was by.

But peaceful was the night
Wherein the Prince of Light
   His reign of peace upon the earth began:
The winds with wonder whist[2]
Smoothly the waters kissed,
   Whispering new joys to the mild ocean,
Who now hath quite forgot to rave,
While birds of calm sit brooding on the charmèd wave.[3]

The stars with deep amaze
Stand fixed in steadfast gaze,
   Bending one way their precious influence,
And will not take their flight
For all the morning light,
   Or Lucifer[4] that often warned them thence;
But in their glimmering orbs did glow,
Until their Lord himself bespake, and bid them go.

And though the shady gloom
Had given day her room,
   The sun himself withheld his wonted speed,
And hid his head for shame,
As his inferior flame
   The new-enlightened world no more should need;
He saw a greater Sun appear
Than his bright throne or burning axletree could bear.

---

[1] *hookèd*: with blades protruding from the wheels [2] *whist*: hushed [3] Halcyons were fabled to nest at the winter solstice (22 December) and bring fair weather and calm at sea [4] *Lucifer*: the morning-star, Venus

The shepherds on the lawn,
Or ere[1] the point of dawn,
    Sat simply chatting in a rustic row;
Full little thought they than[2]
That the mighty Pan
    Was kindly come to live with them below;
Perhaps their loves, or else their sheep,
Was all that did their silly[3] thoughts so busy keep.

When such music sweet
Their hearts and ears did greet,
    As never was by mortal finger strook,
Divinely warbled voice
Answering the stringèd noise,
    As all their souls in blissful rapture took;
The air such pleasure loth to lose,
With thousand echoes still prolongs each heavenly close.

Nature that heard such sound
Beneath the hollow round
    Of Cynthia's seat, the airy region thrilling,
Now was almost won
To think her part was done,
    And that her reign had here its last fulfilling;
She knew such harmony alone
Could hold all heaven and earth in happier union.

At last surrounds their sight
A globe of circular light,
    That with long beams the shamefaced Night arrayed;
The helmèd Cherubim
And swordèd Seraphim
    Are seen in glittering ranks with wings displayed,
Harping in loud and solemn quire
With unexpressive[4] notes to Heaven's new-born heir.

[1] *Or ere*: before [2] *than*: then [3] *silly*: simple, innocent [4] *unexpressive*: inexpressible

Such music (as 'tis said)
Before was never made,
  But when of old the sons of morning sung,
While the Creator great
His constellations set,
  And the well-balanced world on hinges hung,
And cast the dark foundations deep,
And bid the weltering waves their oozy channel keep.

Ring out, ye crystal spheres,
Once bless our human ears
  (If ye have power to touch our senses so),[1]
And let your silver chime
Move in melodious time,
  And let the bass of heaven's deep organ blow;
And with your ninefold harmony
Make up full consort to the angelic symphony.

For if such holy song
Enwrap our fancy long,
  Time will run back and fetch the age of gold,
And speckled Vanity
Will sicken soon and die,
  And leprous Sin will melt from earthly mould,
And hell itself will pass away,
And leave her dolorous mansions to the peering day.

Yea, Truth and Justice then
Will down return to men,
  Orbed in a rainbow; and, like glories wearing,
Mercy will sit between,
Throned in celestial sheen,
  With radiant feet the tissued clouds down steering;
And heaven as at some festival
Will open wide the gates of her high palace hall.

[1] The music made by the nine spheres as they moved was not audible to ears
of flesh but only to disembodied and sinless souls

But wisest Fate says no,
This must not yet be so;
   The Babe lies yet in smiling infancy,
That on the bitter cross
Must redeem our loss,
   So both himself and us to glorify;
Yet first, to those ychained in sleep,
The wakeful trump of doom must thunder through the deep,

With such a horrid clang
As on Mount Sinai rang
   While the red fire and smouldering clouds outbrake;[1]
The aged Earth, aghast
With terror of that blast,
   Shall from the surface to the centre shake,
When at the world's last session
The dreadful Judge in middle air shall spread his throne.

And then at last our bliss
Full and perfect is,
   But now begins; for from this happy day
The old Dragon[2] underground,
In straiter limits bound,
   Not half so far casts his usurpèd sway,
And wroth to see his kingdom fail,
Swinges the scaly horror of his folded tail.

The oracles are dumb,
No voice or hideous hum
   Runs through the archèd roof in words deceiving.
Apollo from his shrine
Can no more divine,
   With hollow shriek the steep of Delphos leaving.
No nightly trance or breathèd spell
Inspires the pale-eyed priest from the prophetic cell.

[1] When Moses received the Law: Exod. 19.16–18 [2] *old Dragon*: Satan: Rev. 12.9, 20.2

The lonely mountains o'er,
And the resounding shore,
   A voice of weeping heard, and loud lament;
From haunted spring and dale
Edged with poplar pale
   The parting Genius is with sighing sent;
With flower-inwoven tresses torn
The nymphs in twilight shade of tangled thickets mourn.

In consecrated earth,
And on the holy hearth,
   The Lars and Lemures[1] moan with midnight plaint;
In urns and altars round,
A drear and dying sound
   Affrights the flamens[2] at their service quaint;
And the chill marble seems to sweat,
While each peculiar power forgoes his wonted seat.

Peor and Baälim
Forsake their temples dim,
   With that twice-battered god of Palestine,
And moonèd Ashtaroth,
Heaven's queen and mother both,
   Now sits not girt with tapers' holy shine;
The Libyc Hammon shrinks his horn,
In vain the Tyrian maids their wounded Thammuz mourn.[3]

And sullen Moloch, fled,
Hath left in shadows dread
   His burning idol all of blackest hue;

[1] *Lares* were Roman tutelary gods of the home; *Lemures* spirits of the dead [2] *flamens*: priests [3] *Baälim* (plural) includes the many names under which the Phoenician sun-god *Baal* was worshipped, one being *Baal-Peor*, from his shrine on Mount Peor. *Dagon*, god of the Philistines, was twice overthrown by the Ark of the Lord: 1 Sam. 5.3-4. *Ashtaroth* (again plural) includes the many names of the female goddess of the Phoenicians, the Syrian Astarte. *Jupiter Ammon* was worshipped in Libya as a ram. *Thammuz*, the Phoenician counterpart of Adonis, slain by a boar, was mourned annually at Biblys, near Tyre.

In vain with cymbals' ring
They call the grisly king,
   In dismal dance about the furnace blue;
The brutish gods of Nile as fast,
Isis and Orus, and the dog Anubis haste.[1]

Nor is Osiris[2] seen
In Memphian grove or green,
   Trampling the unshowered grass with lowings loud;
Nor can he be at rest
Within his sacred chest,
   Naught but profoundest hell can be his shroud;
In vain with timbreled anthems dark
The sable-stolèd sorcerers bear his worshipped ark.

He feels from Judah's land
The dreaded Infant's hand,
   The rays of Bethlehem blind his dusky eyn;
Nor all the gods beside
Longer dare abide,
   Not Typhon[3] huge ending in snaky twine:
Our Babe, to show his Godhead true,
Can in his swaddling bands control the damnèd crew.

So when the sun in bed,
Curtained with cloudy red,
   Pillows his chin upon an orient wave,
The flocking shadows pale
Troop to the infernal jail;
   Each fettered ghost slips to his several grave,
And the yellow-skirted fays
Fly after the night-steeds, leaving their moon-loved maze.

[1] *Moloch*, god of the Ammonites, was worshipped as a brazen idol filled with fire; the cries of the idol's human victims were drowned by the priests' cymbals and trumpets. *Isis*, sister and wife of *Osiris*, was represented with cow's horns; *Horus*, her son, with a hawk's head; *Anubis*, son of *Osiris*, with a dog's or jackal's head [2] *Osiris*: chief of the Egyptian gods, worshipped as a bull. His image in a little wooden gilt casket was carried in procession [3] *Typhon*: Greek hundred-headed monster, a serpent from the waist down

But see, the Virgin blest
Hath laid her Babe to rest.
   Time is our tedious song should here have ending;
Heaven's youngest-teemèd[1] star
Hath fixed her polished car,
   Her sleeping Lord with handmaid lamp attending;
And all about the courtly stable
Bright-harnessed angels sit in order serviceable.

79   On Time

Fly, envious Time, till thou run out thy race,
Call on the lazy leaden-stepping hours,
Whose speed is but the heavy plummet's[2] pace;
And glut thyself with what thy womb devours,
Which is no more than what is false and vain,
And merely mortal dross;
So little is our loss,
So little is thy gain.
For when as each thing bad thou hast entombed,
And last of all thy greedy self consumed,
Then long Eternity shall greet our bliss
With an individual[3] kiss;
And joy shall overtake us as a flood,
When everything that is sincerely[4] good
And perfectly divine,
With Truth, and Peace, and Love shall ever shine
About the supreme throne
Of him, to whose happy-making sight alone
When once our heavenly-guided soul shall climb,
Then all this earthy grossness quit,

---

[1] *youngest-teemèd*: latest born [2] *plummet*: the lead weight that moves the works of a clock [3] *individual*: probably in its modern sense; but, perhaps, undivided, eternal [4] *sincerely*: entirely

Attired with stars, we shall for ever sit,
    Triumphing over Death, and Chance, and thee, O
    Time.

80   At a Solemn Music[1]

Blest pair of Sirens, pledges of heaven's joy,
Sphere-born harmonious sisters, Voice and Verse,
Wed your divine sounds, and mixed power employ
Dead things with inbreathed sense able to pierce,
And to our high-raised phantasy[2] present
That undisturbèd song of pure concent,[3]
Aye sung before the sapphire-coloured throne
To him that sits thereon,
With saintly shout and solemn jubilee,
Where the bright Seraphim in burning row
Their loud uplifted angel-trumpets blow,
And the Cherubic host in thousand quires
Touch their immortal harps of golden wires,
With those just spirits that wear victorious palms,
Hymns devout and holy psalms
Singing everlastingly;
That we on earth with undiscording voice
May rightly answer that melodious noise;
As once we did, till disproportioned sin
Jarred against Nature's chime, and with harsh din
Broke the fair music that all creatures made
To their great Lord, whose love their motion swayed
In perfect diapason, whilst they stood
In first obedience and their state of good.
O may we soon again renew that song,
And keep in tune with heaven, till God ere long
To his celestial consort us unite,
To live with him, and sing in endless morn of light.

[1]At a Concert of Sacred Music [2]*phantasy*: imagination [3]*concent*: harmony

81   [On His Blindness]

When I consider how my light is spent,
   Ere half my days, in this dark world and wide,
   And that one talent which is death to hide
   Lodged with me useless, though my soul more bent
To serve therewith my Maker, and present
   My true account, lest he returning chide,
   'Doth God exact day-labour, light denied?'
   I fondly ask. But Patience, to prevent
That murmur, soon replies: 'God doth not need
   Either man's work or his own gifts; who best
   Bear his mild yoke, they serve him best. His state
Is kingly: thousands at his bidding speed,
   And post o'er land and ocean without rest;
   They also serve who only stand and wait.'

82   [The Ways of God]

(i)

God of our fathers, what is man!
That thou towards him with hand so various —
Or might I say contrarious? —
Temper'st thy providence through his short course,
Not evenly, as thou rul'st
The angelic orders and inferior creatures mute,
Irrational and brute.
Nor do I name of men the common rout,
That wandering loose about
Grow up and perish as the summer fly,
Heads without name no more remembered;
But such as thou hast solemnly elected,

With gifts and graces eminently adorned
To some great work, thy glory,
And people's safety, which in part they effect;
Yet toward these thus dignified, thou oft
Amidst their height of noon
Changest thy countenance and thy hand, with no regard
Of highest favours past
From thee on them, or them to thee of service.
  Nor only dost degrade them, or remit
To life obscured, which were a fair dismission,
But throw'st them lower than thou didst exalt them high,
Unseemly falls in human eye,
Too grievous for the trespass or omission;
Oft leav'st them to the hostile sword
Of heathen and profane, their carcasses
To dogs and fowls a prey, or else captived,
Or to the unjust tribunals, under change of times,
And condemnation of the ingrateful multitude.
If these they 'scape, perhaps in poverty
With sickness and disease thou bow'st them down,
Painful diseases and deformed,
In crude old age;
Though not disordinate, yet causeless suffering
The punishment of dissolute days; in fine
Just or unjust alike seem miserable,
For oft alike, both come to evil end.

(ii)

Oh how comely it is and how reviving
To the spirits of just men long oppressed,
When God into the hands of their deliverer
Puts invincible might
To quell the mighty of the earth, the oppressor,
The brute and boisterous force of violent men,
Hardy and industrious to support
Tyrannic power, but raging to pursue
The righteous and all such as honour truth;

He all their ammunition
And feats of war defeats
With plain heroic magnitude of mind
And celestial vigour armed;
Their armouries and magazines contemns,
Renders them useless, while
With winged expedition
Swift as the lightning glance he executes
His errand on the wicked, who surprised
Lose their defence distracted and amazed.
   But patience is more oft the exercise
Of saints, the trial of their fortitude,
Making them each his own deliverer,
And victor over all
That tyranny or fortune can inflict;
Either of these is in thy lot,
Samson, with might endued
Above the sons of men; but sight bereaved
May chance to number thee with those
Whom patience finally must crown.

83

Hymn

Lord, when the wise men came from far,
Led to thy cradle by a star,
Then did the shepherds too rejoice,
Instructed by thy angel's voice.
Blest were the wise men in their skill,
And shepherds in their harmless will.

Wise men, in tracing Nature's laws,
Ascend unto the highest cause;
Shepherds with humble fearfulness
Walk safely, though their light be less.
Though wise men better know the way,
It seems no honest heart can stray.

There is no merit in the wise
But love, the shepherds' sacrifice.
Wise men, all ways of knowledge passed,
To the shepherds' wonder come at last.
To know can only wonder breed,
And not to know is wonder's seed.

A wise man at the altar bows,
And offers up his studied vows,
And is received. May not the tears,
Which spring too from a shepherd's fears,
And sighs upon his frailty spent,
Though not distinct, be eloquent?

'Tis true, the object sanctifies
All passions which within us rise,
But since no creature comprehends
The cause of causes, end of ends,

He who himself vouchsafes to know
Best pleases his creator so.

When then our sorrows we apply
To our own wants and poverty,
When we look up in all distress,
And our own misery confess,
Sending both thanks and prayers above,
Then, though we do not know, we love.

RICHARD CRASHAW
(1612–1649)

84

An Hymn of the Nativity, Sung as by
the Shepherds

Come, we shepherds, whose blest sight
 Hath met Love's noon in Nature's night,
Come lift we up our loftier song,
 And wake the sun that lies too long.

To all our world of well-stolen joy
 He slept, and dreamed of no such thing;
While we found out Heaven's fairer eye
 And kissed the cradle of our King.
Tell him he rises now too late
To show us ought worth looking at.

Tell him we now can show him more
 Than he e'er showed to mortal sight,
Than he himself e'er saw before,
 Which to be seen needs not his light.
Tell him, Tityrus, where thou'st been,
Tell him, Thyrsis, what thou'st seen.

Tityrus

Gloomy night embraced the place
 Where the noble Infant lay.
The Babe looked up and showed his face;
 In spite of darkness, it was day.
It was thy day, Sweet, and did rise
Not from the East, but from thine eyes.[1]

Thyrsis

Winter chid aloud, and sent
 The angry North to wage his wars

[1] The Chorus throughout repeats the last two lines of each stanza

The North forgot his fierce intent
   And left perfumes instead of scars.
By those sweet eyes' persuasive powers,
Where he meant frost, he scattered flowers.

Both

We saw thee in thy balmy nest,
   Young dawn of our eternal day!
We saw thine eyes break from their East
   And chase the trembling shades away.
We saw thee, and we blessed the sight;
We saw thee by thine own sweet light.

Tityrus

Poor world, said I, what wilt thou do
   To entertain this starry stranger?
Is this the best thou canst bestow,
   A cold, and not too cleanly manger?
Contend, ye powers of heaven and earth,
To fit a bed for this huge birth.

Thyrsis

Proud world, said I, cease your contest,
   And let the mighty Babe alone.
The phoenix builds the phoenix' nest,
   Love's architecture is his own.
The Babe whose birth embraves this morn
Made his own bed ere he was born.

Tityrus

I saw the curled drops, soft and slow,
   Come hovering o'er the place's head,
Offering their whitest sheets of snow,
   To furnish the fair infant's bed.
Forbear, said I, be not too bold;
Your fleece is white, but 'tis too cold.

Thyrsis

I saw the obsequious Seraphins
   Their rosy fleece of fire bestow,
For well they now can spare their wings,
   Since Heaven itself lies here below.
Well done, said I, but are you sure
Your down, so warm, will pass for pure?

Tityrus

No, no, your King's not yet to seek
   Where to repose his royal head;
See, see, how soon his new-bloomed cheek
   'Twixt mother's breasts is gone to bed!
Sweet choice, said we; no way but so,
Not to lie cold, yet sleep in snow.

Both

We saw thee in thy balmy nest,
   Bright dawn of our eternal day!
We saw thine eyes break from their East
   And chase the trembling shades away.
We saw thee and we blessed the sight;
We saw thee by thine own sweet light.

Full Chorus

Welcome, all wonders in one sight!
   Eternity shut in a span,
Summer in winter, day in night,
   Heaven in earth and God in Man;
Great little one! whose all embracing birth
Lifts earth to heaven, stoops heaven to earth.

Welcome! though not to gold nor silk,
   To more than Caesar's birthright is:

Two sister-seas of virgin-milk,
　　With many a rarely-tempered kiss
That breathes at once both Maid and Mother,
Warms in the one, cools in the other. . . .

Welcome! though not to those gay flies
　　Gilded in the beams of earthly kings,
Slippery souls in smiling eyes,
　　But to poor shepherds, home-spun things,
Whose wealth's their flock, whose wit to be
Well read in their simplicity.

Yet when young April's husband showers
　　Shall bless the fruitful Maia's bed,
We'll bring the first-born of her flowers
　　To kiss thy feet and crown thy head.
To thee, dread Lamb! whose love must keep
The shepherds more than they their sheep.

To thee, meek Majesty, soft King
　　Of simple graces and sweet loves,
Each of us his lamb will bring
　　Each his pair of silver doves;
Till burnt at last in fire of thy fair eyes,
Our selves become our own best sacrifice.

85　　　　A Hymn to the Name and Honour of
　　　　　　the Admirable Saint Teresa[1]

Love, thou art absolute, sole Lord
Of life and death. To prove the word,

---

[1] St. Teresa of Avila (1515–1582), foundress of the Order of Discalced (reformed) Carmelites, and mystic. Her childish attempt to court martyrdom by preaching to the Moors is recounted in her autobiography, as is the vision in which a seraph plunged a fiery dart into her heart.

We'll now appeal to none of all
Those thy old soldiers, great and tall,
Ripe men of martyrdom, that could reach down
With strong arms their triumphant crown:
Such as could with lusty breath
Speak loud into the face of death
Their great Lord's glorious name; to none
Of those whose spacious bosoms spread a throne
For Love at large to fill. Spare blood and sweat,
And see him take a private seat,
Making his mansion in the mild
And milky soul of a soft child.
Scarce hath she learnt to lisp the name
Of martyr, yet she thinks it shame
Life should so long play with that breath
Which spent can buy so brave a death.
She never undertook to know
What death with love should have to do;
Nor hath she e'er yet understood
Why to show love, she should shed blood.
Yet though she cannot tell you why,
She can love, and she can die.
Scarce hath she blood enough to make
A guilty sword blush for her sake;
Yet hath she a heart dare hope to prove
How much less strong is death than love.
Be love but there, let poor six years
Be posed with the maturest fears
Man trembles at, you straight shall find
Love knows no nonage, nor the mind.
'Tis love, not years nor limbs, that can
Make the martyr or the man.
Love touched her heart, and lo, it beats
High, and burns with such brave heats,
Such thirsts to die, as dares drink up
A thousand cold deaths in one cup.
Good reason! for she breathes all fire,

Her weak breast heaves with strong desire
Of what she may with fruitless wishes
Seek for amongst her mother's kisses.

Since 'tis not to be had at home,
She'll travel for a martyrdom.
No home for her confesses she,
But where she may a martyr be.
She'll to the Moors and trade with them
For this unvalued Diadem;
She'll offer them her dearest breath,
With Christ's name in't, in change for death.
She'll bargain with them, and will give
Them God, and teach them how to live
In him; or, if they this deny,
For him she'll teach them how to die.
So shall she leave amongst them sown
Her Lord's blood, or at least her own.
Farewell then, all the world adieu!
Teresa is no more for you.
Farewell all pleasures, sports, and joys,
Never till now esteemèd toys!
Farewell whatever dear may be,
Mother's arms or father's knee!
Farewell house, and farewell home!
She's for the Moors and martyrdom.

Sweet, not so fast! Lo, thy fair Spouse,
Whom thou seek'st with so swift vows,
Calls thee back, and bids thee come
To embrace a milder martyrdom.
Blest powers forbid thy tender life
Should bleed upon a barbarous knife,
Or some base hand have power to race[1]
The breast's soft cabinet, and uncase
A soul kept there so sweet. O, no!

[1] *race*: force open

Wise heaven will never have it so.
Thou art Love's victim, and must die
A death more mystical and high.
Into Love's arms thou shalt let fall
A still surviving funeral.
His is the dart must make the death
Whose stroke shall taste thy hallowed breath;
A dart thrice dipped in that rich flame
Which writes thy Spouse's radiant Name
Upon the roof of heaven, where ay
It shines, and with a sovereign ray
Beats bright upon the burning faces
Of souls, which in that Name's sweet graces
Find everlasting smiles. So rare,
So spiritual, pure, and fair,
Must be the immortal instrument
Upon whose choice point shall be sent
A life so loved. And that there be
Fit executioners for thee,
The fairest and first-born sons of fire,
Blest Seraphims, shall leave their quire,
And turn Love's soldiers, upon thee
To exercise their archery.

O how oft shalt thou complain
Of a sweet and subtle pain!
Of intolerable joys!
Of a death, in which who dies
Loves his death, and dies again,
And would forever so be slain;
And lives and dies, and knows not why
To live, but that he thus may never leave to die.
How kindly will thy gentle heart
Kiss the sweetly-killing dart,
And close in his embraces keep
Those delicious wounds that weep
Balsam to heal themselves with! Thus,

When these thy deaths so numerous
Shall all at last die into one,
And melt thy soul's sweet mansion;
Like a soft lump of incense, hasted
By too hot a fire, and wasted
Into perfuming clouds, so fast
Shalt thou exhale to heaven at last,
In a resolving sigh, and then,
O what? Ask not the tongues of men.
Angels cannot tell. Suffice
Thyself shall feel thine own full joys,
And hold them fast forever. There,
So soon as thou shalt first appear,
The Moon of maiden stars, thy white
Mistress, attended by such bright
Souls as thy shining self, shall come,
And in her first ranks make thee room;
Where 'mongst her snowy family
Immortal welcomes wait for thee.

   O what delight, when revealed Life shall
      stand
And teach thy lips heaven with his hand,
On which thou now may'st to thy wishes
Heap up thy consecrated kisses!
What joys shall seize thy soul, when she
Bending her blessed eyes on thee,
Those second smiles of heaven, shall dart
Her mild rays through thy melting heart!
Angels, thy old friends, there shall greet thee,
Glad at their own home now to meet thee.
All thy good works which went before,
And waited for thee at the door,
Shall own thee there, and all in one
Weave a constellation
Of crowns with which the King, thy Spouse,
Shall build up thy triumphant brows.

All thy old woes shall now smile on thee,
And thy pains sit bright upon thee;
All thy sorrows here shall shine,
And thy sufferings be divine.
Tears shall take comfort, and turn gems,
And wrongs repent to diadems.
Even thy deaths shall live, and new
Dress the soul that erst they slew.
Thy wounds shall blush to such bright scars
As keep account of the Lamb's wars.
Those rare works where thou shalt leave writ
Love's noble history, with wit
Taught thee by none but him, while here
They feed our souls, shall clothe thine there.
Each heavenly word, by whose hid flame
Our hard hearts shall strike fire, the same
Shall flourish on thy brows, and be
Both fire to us, and flame to thee;
Whose light shall live bright in thy face
By glory, in our hearts by grace.

Thou shalt look round about, and see
Thousands of crowned souls throng to be
Themselves thy crown; sons of thy vows,
The virgin-births, with which thy sovereign Spouse
Made fruitful thy fair soul. Go now,
And with them all about thee bow
To him. 'Put on', he'll say, 'put on,
My rosy Love, that thy rich zone,
Sparkling with the sacred flames
Of thousand souls, whose happy names
Heaven keeps upon thy score: thy bright
Life brought them first to kiss the light
That kindled them to stars; and so
Thou with the Lamb, thy Lord, shalt go;
And wheresoe'er he sets his white
Steps, walk with him those ways of light,

Which who in death would live to see
Must learn in life to die like thee.'

86   [The Flaming Heart: a Postscript][1]

. . . O thou undaunted daughter of desires!
By all thy dower of lights and fires;
By all the eagle in thee, all the dove;
By all thy lives and deaths of love;
By thy large draughts of intellectual day,
And by thy thirsts of love more large than they;
By all thy brim-filled bowls of fierce desire,
By thy last morning's draught of liquid fire;
By the full kingdom of that final kiss
That seized thy parting soul, and sealed thee his;
By all the heavens thou hast in him
(Fair sister of the Seraphim!);
By all of him we have in thee;
Leave nothing of myself in me.
Let me so read thy life that I
Unto all life of mine may die.

87   *Charitas Nimia*: or the Dear Bargain

Lord, what is man? why should he cost thee
    So dear? what had his ruin lost thee?
Lord, what is man, that thou hast over-bought
    So much a thing of naught?

Love is too kind, I see, and can
Make but a simple merchantman;

[1] 'Upon the Book and Picture of the seraphical Saint Teresa (as She is usually expressed with a Seraphim beside her).'

'Twas for such sorry merchandise
Bold painters have put out his eyes.
Alas, sweet Lord, what were't to thee,
If there were no such worms as we?
    Heaven ne'ertheless still heaven would be,
        Should mankind dwell
        In the deep hell,
    What have his woes to do with thee?
        Let him go weep
        O'er his own wounds;
        Seraphims will not sleep
Nor spheres let fall their faithful rounds;
    Still would the youthful spirits sing,
    And still thy spacious palace ring:
Still would those beauteous ministers of light
        Burn all as bright,
    And bow their flaming heads before thee;
Still Thrones and Dominations would adore thee;
Still would those ever-wakeful sons of fire
        Keep warm thy praise
        Both nights and days,
And teach thy loved name to their noble lyre.
    Let froward dust then do its kind,
And give itself for sport to the proud wind;
Why should a piece of peevish clay plead shares
In the Eternity of thy old cares?
Why should'st thou bow thy awful breast to see
What mine own madnesses have done with me?
    Should not the King still keep his throne
    Because some desperate fool's undone?
    Or will the world's illustrious eyes
    Weep for every worm that dies?
        Will the gallant sun
        E'er the less glorious run?
    Will he hang down his golden head
Or e'er the sooner seek his western bed,
        Because some foolish fly

Grows wanton and will die?
If I was lost in misery,
What was it to thy heaven and thee?
What was it to thy precious blood
If my foul heart called for a flood?
What if my faithless soul and I
 Would needs fall in
 With guilt and sin?
What did the Lamb that he should die?
What did the Lamb that he should need,
When the Wolf sins, himself to bleed?
 If my base lust
Bargained with death and well-beseeming dust,
 Why should the white
 Lamb's bosom write
 The purple name
 Of my sin's shame?
Why should his unstained breast make good
My blushes with his own heart-blood?

O, my Saviour, make me see
How dearly thou hast paid for me,
That lost again my life may prove
As then in death, so now in love.

A Letter to the Countess of Denbigh
88 against Irresolution and Delay in Matters of Religion

What heaven-besiegèd heart is this
Stands trembling at the gate of bliss:
Holds fast the door, yet dares not venture
Fairly to open and to enter?
Whose definition is a doubt
'Twixt life and death, 'twixt in and out.

Ah! linger not, loved soul: a slow
And late consent was a long No.
Who grants at last, a great while tried,
And did his best to have denied.

What magic bolts, what mystic bars
Maintain the will in these strange wars?
What fatal, yet fantastic bands
Keep the free heart from his own hands?
Say, lingering Fair, why comes the birth
Of your brave soul so slowly forth?
Plead your pretences (O, you strong
In weakness!), why you choose so long
In labour of yourself to lie,
Not daring quite to live nor die.
So when the year takes cold we see
Poor waters their own prisoners be;
Fettered and locked up fast they lie
In a cold self-captivity.
The astonished nymphs their flood's strange fate deplore,
To find themselves their own severer shore.
Love, that lends haste to heaviest things,
In you alone hath lost his wings.
Look round and read the world's wide face,
The field of Nature or of Grace;
Where can you fix, to find excuse
Or pattern for the pace you use?
Mark with what faith fruits answer flowers,
And know the call of heaven's kind showers:
Each mindful plant hastes to make good
The hope and promise of his bud.
Seed-time's not all: there should be harvest too.
Alas! and has the year no spring for you?
Both winds and waters urge their way
And murmur if they meet a stay.
Mark how the curled waves work and wind,
All hating to be left behind.

Each big with business thrusts the other
And seems to say, 'Make haste, my brother!'
The airy nation of neat doves,
That draw the chariot of chaste loves,
Chide your delay; yea, those dull things,
Whose ways have least to do with wings,
Make wings at least of their own weight,
And by their love control their fate.
So lumpish steel, untaught to move,
Learned first his lightness by his love.

    Whate'er Love's matter be, he moves
By the even wings of his own doves,
Lives by his own laws, and does hold
In grossest metals his own gold.

    All things swear friends to Fair and Good,
Yea, Suitors. Man alone is wooed,
Tediously wooed and hardly won;
Only not slow to be undone.
As if the bargain had been driven
So hardly betwixt earth and heaven;
Our God would thrive too fast, and be
Too much a gainer by't should we
Our purchased selves too soon bestow
On him who has not loved us so.
When love of us called him to see
If we'd vouchsafe his company,
He left his Father's court, and came,
Lightly as a lambent flame
Leaping upon the hills, to be
The humble King of you and me.
Nor can the cares of his whole crown,
When one poor sigh sends for him down,
Detain him, but he leaves behind
The late wings of the lazy wind,
Spurns the tame laws of Time and Place
And breaks through all ten heavens to our embrace.
    Yield to his siege, wise soul, and see

Your triumph in his victory.
Disband dull fears, give faith the day:
To save your life, kill your delay.
'Tis cowardice that keeps this field,
And want of courage not to yield.
    Yield then, O yield, that Love may win
The fort at last, and let Life in.
Yield quickly, lest perhaps you prove
Death's prey before the prize of Love.
This fort of your fair self, if 't be not won,
He is repulsed indeed, but you're undone.

ANDREW MARVELL
(1621-1678)

89   A Dialogue between
the Resolved Soul and Created Pleasure

Courage, my Soul, now learn to wield
The weight of thine immortal shield,
Close on thy head thy helmet bright,
Balance thy sword against the fight.
See where an army, strong as fair,
With silken banners spreads the air.
Now, if thou be'st that thing divine,
In this day's combat let it shine,
And shew that Nature wants an art
To conquer one resolvèd heart.

Pleasure

Welcome, the Creation's guest,
Lord of Earth and Heaven's heir.
Lay aside that warlike crest,
And of Nature's banquet share,
Where the souls of fruits and flowers
Stand prepared to heighten yours.

Soul

I sup above, and cannot stay
To bait¹ so long upon the way.

Pleasure

On these downy pillows lie,
Whose soft plumes will thither fly;
On these roses strewed so plain,
Lest one leaf thy side should strain.

¹ *bait*: stop for food on a journey

Soul

My gentler rest is on a thought,
Conscious of doing what I ought.

Pleasure

If thou be'st with perfumes pleased,
Such as oft the Gods appeased,
Thou in fragrant clouds shalt show,
Like another God below.

Soul

A soul that knows not to presume
Is Heaven's and its own perfume.

Pleasure

Everything does seem to vie
Which should first attract thine eye;
But since none deserves that grace,
In this crystal view *thy* face.

Soul

When the Creator's skill is prized,
The rest is all but earth disguised.

Pleasure

Hark, how music then prepares
For thy stay these charming airs,
Which the posting winds recall,
And suspend the rivers' fall.

Soul

Had I but any time to lose
On this I would it all dispose.

164

Cease, Tempter! None can chain a mind
Whom this sweet cordage[1] cannot bind.

Chorus

Earth cannot show so brave a sight
As when a single soul does fence
The batteries[2] of alluring sense,
And Heaven views it with delight.
    Then persevere: for still new charges sound,
    And if thou overcom'st, thou shalt be crowned.

Pleasure

All this fair, and soft, and sweet,
    Which scatteringly doth shine,
Shall within one Beauty meet,
    And she be only thine.

Soul

If things of sight such Heavens be,
What Heavens are those we cannot see?

Pleasure

Wheresoe'er thy foot shall go
    The minted gold shall lie;
Till thou purchase all below,
    And want new worlds to buy.

Soul

Were't not a price, who'ld value gold?
And that's worth nought that can be sold.

Pleasure

Wilt thou all the glory have
    That war or peace commend?

[1] *cordage*: the original spelling *chordage* brings out the pun [2] *fence the batteries*: ward off the attacks

Half the world shall be thy slave
The other half thy friend.

Soul

What friends, if to myself untrue?
What slaves, unless I captive you?

Pleasure

Thou shalt know each hidden cause,
And see the future time:
Try what depth the centre[1] draws
And then to Heaven climb.

Soul

None thither mounts by the degree
Of knowledge, but humility.

Chorus

Triumph, triumph, victorious soul!
The world has not one pleasure more;
The rest does lie beyond the Pole
And is thine everlasting store.

90   On a Drop of Dew

See how the orient dew,
Shed from the bosom of the morn,
    Into the blowing roses,
Yet careless of its mansion new,
For[2] the clear region where 'twas born,
    Round in itself encloses;
    And in its little globe's extent,

---

[1] *the centre*: the centre of the earth which exerts attraction [2] *For*: because of

Frames as it can its native element.
   How it the purple flower does slight,
      Scarce touching where it lies,
   But gazing back upon the skies,
      Shines with a mournful light,
        Like its own tear,
Because so long divided from the sphere.
   Restless it rolls and unsecure,
      Trembling lest it grow impure;
   Till the warm sun pity its pain,
And to the skies exhale it back again.
   So the soul, that drop, that ray
Of the clear Fountain of Eternal Day,
Could it within the human flower be seen,
   Remembering still its former height,
   Shuns the sweet leaves and blossoms green,
   And, recollecting its own Light,
Does, in its pure and circling thoughts, express
The greater Heaven in an heaven less.
   In how coy a figure wound,
   Every way it turns away;
   So the world excluding round,
   Yet receiving in the Day.
   Dark beneath, but bright above;
   Here disdaining, there in love.
   How loose and easy hence to go;
   How girt and ready to ascend.
   Moving but on a point below,
   It all about does upwards bend.
Such did the Manna's[1] sacred dew distill,
White and entire, though congealed and chill.
Congealed on earth; but does dissolving run
Into the glories of the Almighty sun.

---

[1] 'And when the dew that lay was gone up, behold, upon the face of the wilderness there lay a small round thing, as small as the hoar-frost on the ground. . . . And when the sun waxed hot it melted' (Exodus xvi)

91   The Coronet

When for the thorns with which I long, too long,
    With many a piercing wound,
    My Saviour's head have crowned,
I seek with garlands to redress that wrong,
    Through every garden, every mead,
I gather flowers (my fruits are only flowers)
    Dismantling all the fragrant towers[1]
That once adorned my Shepherdess's head.
And now when I have summed up all my store,
    Thinking (so I myself deceive)
    So rich a chaplet thence to weave
As never yet the King of Glory wore,
    Alas, I find the Serpent old
    That, twining in his speckled breast,
    About the flowers disguised does fold,
    With wreaths of fame and interest.
Ah, foolish Man, that would'st debase with them,
And mortal glory, Heaven's diadem!
But thou who only could'st the Serpent tame,
Either his slippery knots at once untie,
And disentangle all his winding snare,
Or shatter too with him my curious[2] frame;
And let these wither, so that he may die,
Though set with skill and chosen out with care.
That they, while Thou on both their spoils dost tread,
May crown thy feet, that could not crown thy head.

92   Bermudas

        Where the remote Bermudas ride
        In the ocean's bosom unespied,
        From a small boat, that rowed along,
        The listening winds received this song.

[1] *towers*: high head-dresses worn by women [2] *curious*: elaborately wrought
                            168

'What should we do but sing his praise
That led us through the watery maze,
Unto an isle so long unknown,
And yet far kinder than our own?
Where he the huge sea-monsters wracks,
That lift the deep upon their backs.
He lands us on a grassy stage,
Safe from the storm's and prelates' rage.
He gave us this eternal spring,
Which here enamels everything;
And sends the fowls to us in care,
On daily visits through the air.
He hangs in shades the orange bright,
Like golden lamps in a green night,
And does in the pomegranates close
Jewels more rich than Ormus shows.
He makes the figs our mouths to meet,
And throws the melons at our feet;
But apples[1] plants of such a price
No tree could ever bear them twice.
With cedars, chosen by his hand,
From Lebanon, he stores the land;
And makes the hollow seas that roar
Proclaim the ambergris on shore.
He cast (of which we rather boast)
The Gospel's pearl upon our coast,
And in these rocks for us did frame
A temple, where to sound his Name.
Oh let our voice his praise exalt,
Till it arrive at heaven's vault,
Which thence, perhaps, rebounding may
Echo beyond the Mexique Bay.'
    Thus sung they in the English boat,
An holy and a cheerful note,
And all the way, to guide their chime,
With falling oars they kept the time.

[1] *apples*: pineapples, propagated by planting suckers from the original plant

HENRY VAUGHAN
(1622–1695)

Religion

My God, when I walk in those groves
And leaves thy spirit doth still fan,
I see in each shade that there grows
An angel talking with a man.

Under a juniper some house,
Or the cool myrtle's canopy,
Others beneath an oak's green boughs,
Or at some fountain's bubbling eye;

Here Jacob dreams and wrestles; there
Elias by a raven is fed,
Another time by the angel, where
He brings him water with his bread;

In Abraham's tent the wingèd guests
(O how familiar then was heaven!)
Eat, drink, discourse, sit down, and rest
Until the cool and shady even;

Nay, thou thyself, my God, in fire,
Whirlwinds, and clouds, and the soft voice
Speak'st there so much, that I admire[1]
We have no conference in these days.

Is the truce broke? or 'cause we have
A mediator now with thee,
Dost thou therefore old treaties waive
And by appeals from him decree?

[1] *admire*: am surprised

Or is't so, as some green heads say
That now all miracles must cease?
Though thou hast promised they should stay
The tokens of the Church, and peace.

No, no; religion is a spring
That from some secret, golden mine
Derives her birth, and thence doth bring
Cordials in every drop, and wine;

But in her long and hidden course
Passing through the earth's dark veins,
Grows still from better unto worse,
And both her taste and colour stains,

Then drilling on, learns to increase
False echoes, and confusèd sounds,
And unawares doth often seize
On veins of sulphur underground;

So poisoned, breaks forth in some clime,
And at first sight doth many please,
But drunk, is puddle, or mere slime
And 'stead of physic, a disease;

Just such a tainted sink we have
Like that Samaritan's dead well,
Nor must we for the kernel crave
Because most voices like the shell.

Heal then these waters, Lord; or bring thy flock,
Since these are troubled, to the springing rock,
Look down, great Master of the Feast; O shine,
And turn once more our water into wine!

94   The Morning-Watch

O Joys! Infinite sweetness! with what flowers,
And shoots of glory, my soul breaks, and buds!
                    All the long hours
                    Of night, and rest,
                    Through the still shrouds
                    Of sleep, and clouds,
                This dew fell on my breast;
                    O, how it bloods,
And spirits all my earth! Hark! in what rings,
And hymning circulations the quick world
                    Awakes, and sings;
                    The rising winds
                    And falling springs,
                    Birds, beasts, all things
                Adore him in their kinds.
                    Thus all is hurled
In sacred hymns and order, the great chime
And symphony of nature. Prayer is
                    The world in tune,
                    A spirit-voice,
                    And vocal joys
                Whose echo's heaven's bliss.
                    O, let me climb,
When I lie down. The pious soul by night
Is like a clouded star, whose beams, though said
                    To shed their light
                    Under some cloud,
                    Yet are above,
                    And shine and move
                Beyond that misty shroud.
                    So in my bed,
That curtained grave, though sleep, like ashes, hide
My lamp, and life, both shall in thee abide.

95   Peace

My soul, there is a country
   Far beyond the stars,
Where stands a wingèd sentry
   All skilful in the wars:
There above noise and danger
   Sweet Peace sits crowned with smiles,
And One born in a manger
   Commands the beauteous files.
He is thy gracious friend
   And—O my soul, awake!—
Did in pure love descend
   To die here for thy sake.
If thou canst get but thither,
   There grows the flower of Peace,
The Rose that cannot wither,
   Thy fortress, and thy ease.
Leave then thy foolish ranges,
   For none can thee secure,
But one who never changes,
   Thy God, thy life, thy cure.

96   The Dawning

Ah! what time wilt thou come? when shall that cry,
   'The Bridegroom's coming!' fill the sky?
  Shall it in the evening run
  When our words and works are done?
  Or will thy all-surprising light
    Break at midnight,
When either sleep, or some dark pleasure
Possesseth mad man without measure?

Or shall these early, fragrant hours
    Unlock thy bowers,
And with their blush of light descry
Thy locks crowned with eternity?
Indeed it is the only time
That with thy glory doth best chime:
All now are stirring, every field
    Full hymns doth yield,
The whole creation shakes off night,
And for thy shadow looks, the light;
Stars now vanish without number,
Sleepy planets set, and slumber,
The pursy clouds disband, and scatter,
All expect some sudden matter,
Not one beam triumphs, but from far
    That morning-star.

    O at what time soever thou,
Unknown to us, the heavens wilt bow,
And with thy angels in the van
Descend to judge poor careless man,
Grant, I may not like puddle lie
In a corrupt security,
Where, if a traveller water crave,
He finds it dead, and in a grave.
But as this restless vocal spring
All day and night doth run, and sing,
And though here born, yet is acquainted
Elsewhere, and flowing keeps untainted;
So let me all my busy age
In thy free services engage,
And though, while here, of force I must
Have commerce sometimes with poor dust,
And in my flesh, though vile, and low,
As this doth in her channel, flow,
Yet let my course, my aim, my love,
And chief acquaintance be above;

So when that day and hour shall come
In which thyself will be the sun,
Thou'lt find me dressed and on my way
Watching the break of thy great day.

97   The World

I saw Eternity the other night
Like a great Ring of pure and endless light,
    All calm, as it was bright;
And round beneath it, Time, in hours, days, years,
    Driven by the spheres
Like a vast shadow moved, in which the world
    And all her train were hurled.
The doting Lover in his quaintest strain
    Did there complain;
Near him, his lute, his fancy, and his flights,
    Wit's sour delights;
With gloves and knots, the silly snares of pleasure;
    Yet his dear treasure
All scattered lay, while he his eyes did pour
    Upon a flower.

The darksome Statesman hung with weights and woe,
Like a thick midnight fog, moved there so slow
    He did nor stay nor go;
Condemning thoughts, like sad eclipses, scowl
    Upon his soul,
And clouds of crying witnesses without
    Pursued him with one shout.
Yet digged the mole, and, lest his ways be found,
    Worked underground,
Where he did clutch his prey; but One did see
    That policy.
Churches and altars fed him, perjuries
    Were gnats and flies;
It rained about him blood and tears, but he
    Drank them as free.

The fearful Miser on a heap of rust
Sat pining all his life there, did scarce trust
   His own hands with the dust;
Yet would not place one piece above, but lives
   In fear of thieves.
Thousands there were as frantic as himself,
   And hugged each one his pelf.
The downright Epicure placed heaven in sense
   And scorned pretence;
While others, slipped into a wide excess,
   Said little less;
The weaker sort, slight, trivial wares enslave,
   Who think them brave;
And poor despisèd Truth sat counting by
   Their victory.

Yet some, who all this while did weep and sing,
And sing and weep, soared up into the Ring;
   But most would use no wing.
O fools (said I), thus to prefer dark night
   Before true light,
To live in grots, and caves, and hate the day
   Because it shows the way,
The way which from this dead and dark abode
   Leads up to God,
A way where you might tread the sun, and be
   More bright than he.
But as I did their madness so discuss,
   One whispered thus,
This Ring the Bridegroom did for none provide
   But for his Bride.

98   [Friends Departed]

They are all gone into the world of light!
And I alone sit lingering here;

Their very memory is fair and bright,
    And my sad thoughts doth clear.

It glows and glitters in my cloudy breast
    Like stars upon some gloomy grove,
Or those faint beams in which this hill is dressed,
    After the sun's remove.

I see them walking in an air of glory,
    Whose light doth trample on my days:
My days, which are at best but dull and hoary,
    Mere glimmering and decays.

O holy Hope! and high Humility,
    High as the heavens above!
These are your walks, and you have showed them me,
    To kindle my cold love.

Dear beauteous Death! the jewel of the Just,
    Shining nowhere but in the dark;
What mysteries do lie beyond thy dust,
    Could man outlook that mark!

He that hath found some fledged bird's nest may know,
    At first sight, if the bird be flown;
But what fair well or grove he sings in now,
    That is to him unknown.

And yet, as angels in some brighter dreams
    Call to the soul, when man doth sleep;
So some strange thoughts transcend our wonted themes,
    And into glory peep.

If a star were confined into a tomb
    Her captive flames must needs burn there;
But when the hand that locked her up gives room,
    She'll shine through all the sphere.

O Father of eternal life, and all
    Created glories under thee !
Resume thy spirit from this world of thrall
    Into true liberty.

Either disperse these mists, which blot and fill
    My perspective still as they pass,
Or else remove me hence unto that hill,
    Where I shall need no glass.

99   Night

    Through that pure Virgin-shrine,
That sacred veil drawn o'er thy glorious noon
That men might look and live, as glow-worms shine,
    And face the moon,
  Wise Nicodemus saw such light
  As made him know his God by night.

    Most blest believer he !
Who in that land of darkness and blind eyes
Thy long-expected healing wings could see,
    When thou didst rise,
  And what can never more be done,
  Did at midnight speak with the Sun !

    O who will tell me where
He found thee at that dead and silent hour !
What hallowed solitary ground did bear
    So rare a flower,
  Within whose sacred leaves did lie
  The fullness of the Deity.

No mercy-seat of gold,
No dead and dusty cherub, nor carved stone,
But his own living works did my Lord hold
    And lodge alone;
  Where trees and herbs did watch and peep
  And wonder, while the Jews did sleep.

    Dear night! this world's defeat;
The stop to busy fools; care's check and curb;
The day of spirits; my soul's calm retreat
    Which none disturb!
  Christ's progress, and his prayer time;
  The hours to which high Heaven doth chime.

    God's silent searching flight:
When my Lord's head is filled with dew, and all
His locks are wet with the clear drops of night;
    His still soft call;
  His knocking time; the soul's dumb watch,
  When spirits their fair kindred catch.

    Were all my loud, evil days
Calmed and unhaunted as is thy dark tent,
Whose peace but by some angel's wing or voice
    Is seldom rent,
  Then I in Heaven all the long year
  Would keep and never wander here.

    But living where the sun
Doth all things wake, and where all mix and tire
Themselves and others, I consent and run
    To every mire,
  And by this world's ill-guiding light
  Err more than I can do by night.

    There is in God, some say,
A deep, but dazzling darkness, as men here

Say it is late and dusky, because they
    See not all clear.
  O for that night! where I in him
  Might live invisible and dim.

100   The Waterfall

With what deep murmurs through time's silent stealth
Doth thy transparent, cool, and watery wealth
              Here flowing fall,
              And chide and call,
As if his liquid loose retinue stayed
Lingering, and were of this steep place afraid,
              The common pass
              Where, clear as glass,
              All must descend
              Not to an end;
But quickened by this deep and rocky grave,
Rise to a longer course more bright and brave.

    Dear stream, dear bank, where often I
    Have sat, and pleased my pensive eye,
    Why, since each drop of thy quick store
    Runs thither, whence it flowed before,
    Should poor souls fear a shade or night,
    Who came, sure, from a sea of light?
    Or since those drops are all sent back
    So sure to thee, that none doth lack,
    Why should frail flesh doubt any more
    That what God takes, he'll not restore?
    O useful Element and clear!
    My sacred wash and cleanser here,
    My first consigner unto those
    Fountains of life, where the Lamb goes,
    What sublime truths, and wholesome themes

Lodge in thy mystical, deep streams!
Such as dull man can never find,
Unless that Spirit lead his mind,
Which first upon thy face did move,
And hatched all with his quickening love.
As this loud brook's incessant fall
In streaming rings restagnates all,
Which reach by course the bank, and then
Are no more seen, just so pass men.
O my invisible estate,
My glorious liberty, still late!
Thou art the channel my soul seeks,
Not this with cataracts and creeks.

101   Quickness

False life! a foil and no more, when
                    Wilt thou be gone?
Thou foul deception of all men
That would not have the true come on.

Thou art a moon-like toil; a blind
                    Self-posing state;
A dark contest of waves and wind;
A mere tempestuous debate.

Life is a fixed, discerning light,
                    A knowing joy;
No chance, or fit; but ever bright,
And calm and full, yet doth not cloy.

'Tis such a blissful thing, that still
                    Doth vivify,
And shine and smile, and hath the skill
To please without Eternity.

Thou art a toilsome mole, or less,
    A moving mist;
But life is what none can express,
A quickness which my God hath kissed.

102   The Revival

Unfold, unfold! take in his light,
Who makes thy cares more short than night.
The joys, which with his day-star rise,
He deals to all but drowsy eyes;
And what the men of this world miss,
Some drops and dews of future bliss.
 Hark how his winds have changed their note,
And with warm whispers call thee out.
The frosts are past, the storms are gone;
And backward life at last comes on.
The lofty groves in express joys
Reply unto the Turtle's voice,
And here in dust and dirt, O here
The lilies of his love appear!

JOHN DRYDEN
(1631–1700)

[Reason and Religion]

Dim as the borrowed beams of moon and stars
To lonely, weary, wandering travellers,
Is Reason to the soul; and, as on high
Those rolling fires discover but the sky,
Not light us here, so Reason's glimmering ray
Was lent, not to assure our doubtful way,
But guide us upward to a better day.
And as those nightly tapers disappear,
When day's bright lord ascends our hemisphere,
So pale grows Reason at Religion's sight;
So dies, and so dissolves in supernatural light.
Some few, whose lamp shone brighter, have been led
From cause to cause, to nature's secret head;
And found that one first principle must be:
But what, or who, that UNIVERSAL HE;
Whether some soul encompassing this ball,
Unmade, unmoved; yet making, moving all;
Or various atoms' interfering dance
Leapt into form, the noble work of chance;
Or this great All was from eternity;
Not even the Stagirite[1] himself could see,
And Epicurus guessed as well as he:
As blindly groped they for a future state;
As rashly judged of providence and fate:
But least of all could their endeavours find
What most concerned the good of humankind;
For happiness was never to be found,
But vanished from them like enchanted ground.
One thought content the good to be enjoyed;
This every little accident destroyed:

[1] *the Stagirite*: Aristotle

The wiser madmen did for virtue toil,
A thorny, or at best, a barren soil;
In pleasure some their glutton souls would steep,
But found their line too short, the well too deep,
And leaky vessels which no bliss could keep.
Thus anxious thoughts in endless circles roll,
Without a centre where to fix the soul;
In this wild maze their vain endeavours end:
How can the less the greater comprehend?
Or finite reason reach Infinity?
For what could fathom God were more than he.

104   [Revelation]

What weight of ancient witness can prevail,
If private reason hold the public scale?
But, gracious God, how well dost thou provide
For erring judgements an unerring guide!
Thy throne is darkness in the abyss of light,
A blaze of glory that forbids the sight.
O teach me to believe thee thus concealed,
And search no farther than thyself revealed;
But her alone for my director take,
Whom thou hast promised never to forsake!
My thoughtless youth was winged with vain desires,
My manhood, long misled by wandering fires,
Followed false lights; and, when their glimpse was gone,
My pride struck out new sparkles of her own.
Such was I, such by nature still I am;
Be thine the glory, and be mine the shame.
Good life be now my task: my doubts are done;
(What more could fright my faith than Three in One?)
Can I believe eternal God could lie
Disguised in mortal mould and infancy?
That the great Maker of the world could die?

And after that trust my imperfect sense,
Which calls in question his omnipotence?
Can I my reason to my faith compel,
And shall my sight, and touch, and taste rebel?
Superior faculties are set aside;
Shall their subservient organs be my guide?
Then let the moon usurp the rule of day,
And winking tapers shew the sun his way;
For what my senses can themselves perceive,
I need no revelation to believe.
Can they who say the Host should be descried
By sense, define a body glorified,
Impassible, and penetrating parts?
Let them declare by what mysterious arts
He shot that body through the opposing might
Of bolts and bars impervious to the light,
And stood before his train confessed in open sight.

   For since thus wondrously he passed, 'tis plain,
One single place two bodies did contain;
And sure the same Omnipotence as well
Can make one body in more places dwell.
Let Reason then at her own quarry fly,
But how can finite grasp infinity?
   'Tis urged again that faith did first commence
By miracles, which are appeals to sense,
And thence concluded, that our sense must be
The motive still of credibility.
For latter ages must on former wait,
And what began belief must propagate.

   But winnow well this thought, and you shall find
'Tis light as chaff that flies before the wind.
Were all those wonders wrought by power divine
As means or ends of some more deep design?
Most sure as means, whose end was this alone,
To prove the Godhead of the eternal Son.
God thus asserted: man is to believe
Beyond what sense and reason can conceive,

And for mysterious things of faith rely
On the proponent, Heaven's authority.
If then our faith we for our guide admit,
Vain is the farther search of human wit;
As, when the building gains a surer stay,
We take the unuseful scaffolding away.
Reason by sense no more can understand;
The game is played into another hand.
Why choose we then like *bilanders*[1] to creep
Along the coast, and land in view to keep,
When safely we may launch into the deep?
In the same vessel which our Saviour bore,
Himself the pilot, let us leave the shore
And with a better guide a better world explore.
Could he his Godhead veil with flesh and blood,
And not veil these again to be our food?
His grace in both is equal in extent,
The first affords us life, the second nourishment.
And if he can, why all this frantic pain
To construe[2] what his clearest words contain,
And make a riddle what he made so plain?
To take up half on trust, and half to try,
Name it not faith, but bungling bigotry.
Both knave and fool the merchant we may call,
To pay great sums, and to compound the small:
For who would break[3] with Heaven, and would not break
    for all?
Rest, then, my soul, from endless anguish freed:
Nor sciences thy guide, nor sense thy creed.
Faith is the best ensurer of thy bliss;
The bank above must fail before the venture miss.

[1] *bilanders*: coasting vessels (Dutch)   [2] *construe*: pronounced *conster*   [3] *break*: go bankrupt

105

Veni Creator Spiritus

Creator Spirit, by whose aid
The world's foundations first were laid,
Come visit every pious mind;
Come pour thy joys on humankind;
From sin and sorrow set us free,
And make thy temples worthy thee.
  O source of uncreated light,
The Father's promised Paraclete!
Thrice holy fount, thrice holy fire,
Our hearts with heavenly love inspire;
Come, and thy sacred unction bring
To sanctify us while we sing!
  Plenteous of grace, descend from high,
Rich in thy sevenfold energy,
Thou strength of his almighty hand,
Whose power does heaven and earth command!
Proceeding Spirit, our defence,
Who dost the gift of tongues dispense,
And crownst thy gift with eloquence!
  Refine and purge our earthy parts;
But, O, inflame and fire our hearts!
Our frailties help, our vice control,
Submit the senses to the soul;
And when rebellious they are grown,
Then lay thy hand and hold them down.
  Chase from our minds the infernal foe,
And peace, the fruit of love, bestow;
And lest our feet should step astray,
Protect and guide us in the way.
  Make us eternal truths receive,
And practise all that we believe:
Give us thyself that we may see
The Father and the Son, by thee.

Immortal honour, endless fame,
Attend the Almighty Father's Name:
The Saviour Son be glorified,
Who for lost man's redemption died;
And equal adoration be,
Eternal Paraclete, to thee.

NATHANIEL WANLEY
(1634–1680)

The Invitation

Lord, what unvalued[1] pleasures crowned
    The times of old!
When thou wert so familiar found,
    Those days were gold.

When Abram wished, thou couldst afford
    With him to feast;
When Lot but said, 'Turn in, my Lord',
    Thou wert his guest.

But, ah, this heart of mine doth pant
    And beat for thee;
Yet thou art strange, and wilt not grant
    Thyself to me.

What, shall thy people be so dear
    To thee no more?
Or is not heaven to earth as near
    As heretofore?

The famished raven's hoarser cry
    Finds out thine ear;
My soul is famished, and I die
    Unless thou hear.

O thou great ALPHA, King of Kings,
    Or bow to me.
Or lend my soul seraphic wings
    To get to thee.

---

[1] *unvalued*: inestimable

THOMAS TRAHERNE
(1637–1674)

Wonder

How like an angel came I down!
　　How bright are all things here!
When first among his works I did appear,
　　Oh, how their Glory me did crown!
The world resembled his Eternity,
　　　　In which my soul did walk;
　　And every thing that I did see
　　　　Did with me talk.

The skies in their magnificence,
　　The lively, lovely air;
Oh, how divine, how soft, how sweet, how fair!
　　The stars did entertain my sense,
And all the works of God so bright and pure,
　　　　So rich and great did seem
　　As if they ever must endure
　　　　In my esteem.

A native health and innocence
　　Within my bones did grow,
And while my God did all his glories show,
　　I felt a vigour in my sense
That was all spirit. I within did flow
　　　　With seas of life, like wine;
　　I nothing in the world did know,
　　　　But 'twas divine.

Harsh, ragged objects were concealed,
　　Oppressions, tears, and cries,
Sins, griefs, complaints, dissentions, weeping eyes,
　　Were hid: and only things revealed
Which heavenly spirits and the angels prize.

The State of Innocence
And Bliss, not trades and poverties,
    Did fill my sense.

The streets were paved with golden stones,
    The boys and girls were mine;
Oh, how did all their lovely faces shine!
The Sons of Men were Holy Ones,
Joy, Beauty, Welfare did appear to me,
    And every thing which here I found,
While like an angel I did see,
    Adorned the ground.

Rich diamond, and pearl, and gold
    In every place was seen;
Rare splendours, yellow, blue, red, white, and green,
    Mine eyes did everywhere behold;
Great Wonders clothed with Glory did appear,
    Amazement was my Bliss.
    That and my wealth was everywhere:
        No Joy to this. . . .

108   Shadows in the Water

In unexperienced infancy
Many a sweet mistake doth lie–
Mistake, though false, intending true,
A seeming somewhat more than view–
    That doth instruct the mind
    In things that lie behind
And many secrets to us show
Which afterwards we come to know.

Thus did I by the water's brink
Another world beneath me think;

And while the lofty spacious skies
Reversèd there abused mine eyes,
   I fancied other feet
   Came mine to touch and meet;
As by some puddle I did play
Another world within it lay.

Beneath the water people drowned;
Yet with another heaven crowned,
In spacious regions seemed to go,
Freely moving to and fro.
   In bright and open space
   I saw their very face;
Eyes, hands, and feet they had like mine;
Another sun did with them shine.

'Twas strange that people there should walk,
And yet I could not hear them talk;
That through a little watery chink,
Which one dry ox or horse might drink,
   We other worlds should see,
   Yet not admitted be;
And other confines there behold
Of light and darkness, heat and cold.

I called them oft, but called in vain;
No speeches we could entertain;
Yet did I there expect to find
Some other world, to please my mind.
   I plainly saw by these
   A new Antipodes,
Whom, though they were so plainly seen,
A film kept off that stood between.

By walking men's reversèd feet
I chanced another world to meet;
Though it did not to view exceed

A phantasm, 'tis a world indeed,
  Where skies beneath us shine,
  And earth by art divine
Another face presents below,
Where people's feet against ours go.

Within the regions of the air,
Compassed about with heavens fair,
Great tracts of land there may be found
Enriched with fields and fertile ground;
  Where many numerous hosts
  In those far distant coasts,
For other great and glorious ends,
Inhabit, my yet unknown Friends.

Oh ye that stand upon the brink,
Whom I so near me, through the chink,
With wonder see, what faces there,
Whose feet, whose bodies, do ye wear?
  I my companions see
  In you, another me.
They seemèd others, but are we;
Our second selves those shadows be.

Look, how far off those lower skies
Extend themselves! Scarce with mine eyes
I can them reach. Oh ye my friends,
What Secret borders on those ends?
  Are lofty heavens hurled
  'Bout your inferior world?
Are ye the representatives
Of other people's distant lives?

Of all the playmates which I knew
That here I do the image view
In other selves, what can it mean?
But that below the purling stream

Some unknown Joys there be
Laid up in store for me;
To which I shall, when that thin skin
Is broken, be admitted in.

109   On News

News from a foreign country came,
As if my treasure and my wealth lay there:
So much it did my heart inflame,
'Twas wont to call my Soul into mine ear;
Which thither went to meet
The approaching Sweet,
And on the threshold stood,
To entertain the unknown Good.
It hovered there
As if 'twould leave mine ear,
And was so eager to embrace
The joyful tidings as they came,
'Twould almost leave its dwelling-place,
To entertain the same.

As if the tidings were the things,
My very Joys themselves, my foreign treasure,
Or else did bear them on their wings,
With so much joy they came, with so much pleasure.
My Soul stood at the gate
To recreate
Itself with Bliss, and to
Be pleased with speed. A fuller view
It fain would take,
Yet journeys back would make
Unto my heart; as if 'twould fain
Go out to meet, yet stay within
To fit a place, to entertain
And bring the tidings in.

What sacred instinct did inspire
My Soul in childhood with a hope so strong?
   What secret force moved my desire
To expect my Joys beyond the seas, so young?
      Felicity I knew
         Was out of view:
      And being here alone,
   I saw that happiness was gone,
      From me! For this,
      I thirsted absent Bliss,
   And thought that sure beyond the seas,
   Or else in something near at hand
   I knew not yet–since naught did please
      I knew–my Bliss did stand.

But little did the infant dream
That all the treasures of the world were by;
   And that himself was so the cream
And crown of all which round about did lie.
      Yet thus it was. The Gem,
         The Diadem,
      The Ring enclosing all
   That stood upon this earthy ball,
      The Heavenly Eye,
      Much wider than the sky,
   Wherein they all included were,
   The glorious Soul that was the King
Made to possess them, did appear
      A small and little thing.

JOSEPH ADDISON
(1672–1719)

110   Ode

The spacious firmament on high
With all the blue ethereal sky,
And spangled heavens, a shining frame,
Their great Original proclaim:
The unwearied sun, from day to day,
Does his Creator's power display,
And publishes to every land
The work of an almighty hand.

Soon as the evening shades prevail,
The moon takes up the wondrous tale,
And nightly to the listening earth
Repeats the story of her birth:
Whilst all the stars that round her burn,
And all the planets in their turn,
Confirm the tidings as they roll,
And spread the truth from pole to pole.

What though, in solemn silence, all
Move round the dark, terrestrial ball?
What though nor real voice nor sound
Amid their radiant orbs be found?
In reason's ear they all rejoice,
And utter forth a glorious voice,
For ever singing, as they shine,
'The hand that made us is divine'.

'When rising from the bed of death'

111   When rising from the bed of death,
              O'erwhelmed with guilt and fear,

I see my Maker face to face,
　O how shall I appear?

If yet, while pardon may be found,
　And mercy may be sought,
My heart with inward horror shrinks,
　And trembles at the thought;

When thou, O Lord, shalt stand disclosed
　In majesty severe,
And sit in judgement on my soul,
　O how shall I appear?

But thou hast told the troubled mind,
　Who does her sins lament,
The timely tribute of her tears
　Shall endless woe prevent.

Then see the sorrows of my heart
　Ere yet it be too late;
And hear my Saviour's dying groans,
　To give those sorrows weight.

For never shall my soul despair
　Her pardon to procure,
Who knows thine only Son has died
　To make her pardon sure.

ISAAC WATTS
(1674–1748)

112   'When I survey the wondrous Cross'

When I survey the wondrous Cross
On which the Prince of Glory died,
My richest gain I count but loss,
And pour contempt on all my pride.

Forbid it, Lord, that I should boast
Save in the death of Christ, my God;
All the vain things that charm me most,
I sacrifice them to his blood.

See from his head, his hands, his feet,
Sorrow and love flow mingled down;
Did e'er such love and sorrow meet?
Or thorns compose so rich a crown?

His dying crimson like a robe
Spreads o'er his body on the Tree,
Then am I dead to all the globe,
And all the globe is dead to me.

Were the whole realm of nature mine,
That were a present far too small;
Love so amazing, so divine,
Demands my soul, my life, my all.

113   'There is a land of pure delight'

There is a land of pure delight
 Where saints immortal reign;
Infinite day excludes the night,
 And pleasures banish pain.

There everlasting spring abides,
    And never-withering flowers:
Death like a narrow sea divides
    This heavenly land from ours.

Sweet fields beyond the swelling flood
    Stand dressed in living green:
So to the Jews old Canaan stood,
    While Jordan rolled between.

But timorous mortals start and shrink
    To cross this narrow sea,
And linger shivering on the brink
    And fear to launch away.

O could we make our doubts remove,
    These gloomy doubts that rise,
And see the Canaan that we love,
    With unbeclouded eyes.

Could we but climb where Moses stood,
    And view the landscape o'er,
Not Jordan's stream, nor Death's cold flood,
    Should fright us from the shore.

114   'Our God, our help in ages past'

        Our God, our help in ages past,
            Our hope for years to come,
        Our shelter from the stormy blast,
            And our eternal home.

        Under the shadow of thy throne
            Thy saints have dwelt secure;

Sufficient is thine arm alone,
   And our defence is sure.

Before the hills in order stood,
   Or earth received her frame,
From everlasting thou art God,
   To endless years the same.

Thy Word commands our flesh to dust,
   'Return, ye sons of men':
All nations rose from earth at first,
   And turn to earth again.

A thousand ages in thy sight
   Are like an evening gone;
Short as the watch that ends the night
   Before the rising sun.

The busy tribes of flesh and blood
   With all their lives and cares
Are carried downwards by thy flood
   And lost in following years.

Time like an ever-rolling stream
   Bears all its sons away;
They fly forgotten as a dream
   Dies at the opening day.

Like flowery fields the nations stand
   Pleased with the morning light;
The flowers beneath the mower's hand
   Lie withering ere 'tis night.

Our God, our help in ages past,
   Our hope for years to come,
Be thou our guard while troubles last,
   And our eternal home.

115   'Sweet Muse, descend'

Sweet Muse, descend and bless the shade,
    And bless the evening grove;
Business, and noise, and day are fled,
    And every care but love.

But hence, ye wanton young and fair,
    Mine is a purer flame;
No Phyllis shall infect the air,
    With her unhallowed name.

Jesus has all my powers possessed,
    My hopes, my fears, my joys:
He, the dear Sovereign of my breast,
    Shall still command my voice.

Some of the fairest choirs above
    Shall flock around my song,
With joy to hear the name they love
    Sound from a mortal tongue.

His charms shall make my numbers flow,
    And hold the falling floods,
While silence sits on every bough,
    And bends the listening woods.

I'll carve our passion on the bark,
    And every wounded tree
Shall drop and bear some mystic mark,
    That Jesus died for me.

The swains shall wonder when they read,
    Inscribed on all the grove,
That Heaven itself came down, and bled
    To win a mortal's love.

EDWARD YOUNG
(1683–1765)

116 [Lavinia at Church]

Lavinia is polite, but not profane;
To church as constant as to Drury Lane.
She decently, in form, pays heaven its due;
And makes a civil visit to her pew.
Her lifted fan, to give a solemn air,
Conceals her face, which passes for a prayer:
Curtsies to curtsies, then, with grace, succeed;
Not one the fair omits, but at the creed.
Or if she joins the service, 'tis to speak;
Through dreadful silence the pent heart might break;
Untaught to bear it, women talk away
To God himself, and fondly think they pray.
But sweet their accent, and their air refined;
For they're before their Maker–and mankind:
When ladies once are proud of praying well,
Satan himself will toll the parish bell.

ALEXANDER POPE
(1688-1744)

[A Sad Story]

Where London's column, pointing at the skies,
Like a tall bully, lifts the head and lies,[1]
There dwelt a citizen of sober fame,
A plain good man, and Balaam was his name;
Religious, punctual, frugal, and so forth;
His word would pass for more than he was worth.
One solid dish his week-day meal affords,
An added pudding solemnized the Lord's:
Constant at Church and Change; his gains were sure,
His givings rare, save farthings to the poor.

    The Devil was piqued such saintship to behold,
And longed to tempt him like good Job of old:
But Satan now is wiser than of yore,
And tempts by making rich, not making poor.

    Roused by the Prince of Air, the whirlwinds sweep
The surge and plunge his father in the deep;
Then full against his Cornish lands they roar,
And two rich ship-wrecks bless the lucky shore.

    Sir Balaam now, he lives like other folks,
He takes his chirping pint, and cracks his jokes·
'Live like yourself', was soon my Lady's word;
And lo! two puddings smoked upon the board.

    Asleep and naked as an Indian lay,
An honest factor stole a gem away:
He pledged it to the knight; the knight had wit,
So kept the diamond, but the rogue was bit.
Some scruple rose, but thus he eased his thought,
'I'll now give sixpence where I gave a groat,
Where once I went to church, I'll now go twice—
And am so clear too of all other vice.'

[1] The Monument ascribed the Great Fire of 1666 to the Papists

The Tempter saw his time; the work he plied;
Stocks and subscriptions pour on every side,
Till all the Demon makes his full descent
In one abundant shower of cent per cent,
Sinks deep within him, and possesses whole,
Then dubs Director, and secures his soul.

Behold Sir Balaam, now a man of spirit,
Ascribes his gettings to his parts and merit,
What late he called a blessing, now was wit,
And God's good Providence, a lucky hit.
Things change their titles, as our manners turn:
His counting-house employed the Sunday-morn:
Seldom at church ('twas such a busy life)
But duly sent his family and wife.
There (so the Devil ordained) one Christmas-tide
My good old Lady catched a cold, and died.

A Nymph of Quality admires our Knight;
He marries, bows at Court, and grows polite:
Leaves the dull City, and joins (to please the fair)
The well-bred cuckolds in St. James's air:
First, for his son, a gay commission buys,
Who drinks, whores, fights, and in a duel dies:
His daughter flaunts, a Viscount's tawdry wife;
She bears a coronet and pox for life.
In Britain's senate he a seat obtains,
And one more pensioner St. Stephen gains.
My Lady falls to play; so bad her chance,
He must repair it; takes a bribe from France;
The House impeach him; Coningsby harangues;
The Court forsake him, and Sir Balaam hangs:
Wife, son, and daughter, Satan, are thy own,
His wealth, yet dearer, forfeit to the Crown:
The Devil and the King divide the prize,
And sad Sir Balaam curses God and dies.

JOHN BYROM
(1692–1763)

118   'My spirit longeth for thee'

My spirit longeth for thee
   Within my troubled breast;
Although I be unworthy
   Of so divine a Guest.

Of so divine a Guest,
   Unworthy though I be;
Yet has my heart no rest,
   Unless it come from thee.

Unless it come from thee,
   In vain I look around;
In all that I can see,
   No rest is to be found.

No rest is to be found,
   But in thy blessed love;
O, let my wish be crowned,
   And send it from above.

119   A Hymn for Christmas Day

Christians awake, salute the happy morn
Whereon the Saviour of the world was born;
Rise, to adore the Mystery of Love,
Which hosts of angels chanted from above:
With them the joyful tidings first begun
Of God incarnate and the Virgin's Son.
Then to the watchful shepherds it was told,
Who heard the angelic herald's voice: 'Behold!
I bring good tidings of a Saviour's birth
To you, and all the nations upon earth;
This day hath God fulfilled his promised word;

This day is born a Saviour, Christ, the Lord:
In David's city, Shepherds, ye shall find
The long foretold Redeemer of mankind;
Wrapped up in swaddling clothes, the Babe divine
Lies in a manger; this shall be your sign.'
He spake, and straightway the celestial choir
In hymns of joy, unknown before, conspire:
The praises of redeeming Love they sung,
And Heaven's whole orb with Hallelujahs rung:
God's highest glory was their anthem still;
Peace upon earth, and mutual good will.
To Bethlehem straight the enlightened shepherds ran,
To see the wonder God had wrought for man;
And found, with Joseph and the blessed Maid,
Her Son, the Saviour, in a manger laid.
Amazed, the wondrous story they proclaim,
The first apostles of his infant fame.
While Mary keeps, and ponders in her heart
The heavenly vision, which the swains impart,
They to their flocks, still praising God, return,
And their glad hearts within their bosoms burn.
  Let us, like these good shepherds then, employ
Our grateful voices to proclaim the joy:
Like Mary, let us ponder in our mind
God's wondrous love in saving lost mankind.
Artless, and watchful, as these favoured swains,
While virgin meekness in the heart remains,
Trace we the Babe, who has retrieved our loss,
From his poor manger to his bitter cross;
Treading his steps, assisted by his grace,
Till man's first heavenly state again takes place:
Then may we hope, the angelic thrones among,
To sing, redeemed, a glad triumphal song.
He that was born, upon this joyful day,
Around us all his glory shall display;
Saved by his love, incessant we shall sing
Of angels, and of angel-men, the King.

CHARLES WESLEY
(1707–1788)

Wrestling Jacob

Come, O thou Traveller unknown,
    Whom still I hold, but cannot see,
My company before is gone,
    And I am left alone with thee,
With thee all night I mean to stay,
And wrestle till the break of day.

I need not tell thee who I am,
    My misery, or sin declare,
Thyself hast called me by my name,
    Look on thy hands, and read it there,
But who, I ask thee, who art thou?
Tell me thy name, and tell me now.

In vain thou strugglest to get free,
    I never will unloose my hold:
Art thou the Man that died for me?
    The secret of thy love unfold.
Wrestling I will not let thee go,
Till I thy name, thy nature know.

Wilt thou not yet to me reveal
    Thy new, unutterable name?
Tell me, I still beseech thee, tell;
    To know it now resolved I am.
Wrestling I will not let thee go,
Till I thy name, thy nature know.

'Tis all in vain to hold thy tongue,
    Or touch the hollow of my thigh:
Though every sinew be unstrung,
    Out of my arms thou shalt not fly.

Wrestling I will not let thee go,
Till I thy name, thy nature know.

What though my shrinking flesh complain,
   And murmur to contend so long,
I rise superior to my pain,
   When I am weak then I am strong,
And when my all of strength shall fail,
I shall with the God-Man prevail.

My strength is gone, my nature dies,
   I sink beneath thy weighty hand,
Faint to revive, and fall to rise;
   I fall, and yet by faith I stand,
I stand, and will not let thee go,
Till I thy name, thy nature know.

Yield to me now–for I am weak;
   But confident in self-despair:
Speak to my heart, in blessings speak,
   Be conquered by my instant prayer,
Speak, or thou never hence shalt move,
And tell me, if thy name is Love.

'Tis Love, 'tis Love! Thou diedst for me,
   I hear thy whisper in my heart.
The morning breaks, the shadows flee:
   Pure Universal Love thou art;
To me, to all, thy bowels move,
Thy nature and thy name is Love.

My prayer hath power with God; the Grace
   Unspeakable I now receive,
Through Faith I see thee face to face,
   I see thee face to face, and live:
In vain I have not wept, and strove,
Thy nature and thy name is Love.

I know thee, Saviour, who thou art,
   Jesus, the feeble sinner's friend;
Nor wilt thou with the night depart,
   But stay, and love me to the end;
Thy mercies never shall remove,
Thy nature and thy name is Love.

The Sun of Righteousness on me
   Hath rose with healing in his wings,
Withered my nature's strength; from thee
   My soul its life and succour brings,
My help is all laid up above;
Thy nature and thy name is Love.

Contented now upon my thigh
   I halt, till life's short journey end;
All helplessness, all weakness I,
   On thee alone for strength depend,
Nor have I power, from thee, to move;
Thy nature and thy name is Love.

Lame as I am, I take the prey,
   Hell, earth, and sin with ease o'ercome;
I leap for joy, pursue my way,
   And as a bounding hart fly home,
Through all eternity to prove
Thy nature and thy name is Love.

121   Free Grace

And can it be, that I should gain
   An interest in the Saviour's blood?
Died he for me, who caused his pain,
   For me, who him to death pursued?
Amazing Love! How can it be
That thou, my God, shouldst die for me?

'Tis Mystery all! the Immortal dies!
   Who can explore his strange design?
In vain the first-born seraph tries
   To sound the depths of Love divine.
'Tis Mercy all! Let earth adore;
Let angel minds enquire no more.

He left his Father's throne above,
   (So free, so infinite his Grace!)
Emptied himself of all but Love,
   And bled for Adam's helpless race:
'Tis Mercy all, immense and free!
For, O my God, it found out me!

Long my imprisoned spirit lay,
   Fast bound in sin and nature's night:
Thine eye diffused a quickening ray;
   I woke; the dungeon flamed with light;
My chains fell off, my heart was free,
I rose, went forth, and followed thee.

Still the small inward voice I hear
   That whispers all my sins forgiven;
Still the atoning blood is near
   That quenched the wrath of hostile heaven:
I feel the life his wounds impart;
I feel my Saviour in my heart.

No condemnation now I dread,
   Jesus, and all in him, is mine:
Alive in him, my living Head,
   And clothed in Righteousness divine,
Bold I approach the eternal throne,
And claim the crown, through Christ, my own.

122   Morning Hymn

Christ, whose glory fills the skies,
    Christ the true, the only Light,
Sun of Righteousness, arise,
    Triumph o'er the shades of night!
Day-spring from on high, be near!
Day-star, in my heart appear!

Dark and cheerless is the morn
    Unaccompanied by thee;
Joyless is the day's return,
    Till thy mercy's beams I see;
Till they inward light impart,
Glad my eyes, and warm my heart.

Visit then this soul of mine,
    Pierce the gloom of sin and grief!
Fill me, Radiancy Divine,
    Scatter all my unbelief!
More and more thyself display,
Shining to the perfect day.

SAMUEL JOHNSON
(1709–1784)

[Prayer]

Where then shall Hope and Fear their objects find?
Must dull suspense corrupt the stagnant mind?
Must helpless man, in ignorance sedate,
Roll darkling down the torrent of his fate?
Must no dislike alarm, no wishes rise,
No cries attempt the mercies of the skies?
Enquirer, cease, petitions yet remain,
Which Heaven may hear, nor deem Religion vain.
Still raise for good the supplicating voice,
But leave to Heaven the measure and the choice:
Safe in his power, whose eyes discern afar
The secret ambush of a specious prayer.
Implore his aid, in his decisions rest,
Secure, whate'er he gives, he gives the best.
Yet when the sense of sacred Presence fires,
And strong devotion to the skies aspires,
Pour forth thy fervours for a healthful mind,
Obedient passions, and a will resigned;
For love, which scarce collective man can fill;
For patience, sovereign o'er transmuted ill;
For faith, that panting for a happier seat,
Counts death kind Nature's signal of retreat.
These goods for man the laws of Heaven ordain,
These goods he grants, who grants the power to gain;
With these celestial Wisdom calms the mind,
And makes the happiness she does not find.

124   On the Death of Mr. Robert Levet
            A Practiser in Physic

Condemned to Hope's delusive mine,
    As on we toil from day to day,
By sudden blasts, or slow decline,
    Our social comforts drop away.

Well tried through many a varying year,
    See Levet to the grave descend;
Officious, innocent, sincere,
    Of every friendless name the friend.

Yet still he fills affection's eye,
    Obscurely wise, and coarsely kind;
Nor, lettered arrogance, deny
    Thy praise to merit unrefined.

When fainting nature called for aid,
    And hovering death prepared the blow,
His vigorous remedy displayed
    The power of art without the show.

In misery's darkest caverns known,
    His useful care was ever nigh,
Where hopeless anguish poured his groan,
    And lonely want retired to die.

No summons mocked by chill delay,
    No petty gain disdained by pride,
The modest wants of every day
    The toil of every day supplied.

His virtues walked their narrow round,
    Nor made a pause, nor left a void;

And sure the Eternal Master found
   The single talent well employed.

The busy day, the peaceful night,
   Unfelt, uncounted, glided by;
His frame was firm, his powers were bright,
   Though now his eightieth year was nigh.

Then with no fiery throbbing pain,
   No cold gradations of decay,
Death broke at once the vital chain,
   And freed his soul the nearest way.

CHRISTOPHER SMART*
(1722–1771)

A Song to David

O thou that sit'st upon a throne,
With harp of high majestic tone,
   To praise the Kings of Kings;
And voice of heaven-ascending swell,
Which, while its deeper notes excel,
   Clear as a clarion, rings:

To bless each valley, grove and coast,
And charm the cherubs to the post
   Of gratitude in throngs;
To keep the days on Zion's mount,
And send the year to his account,
   With dances and with songs:

O Servant of God's holiest charge,
The minister of praise at large,
   Which thou mayst now receive;
From thy blest mansion hail and hear,
From topmost eminence appear
   To this the wreath I weave. . . .

O DAVID, highest in the list
Of worthies, on God's ways insist,
   The genuine word repeat:
Vain are the documents of men,
And vain the flourish of the pen
   That keeps the fool's conceit.

PRAISE above all—for praise prevails;
Heap up the measure, load the scales,
   And good to goodness add:

* See note, p. 348

The generous soul her Saviour aids,
But peevish obloquy degrades;
　　The Lord is great and glad.

For ADORATION all the ranks
Of angels yield eternal thanks,
　　And DAVID in the midst;
With God's good poor, which, last and least
In man's esteem, thou to thy feast,
　　O blessed bride-groom, bidst.

For ADORATION seasons change,
And order, truth, and beauty range,
　　Adjust, attract, and fill:
The grass the polyanthus cheques;
And polished porphyry reflects,
　　By the descending rill.

Rich almonds colour to the prime
For ADORATION; tendrils climb,
　　And fruit-trees pledge their gems;
And Ivis[1] with her gorgeous vest
Builds for her eggs her cunning nest,
　　And bell-flowers bow their stems.

With vinous syrup cedars spout;
From rocks pure honey gushing out,
　　For ADORATION springs:
All scenes of painting crowd the map
Of nature; to the mermaid's pap
　　The scalèd infant clings.

The spotted ounce and playsome cubs
Run rustling 'mongst the flowering shrubs,
　　And lizards feed the moss;

[1] *Ivis*: the humming-bird

216

For ADORATION beasts embark,[1]
While waves upholding halcyon's ark
  No longer roar and toss.

While Israel sits beneath his fig,
With coral root and amber sprig
  The weaned adventurer sports;
Where to the palm the jasmin cleaves,
For ADORATION 'mongst the leaves
  The gale his peace reports.

Increasing days their reign exalt,
Nor in the pink and mottled vault
  The opposing spirits tilt;
And, by the coasting reader spied,
The silverlings and crusions glide
  For ADORATION gilt.

For ADORATION ripening canes
And cocoa's purest milk detains
  The western pilgrim's staff;
Where rain in clasping boughs inclosed,
And vines with oranges disposed,
  Embower the social laugh.

Now labour his reward receives,
For ADORATION counts his sheaves
  To peace, her bounteous prince;
The nectarine his strong tint imbibes,
And apples of ten thousand tribes,
  And quick peculiar quince.

The wealthy crops of whitening rice,
'Mongst thyine woods and groves of spice,
  For ADORATION grow;

[1] 'There is a large quadruped that preys upon fish, and provides himself with a species of timber for that purpose with which he is very handy' (Note in edition of 1765)

And, marshalled in the fencèd land,
The peaches and pomegranates stand,
  Where wild carnations blow.

The laurels with the winter strive;
The crocus burnishes alive
  Upon the snow-clad earth:
For ADORATION myrtles stay
To keep the garden from dismay,
  And bless the sight from dearth.

The pheasant shows his pompous neck;
And ermine, jealous of a speck,
  With fear eludes offence:
The sable, with his glossy pride,
For ADORATION is descried,
  Where frosts the wave condense.

The cheerful holly, pensive yew,
And holy thorn, their trim renew;
  The squirrel hoards his nuts:
All creatures batten o'er their stores,
And careful nature all her doors
  For ADORATION shuts.

For ADORATION, DAVID's psalms
Lift up the heart to deeds of alms;
  And he, who kneels and chants,
Prevails his passions to control,
Finds meat and medicine to the soul,
  Which for translation pants.

For ADORATION, beyond match,
The scholar bulfinch aims to catch
  The soft flute's ivory touch;
And, careless on the hazel spray,
The daring redbreast keeps at bay
  The damsel's greedy clutch.

For ADORATION, in the skies,
The Lord's philosopher espies
　　The Dog, the Ram, and Rose;
The planets ring, Orion's sword;
Nor is his greatness less adored
　　In the vile worm that glows.

For ADORATION, on the strings[1]
The western breezes work their wings,
　　The captive ear to sooth.
Hark! 'tis a voice–how still, and small–
That makes the cataracts to fall,
　　Or bids the sea be smooth.

For ADORATION, incense comes
From bezoar, and Arabian gums:
　　And from the civet's fur.
But as for prayer, or ere it faints,
Far better is the breath of saints
　　Than galbanum and myrrh.

For ADORATION, from the down
Of damsons to the anana's[2] crown,
　　God sends to tempt the taste;
And while the luscious zest invites,
The sense, that in the scene delights,
　　Commands desire be chaste.

For ADORATION, all the paths
Of grace are open, all the baths
　　Of purity refresh;
And all the rays of glory beam
To deck the man of God's esteem,
　　Who triumphs o'er the flesh.

---

[1] Æolian harp　[2] *anana*: pineapple

For ADORATION, in the dome
Of Christ the sparrows find an home;
   And on his olives perch:
The swallow also dwells with thee,
O man of God's humility,
   Within his Saviour's CHURCH.

Sweet is the dew that falls betimes,
And drops upon the leafy limes;
   Sweet Hermon's fragrant air:
Sweet is the lily's silver bell,
And sweet the wakeful tapers smell
   That watch for early prayer.

Sweet the young nurse with love intense,
Which smiles o'er sleeping innocence;
   Sweet when the lost arrive:
Sweet the musician's ardour beats,
While his vague mind's in quest of sweets,
   The choicest flowers to hive.

Sweeter in all the strains of love,
The language of thy turtle dove,
   Paired to thy swelling chord;
Sweeter with every grace endued,
The glory of thy gratitude,
   Respired unto the Lord.

Strong is the horse upon his speed;
Strong in pursuit the rapid glede,[1]
   Which makes at once his game:
Strong the tall ostrich on the ground;
Strong through the turbulent profound
   Shoots xiphias[2] to his aim.

---

[1] *glede*: kite   [2] *xiphias*: swordfish

220

Strong is the lion—like a coal
His eye-ball—like a bastion's mole
   His chest against the foes:
Strong the gier-eagle on his sail,
Strong against tide, the enormous whale
   Emerges as he goes.

But stronger still, in earth and air,
And in the sea, the man of prayer;
   And far beneath the tide;
And in the seat to faith assigned,
Where ask is have, where seek is find,
   Where knock is open wide.

Beauteous the fleet before the gale;
Beauteous the multitudes in mail,
   Ranked arms and crested heads:
Beauteous the garden's umbrage mild,
Walk, water, meditated wild,
   And all the bloomy beds.

Beauteous the moon full on the lawn;
And beauteous, when the veil's withdrawn,
   The virgin to her spouse:
Beauteous the temple decked and filled,
When to the heaven of heavens they build
   Their heart-directed vows.

Beauteous, yea, beauteous more than these,
The shepherd king upon his knees,
   For his momentous trust;
With wish of infinite conceit,
For man, beast, mute, the small and great,
   And prostrate dust to dust.

Precious the bounteous widow's mite;
And precious, for extreme delight,
   The largess from the churl:[1]
Precious the ruby's blushing blaze,
And alba's[2] blest imperial rays,
   And pure cerulean pearl.

Precious the penitential tear;
And precious is the sigh sincere,
   Acceptable to God:
And precious are the winning flowers,
In gladsome Israel's feast of bowers,
   Bound on the hallowed sod.

More precious that diviner part
Of David, even the Lord's own heart,
   Great, beautiful, and new:
In all things where it was intent,
In all extremes in each event,
   Proof–answering true to true.

Glorious the sun in mid career;
Glorious the assembled fires appear;
   Glorious the comet's train:
Glorious the trumpet and alarm;
Glorious the almighty stretched–out arm;
   Glorious the enraptured main:

Glorious the northern lights astream;
Glorious the song, when God's the theme
   Glorious the thunder's roar:
Glorious hosanna from the den;
Glorious the catholic amen;
   Glorious the martyr's gore:

[1] Abigail who brought largess to David, in place of her churlish husband
(1. Sam. 25) [2] *alba*: a white precious stone, usually taken as a pearl

Glorious—more glorious is the crown
Of Him that brought salvation down
    By meekness called thy Son;
Thou that stupendous truth believed,
And now the matchless deed's achieved,
    DETERMINED, DARED, and DONE.

126   The Nativity of Our Lord and Saviour
                            Jesus Christ

Where is this stupendous stranger?
    Swains of Solyma, advise,
Lead me to my Master's manger,
    Shew me where my Saviour lies.

O most Mighty! O most Holy!
    Far beyond the seraph's thought,
Art thou then so mean and lowly,
    As unheeded prophets taught?

O the magnitude of meekness!
    Worth from worth immortal sprung;
O the strength of infant weakness,
    If eternal is so young!

If so young and thus eternal,
    Michael tune the shepherd's reed,
Where the scenes are ever vernal,
    And the loves be love indeed!

See the God blasphemed and doubted
    In the schools of Greece and Rome,
See the powers of darkness routed,
    Taken at their utmost gloom.

Nature's decorations glisten
  Far above their usual trim;
Birds on box and laurels listen,
  As so near the cherubs hymn.

Boreas now no longer winters
  On the desolated coast;
Oaks no more are riven in splinters
  By the whirlwind and his host.

Spinks and ouzels sing sublimely
  'We too have a Saviour born';
Whiter blossoms burst untimely
  On the blest Mosaic thorn.

God all-bounteous, all creative,
  Whom no ills from good dissuade,
Is incarnate and a native
  Of the very world he made.

JOHN NEWTON
(1725–1807)

The Name of Jesus

How sweet the name of Jesus sounds
    In a believer's ear!
It soothes his sorrows, heals his wounds,
    And drives away his fear.

It makes the wounded spirit whole,
    And calms the troubled breast;
'Tis manna to the hungry soul,
    And to the weary rest.

Dear Name! the rock on which I build,
    My shield and hiding-place,
My never-failing treasury filled
    With boundless stores of grace.

By thee my prayers acceptance gain,
    Although with sin defiled;
Satan accuses me in vain,
    And I am owned a child.

Jesus! my Shepherd, Husband, Friend,
    My Prophet, Priest, and King;
My Lord, my Life, my Way, my End,
    Accept the praise I bring.

Weak is the effort of my heart
    And cold my warmest thought;
But, when I see thee as thou art,
    I'll praise thee as I ought.

Till then I would thy love proclaim
    With every fleeting breath;
And may the music of thy name
    Refresh my soul in death.

WILLIAM COWPER
(1731–1800)

128   Walking with God

Oh! for a closer walk with God,
    A calm and heavenly frame;
A light to shine upon the road
    That leads me to the Lamb!

Where is the blessedness I knew
    When first I saw the Lord?
Where is the soul-refreshing view
    Of Jesus and his word?

What peaceful hours I once enjoyed!
    How sweet their memory still!
But they have left an aching void,
    The world can never fill.

Return, O holy Dove, return,
    Sweet messenger of rest;
I hate the sins that made thee mourn,
    And drove thee from my breast.

The dearest idol I have known,
    Whate'er that idol be;
Help me to tear it from thy throne,
    And worship only thee.

So shall my walk be close with God,
    Calm and serene my frame;
So purer light shall mark the road
    That leads me to the Lamb.

129   Lovest Thou Me?

Hark, my soul! it is the Lord;
'Tis thy Saviour, hear his word;
Jesus speaks, and speaks to thee:
'Say, poor sinner, lov'st thou me?

I delivered thee when bound,
And, when wounded, healed thy wound;
Sought thee wandering, set thee right,
Turned thy darkness into light.

Can a woman's tender care
Cease towards the child she bare?
Yes, she may forgetful be,
Yet will I remember thee.

Mine is an unchanging love,
Higher than the heights above;
Deeper than the depths beneath,
Free and faithful, strong as death.

Thou shalt see my glory soon,
When the work of grace is done;
Partner of my throne shalt be;
Say, poor sinner, lov'st thou me?'

Lord, it is my chief complaint
That my love is weak and faint;
Yet I love thee and adore,
Oh for grace to love thee more!

130   Light Shining out of Darkness

God moves in a mysterious way
  His wonders to perform;

He plants his footsteps in the sea,
    And rides upon the storm.

Deep in unfathomable mines
    Of never-failing skill
He treasures up his bright designs,
    And works his sovereign will.

Ye fearful saints fresh courage take;
    The clouds ye so much dread
Are big with mercy, and shall break
    In blessings on your head.

Judge not the Lord by feeble sense,
    But trust him for his grace;
Behind a frowning providence
    He hides a smiling face.

His purposes will ripen fast
    Unfolding every hour;
The bud may have a bitter taste,
    But sweet will be the flower.

Blind unbelief is sure to err,
    And scan his work in vain;
God is his own interpreter,
    And he will make it plain.

WILLIAM BLAKE
(1757–1827)

131   The Divine Image

To Mercy, Pity, Peace, and Love
All pray in their distress;
And to these virtues of delight
Return their thankfulness.

For Mercy, Pity, Peace, and Love
Is God, our father dear,
And Mercy, Pity, Peace, and Love
Is Man, his child and care.

For Mercy has a human heart,
Pity a human face,
And Love, the human form divine,
And Peace, the human dress.

Then every man, of every clime,
That prays in his distress,
Prays to the human form divine,
Love, Mercy, Pity, Peace.

And all must love the human form,
In Heathen, Turk, or Jew;
Where Mercy, Love, and Pity dwell
There God is dwelling too.

132   Holy Thursday

'Twas on a Holy Thursday, their innocent faces clean,
The children walking two and two, in red and blue and green,

Grey-headed beadles walked before with wands as white as snow,
Till into the high dome of Paul's they like Thames' waters flow.

O what a multitude they seemed, these flowers of London town!
Seated in companies they sit with radiance all their own.
The hum of multitudes was there, but multitudes of lambs,
Thousands of little boys and girls raising their innocent hands.

Now like a mighty wind they raise to heaven the voice of song,
Or like harmonious thunderings the seats of Heaven among.
Beneath them sit the aged men, wise guardians of the poor;
Then cherish pity, lest you drive an angel from your door.

133   The Tyger

        Tyger! Tyger! burning bright
        In the forests of the night,
        What immortal hand or eye
        Could frame thy fearful symmetry?

        In what distant deeps or skies
        Burnt the fire of thine eyes?
        On what wings dare he aspire?
        What the hand dare seize the fire?

        And what shoulder, and what art,
        Could twist the sinews of thy heart?
        And when thy heart began to beat,
        What dread hand? and what dread feet?

        What the hammer? what the chain?
        In what furnace was thy brain?
        What the anvil? what dread grasp
        Dare its deadly terrors clasp?

When the stars threw down their spears,
And watered heaven with their tears,
Did he smile his work to see?
Did he who made the Lamb make thee?

Tyger! Tyger! burning bright
In the forests of the night,
What immortal hand or eye,
Dare frame thy fearful symmetry?

134   To Tirzah

Whate'er is born of mortal birth
Must be consumèd with the earth
To rise from generation free:
Then what have I to do with thee?

The sexes sprung from shame and pride,
Blowed in the morn; in evening died;
But mercy changed death into sleep;
The sexes rose to work and weep.

Thou, Mother of my mortal part,
With cruelty didst mould my heart,
And with false self-deceiving tears
Didst bind my nostrils, eyes, and ears:

Didst close my tongue in senseless clay,
And me to mortal life betray.
The death of Jesus set me free:
Then what have I to do with thee?

135   Eternity

> He who bends to himself a joy
> Does the wingèd life destroy;
> But he who kisses the joy as it flies
> Lives in eternity's sunrise.

136   'Mock on! Mock on!'

> Mock on, mock on, Voltaire, Rousseau:
> Mock on, mock on: 'tis all in vain!
> You throw the sand against the wind,
> And the wind blows it back again.
>
> And every sand becomes a gem
> Reflected in the beams divine;
> Blown back they blind the mocking eye,
> But still in Israel's paths they shine.
>
> The atoms of Democritus
> And Newton's particles of light
> Are sands upon the Red Sea shore,
> Where Israel's tents do shine so bright.

ROBERT BURNS
(1759–1796)

137

Holy Willie's Prayer

O thou that in the heavens does dwell!
Wha, as it pleases best thysel,
Sends ane to heaven and ten to hell,
              A' for thy glory!
And no for ony gude or ill
              They've done before thee.–

I bless and praise thy matchless might,
When thousands thou has left in night,
That I am here before thy sight,
              For gifts and grace,
A burning and a shining light
              To a' this place.–

What was I, or my generation,
That I should get such exaltation?
I, wha deserved most just damnation,
              For broken laws
Sax thousand years ere my creation,
              Thro' Adam's cause!

When from my mother's womb I fell,
Thou might hae plunged me deep in hell,
To gnash my gooms, and weep, and wail,
              In burning lakes,
Where damnèd devils roar and yell
              Chained to their stakes.–

Yet I am here, a chosen sample,
To shew thy grace is great and ample:
I'm here, a pillar o' thy temple
              Strong as a rock,

A guide, a ruler and example
        To a' thy flock.-

O Lord thou kens what zeal I bear,
When drinkers drink, and swearers swear,
And singin' there, and dancin' here,
        Wi' great an' sma';
For I am keepet by thy fear,
        Free frae them a'.-

But yet-O Lord-confess I must-
At times I'm fashed wi' fleshly lust;
And sometimes too, in warldly trust
        Vile Self gets in;
But thou remembers we are dust,
        Defiled wi' sin.-

O Lord-yestreen-thou kens-wi' Meg-
Thy pardon I sincerely beg!
O may't ne'er be a living plague,
        To my dishonor,
And I'll ne'er lift a lawless leg
        Again upon her.-

Besides, I farther maun avow,
Wi' Leezie's lass, three times-I trow-
But Lord, that Friday I was fou
        When I cam near her;
Or else, thou kens, thy servant true
        Wad never steer her.-

Maybe thou lets this fleshly thorn
Buffet thy servant e'en and morn,
Lest he o'er proud and high should turn,
        That he's sae gifted;
If sae, thy hand maun e'en be borne
        Untill thou lift it.-

Lord bless thy Chosen in this place,
For here thou has a chosen race:
But God, confound their stubborn face,
                    And blast their name,
Wha bring thy rulers to disgrace
                    And open shame.–

Lord mind Gaun Hamilton's deserts!
He drinks, and swears, and plays at cartes,
Yet has sae mony taking arts
                    Wi' Great and Sma',
Frae God's ain priest the people's hearts
                    He steals awa.–

And when we chastened him therefore,
Thou kens how he bred sic a splore,
And set the warld in a roar
                    O' laughin at us:
Curse thou his basket and his store,
                    Kail and potatoes.–

Lord hear my earnest cry and prayer
Against that Presbytry of Ayr!
Thy strong right hand, Lord, make it bare
                    Upon their heads!
Lord visit them, and dinna spare,
                    For their misdeeds!

O Lord my God, that glib-tongued Aiken!
My very heart and flesh are quaking
To think how I sat, sweating, shaking,
                    And pissed wi' dread,
While Auld wi' hingin lip gaed sneaking
                    And hid his head!

Lord, in thy day o' vengeance try him!
Lord visit him that did employ him!

And pass not in thy mercy by them,
    Nor hear their prayer;
But for thy people's sake destroy them,
    And dinna spare!

But Lord, remember me and mine
Wi' mercies temporal and divine!
That I for grace and gear may shine,
    Excelled by nane!
And a' the glory shall be thine!
    Amen! Amen!

WILLIAM WORDSWORTH
(1770–1850)

138

[Guilt]

One evening (surely I was led by her)
I went alone into a shepherd's boat,
A skiff that to a willow tree was tied
Within a rocky cave, its usual home.
'Twas by the shores of Patterdale, a vale
Wherein I was a stranger, thither come
A school-boy traveller, at the holidays.
Forth rambled from the village inn alone
No sooner had I sight of this small skiff,
Discovered thus by unexpected chance,
Than I unloosed her tether and embarked.
The moon was up, the lake was shining clear
Among the hoary mountains; from the shore
I pushed, and struck the oars and struck again
In cadence, and my little boat moved on
Even like a man who walks with stately step
Though bent on speed. It was an act of stealth
And troubled pleasure; not without the voice
Of mountain-echoes did my boat move on,
Leaving behind her still on either side
Small circles glittering idly in the moon,
Until they melted all into one track
Of sparkling light. A rocky steep uprose
Above the cavern of the willow tree
And now, as suited one who proudly rowed
With his best skill, I fixed a steady view
Upon the top of that same craggy ridge,
The bound of the horizon, for behind
Was nothing but the stars and the grey sky.
She was an elfin pinnace; lustily
I dipped my oars into the silent lake,
And, as I rose upon the stroke, my boat

Went heaving through the water, like a swan;
When from behind that craggy steep, till then
The bound of the horizon, a huge cliff,
As if with voluntary power instinct,
Upreared its head. I struck, and struck again,
And, growing still in stature, the huge cliff
Rose up between me and the stars, and still,
With measured motion, like a living thing,
Strode after me. With trembling hands I turned,
And through the silent water stole my way
Back to the cavern of the willow tree.
There, in her mooring-place, I left my bark,
And, through the meadows homeward went, with grave
And serious thoughts; and after I had seen
That spectacle, for many days my brain
Worked with a dim and undetermined sense
Of unknown modes of being; in my thoughts
There was a darkness, call it solitude,
Or blank desertion, no familiar shapes
Of hourly objects, images of trees,
Of sea or sky, no colours of green fields;
But huge and mighty Forms that do not live
Like living men moved slowly through my mind
By day and were the trouble of my dreams.

139   ['I saw one life, and felt that it was joy']

Thus did my days pass on, and now at length
From Nature and her overflowing soul
I had received so much that all my thoughts
Were steeped in feeling; I was only then
Contented when with bliss ineffable
I felt the sentiment of Being spread
O'er all that moves, and all that seemeth still,

O'er all, that, lost beyond the reach of thought
And human knowledge, to the human eye
Invisible, yet liveth to the heart,
O'er all that leaps, and runs, and shouts, and sings,
Or beats the gladsome air, o'er all that glides
Beneath the wave, yea, in the wave itself
And mighty depth of waters. Wonder not
If such my transports were; for in all things
I saw one life, and felt that it was joy.
One song they sang, and it was audible,
Most audible then, when the fleshly ear,
O'ercome by grosser prelude of that strain,
Forgot its functions, and slept undisturbed.

140   [Dedication]

The memory of one particular hour
Doth here rise up against me. In a throng,
A festal company of maids and youths,
Old men, and matrons staid, promiscuous rout,
A medley of all tempers, I had passed
The night in dancing, gaiety and mirth;
 With din of instruments, and shuffling feet,
And glancing forms, and tapers glittering,
And unaimed prattle flying up and down,
Spirits upon the stretch, and here and there
Slight shocks of young love-liking interspersed,
That mounted up like joy into the head,
And tingled through the veins. Ere we retired,
The cock had crowed, the sky was bright with day.
Two miles I had to walk along the fields
Before I reached my home. Magnificent
The morning was, a memorable pomp,
More glorious than I ever had beheld.
The sea was laughing at a distance; all

The solid mountains were as bright as clouds,
Grain-tinctured, drenched in empyrean light;
And, in the meadows and the lower grounds,
Was all the sweetness of a common dawn,
Dews, vapours, and the melody of birds,
And labourers going forth into the fields.
— Ah! need I say, dear Friend, that to the brim
My heart was full; I made no vows, but vows
Were then made for me; bond unknown to me
Was given, that I should be, else sinning greatly,
A dedicated Spirit. On I walked
In blessedness, which even yet remains.

141   [Authentic Tidings]

                                   Upturning with a band
Of travellers, from the Valais we had clomb
Along the road that leads to Italy;
A length of hours, making of these our guides
Did we advance, and having reached an inn
Among the mountains, we together ate
Our noon's repast, from which the travellers rose,
Leaving us at the board. Ere long we followed,
Descending by the beaten road that led
Right to a rivulet's edge, and there broke off.
The only track now visible was one
Upon the further side, right opposite,
And up a lofty mountain. This we took
After a little scruple, and short pause,
And climbed with eagerness, though not, at length
Without surprise, and some anxiety
On finding that we did not overtake
Our comrades gone before. By fortunate chance,
While every moment now encreased our doubts,

A peasant met us, and from him we learned
That to the place which had perplexed us first
We must descend, and there should find the road
Which in the stony channel of the stream
Lay a few steps, and then along its banks;
And further, that thenceforward all our course
Was downwards, with the current of that stream.
Hard of belief, we questioned him again,
And all the answers which the man returned
To our inquiries, in their sense and substance,
Translated by the feelings which we had
Ended in this; *that we had crossed the Alps.*

    Imagination! lifting up itself
Before the eye and progress of my Song
Like an unfathered vapour; here that Power,
In all the might of its endowments, came
Athwart me; I was lost as in a cloud,
Halted, without a struggle to break through.
And now recovering, to my soul I say
I recognise thy glory; in such strength
Of usurpation, in such visitings
Of awful promise, when the light of sense
Goes out in flashes that have shewn to us
The invisible world, doth greatness make abode,
There harbours whether we be young or old.
Our destiny, our nature, and our home
Is with infinitude, and only there;
With hope it is, hope that can never die,
Effort, and expectation, and desire,
And something evermore about to be.
The mind beneath such banners militant
Thinks not of spoils or trophies, nor of aught
That may attest its prowess, blest in thoughts
That are their own perfection and reward,
Strong in itself, and in the access of joy
Which hides it like the overflowing Nile.

The dull and heavy slackening that ensued
Upon those tidings by the peasant given
Was soon dislodged; downwards we hurried fast,
And entered with the road which we had missed
Into a narrow chasm; the brook and road
Were fellow-travellers in this gloomy pass,
And with them did we journey several hours
At a slow step. The immeasurable height
Of woods decaying, never to be decayed,
The stationary blasts of water-falls,
And everywhere along the hollow rent
Winds thwarting winds, bewildered and forlorn,
The torrents shooting from the clear blue sky,
The rocks that muttered close upon our ears,
Black drizzling crags that spake by the way-side
As if a voice were in them, the sick sight
And giddy prospect of the raving stream,
The unfettered clouds, and region of the Heavens,
Tumult and peace, the darkness and the light
Were all like workings of one mind, the features
Of the same face, blossoms upon one tree,
Characters of the great Apocalypse,
The types and symbols of Eternity,
Of first and last, and midst, and without end.

SAMUEL TAYLOR COLERIDGE
(1772–1834)

142

Hymn Before Sunrise in the Vale of
Chamouni

Hast thou a charm to stay the morning-star
In his steep course? So long he seems to pause
On thy bald awful head, O sovran Blanc,
The Arve and Arveiron at thy base
Rave ceaselessly; but thou, most awful Form!
Risest from forth thy silent sea of pines,
How silently! Around thee and above
Deep is the air and dark, substantial, black,
An ebon mass: methinks thou piercest it,
As with a wedge! But when I look again,
It is thine own calm home, thy crystal shrine,
Thy habitation from eternity!
O dread and silent Mount! I gazed upon thee,
Till thou, still present to the bodily sense,
Didst vanish from my thought: entranced in prayer
I worshipped the Invisible alone.

Yet, like some sweet beguiling melody,
So sweet, we know not we are listening to it,
Thou, the meanwhile, wast blending with my Thought,
Yea, with my Life and Life's own secret joy:
Till the dilating Soul, enrapt, transfused,
Into the mighty vision passing—there
As in her natural form, swelled vast to Heaven!

Awake, my soul! not only passive praise
Thou owest! not alone these swelling tears,
Mute thanks and secret ecstasy! Awake,
Voice of sweet song! Awake, my heart, awake!
Green vales and icy cliffs, all join my Hymn.

Thou first and chief, sole sovereign of the Vale!
O struggling with the darkness all the night,
And visited all night by troops of stars,
Or when they climb the sky or when they sink:
Companion of the morning-star at dawn,
Thyself Earth's rosy star, and of the dawn
Co-herald: wake, O wake, and utter praise!
Who sank thy sunless pillars deep in Earth?
Who filled thy countenance with rosy light?
Who made thee parent of perpetual streams?

And you, ye five wild torrents fiercely glad!
Who called you forth from night and utter death,
From dark and icy caverns called you forth,
Down those precipitous, black, jagged rocks,
For ever shattered and the same for ever?
Who gave you your invulnerable life,
Your strength, your speed, your fury, and your joy,
Unceasing thunder and eternal foam?
And who commanded (and the silence came)
Here let the billows stiffen, and have rest?

Ye Ice-falls! ye that from the mountain's brow
Adown enormous ravines slope amain—
Torrents, methinks, that heard a mighty voice,
And stopped at once amid their maddest plunge!
Motionless torrents! silent cataracts!
Who made you glorious as the Gates of Heaven
Beneath the keen full moon? Who bade the sun
Clothe you with rainbows? Who, with living flowers
Of loveliest blue, spread garlands at your feet?—
God! let the torrents, like a shout of nations,
Answer! and let the ice-plains echo, God!
God! sing ye meadow-streams with gladsome voice!
Ye pine-groves, with your soft and soul-like sounds!
And they too have a voice, yon piles of snow,
And in their perilous fall shall thunder, God!

Ye living flowers that skirt the eternal frost!
Ye wild goats sporting round the eagle's nest!
Ye eagles, play-mates of the mountain-storm!
Ye lightnings, the dread arrows of the clouds!
Ye signs and wonders of the element!
Utter forth God, and fill the hills with praise!

Thou too, hoar Mount! with thy sky-pointing peaks,
Oft from whose feet the avalanche, unheard,
Shoots downward, glittering through the pure serene
Into the depth of clouds, that veil thy breast—
Thou too again, stupendous Mountain! thou
That as I raise my head, awhile bowed low
In adoration, upward from thy base
Slow travelling with dim eyes suffused with tears,
Solemnly seemest, like a vapoury cloud,
To rise before me—Rise, O ever rise,
Rise like a cloud of incense from the Earth!
Thou kingly Spirit throned among the hills,
Thou dread ambassador from Earth to Heaven,
Great Hierarch! tell thou the silent sky,
And tell the stars, and tell yon rising sun
Earth, with her thousand voices, praises God.

PERCY BYSSHE SHELLEY
(1792–1822)

143

Hymn to Intellectual Beauty

I

The awful shadow of some unseen Power
  Floats though unseen among us,–visiting
  This various world with as inconstant wing
As summer winds that creep from flower to flower,–
Like moonbeams that behind some piny mountain shower,
    It visits with inconstant glance
    Each human heart and countenance;
Like hues and harmonies of evening,–
    Like clouds in starlight widely spread,–
    Like memory of music fled,–
    Like aught that for its grace may be
Dear, and yet dearer for its mystery.

II

Spirit of Beauty, that dost consecrate
  With thine own hues all thou dost shine upon
  Of human thought or form,–where art thou gone?
Why dost thou pass away and leave our state,
This dim vast vale of tears, vacant and desolate?
    Ask why the sunlight not for ever
    Weaves rainbows o'er yon mountain-river,
Why aught should fail and fade that once is shown,
    Why fear and dream and death and birth
    Cast on the daylight of this earth
    Such gloom,–why man has such a scope
For love and hate, despondency and hope?

III

No voice from some sublimer world hath ever
  To sage or poet these responses given–
  Therefore the names of Demon, Ghost, and Heaven,

Remain the records of their vain endeavour,
Frail spells–whose uttered charm might not avail to sever,
    From all we hear and all we see,
    Doubt, chance, and mutability.
Thy light alone–like mist o'er mountains driven,
    Or music by the night-wind sent
    Through strings of some still instrument,
    Or moonlight on a midnight stream,
Gives grace and truth to life's unquiet dream.

IV

Love, Hope, and Self-esteem, like clouds depart
    And come, for some uncertain moments lent.
    Man were immortal, and omnipotent,
Didst thou, unknown and awful as thou art,
Keep with thy glorious train firm state within his heart.
    Thou messenger of sympathies,
    That wax and wane in lovers' eyes–
Thou–that to human thought art nourishment,
    Like darkness to a dying flame!
    Depart not as thy shadow came,
    Depart not–lest the grave should be,
Like life and fear, a dark reality.

V

While yet a boy I sought for ghosts, and sped
    Through many a listening chamber, cave and ruin,
    And starlight wood, with fearful steps pursuing
Hopes of high talk with the departed dead.
I called on poisonous names with which our youth is fed;
    I was not heard–I saw them not–
    When musing deeply on the lot
Of life, at that sweet time when winds are wooing
    All vital things that wake to bring
    News of birds and blossoming,–
    Sudden, thy shadow fell on me;
I shrieked, and clasped my hands in ecstasy!

VI

I vowed that I would dedicate my powers
  To thee and thine—have I not kept the vow?
  With beating heart and streaming eyes, even now
I call the phantoms of a thousand hours
Each from his voiceless grave: they have in visioned bowers
    Of studious zeal or love's delight
    Outwatched with me the envious night—
They know that never joy illumed my brow
    Unlinked with hope that thou wouldst free
    This world from its dark slavery,
    That thou—O awful Loveliness,
Wouldst give whate'er these words cannot express.

VII

The day becomes more solemn and serene
  When noon is past—there is a harmony
  In autumn, and a lustre in its sky,
Which through the summer is not heard or seen,
As if it could not be, as if it had not been!
    Thus let thy power, which like the truth
    Of nature on my passive youth
Descended, to my onward life supply
    Its calm—to one who worships thee,
    And every form containing thee,
    Whom, Spirit fair, thy spells did bind
To fear himself, and love all human kind.

144   ['Mourn not for Adonais']

Peace, peace! he is not dead, he doth not sleep—
He hath awakened from the dream of life—
'Tis we, who lost in stormy visions, keep

With phantoms an unprofitable strife,
And in mad trance, strike with our spirit's knife
Invulnerable nothings. – *We* decay
Like corpses in a charnel; fear and grief
Convulse us and consume us day by day,
And cold hopes swarm like worms within our living clay.

He has outsoared the shadow of our night;
Envy and calumny and hate and pain,
And that unrest which men miscall delight,
Can touch him not and torture not again;
From the contagion of the world's slow stain
He is secure, and now can never mourn
A heart grown cold, a head grown gray in vain;
Nor, when the spirit's self has ceased to burn,
With sparkless ashes load an unlamented urn.

He lives, he wakes – 'tis Death is dead, not he;
Mourn not for Adonais. – Thou young Dawn,
Turn all thy dew to splendour, for from thee
The spirit thou lamentest is not gone;
Ye caverns and ye forests, cease to moan!
Cease, ye faint flowers and fountains, and thou Air,
Which like a mourning veil thy scarf hadst thrown
O'er the abandoned Earth, now leave it bare
Even to the joyous stars which smile on its despair!

He is made one with Nature: there is heard
His voice in all her music, from the moan
Of thunder, to the song of night's sweet bird;
He is a presence to be felt and known
In darkness and in light, from herb and stone,
Spreading itself where'er that Power may move
Which has withdrawn his being to its own;
Which wields the world with never-wearied love,
Sustains it from beneath, and kindles it above.

He is a portion of the loveliness
Which once he made more lovely: he doth bear
His part, while the one Spirit's plastic stress
Sweeps through the dull dense world, compelling there,
All new successions to the forms they wear;
Torturing th'unwilling dross that checks its flight
To its own likeness, as each mass may bear;
And bursting in its beauty and its might
From trees and beasts and men into the Heaven's light.

The splendours of the firmament of time
May be eclipsed, but are extinguished not;
Like stars to their appointed height they climb,
And death is a low mist which cannot blot
The brightness it may veil. When lofty thought
Lifts a young heart above its mortal lair,
And love and life contend in it, for what
Shall be its earthly doom, the dead live there
And move like winds of light on dark and stormy air.

*   *   *

The One remains, the many change and pass;
Heaven's light forever shines, Earth's shadows fly;
Life, like a dome of many-coloured glass,
Stains the white radiance of Eternity,
Until Death tramples it to fragments.–Die,
If thou wouldst be with that which thou dost seek!
Follow where all is fled!–Rome's azure sky,
Flowers, ruins, statues, music, words, are weak
The glory they transfuse with fitting truth to speak.

Why linger, why turn back, why shrink, my Heart?
Thy hopes are gone before: from all things here
They have departed; thou shouldst now depart!
A light is passed from the revolving year,
And man, and woman; and what still is dear

Attracts to crush, repels to make thee wither.
The soft sky smiles,–the low wind whispers near:
'Tis Adonais calls! oh, hasten thither,
No more let Life divide what Death can join together.

That Light whose smile kindles the Universe,
That Beauty in which all things work and move,
That Benediction which the eclipsing Curse
Of birth can quench not, that sustaining Love
Which through the web of being blindly wove
By man and beast and earth and air and sea,
Burns bright or dim, as each are mirrors of
The fire for which all thirst; now beams on me,
Consuming the last clouds of cold mortality.

The breath whose might I have invoked in song
Descends on me; my spirit's bark is driven,
Far from the shore, far from the trembling throng
Whose sails were never to the tempest given;
The massy earth and spherèd skies are riven!
I am borne darkly, fearfully, afar;
Whilst, burning through the inmost veil of Heaven,
The soul of Adonais, like a star,
Beacons from the abode where the Eternal are.

ALFRED, LORD TENNYSON
(1809–1892)

'Strong Son of God'

Strong Son of God, immortal Love,
 Whom we, that have not seen thy face,
 By faith, and faith alone, embrace,
Believing where we cannot prove;

Thine are these orbs of light and shade;
 Thou madest Life in man and brute;
 Thou madest Death; and lo, thy foot
Is on the skull which thou hast made.

Thou wilt not leave us in the dust:
 Thou madest man, he knows not why,
 He thinks he was not made to die;
And thou hast made him: thou art just.

Thou seemest human and divine,
 The highest, holiest manhood, thou:
 Our wills are ours, we know not how;
Our wills are ours, to make them thine.

Our little systems have their day;
 They have their day and cease to be:
 They are but broken lights of thee,
And thou, O Lord, art more than they.

We have but faith: we cannot know;
 For knowledge is of things we see;
 And yet we trust it comes from thee,
A beam in darkness: let it grow.

Let knowledge grow from more to more,
 But more of reverence in us dwell;
 That mind and soul, according well,
May make one music as before,

But vaster. We are fools and slight;
  We mock thee when we do not fear:
  But help thy foolish ones to bear;
Help thy vain worlds to bear thy light.

Forgive what seemed my sin in me;
  What seemed my worth since I began;
  For merit lives from man to man,
And not from man, O Lord, to thee.

Forgive my grief for one removed,
  Thy creature, whom I found so fair.
  I trust he lives in thee, and there
I find him worthier to be loved.

Forgive these wild and wandering cries,
  Confusions of a wasted youth;
  Forgive them where they fail in truth,
And in thy wisdom make me wise.

146   'O yet we trust'

O yet we trust that somehow good
  Will be the final goal of ill,
  To pangs of nature, sins of will,
Defects of doubt, and taints of blood;

That nothing walks with aimless feet;
  That not one life shall be destroyed,
  Or cast as rubbish to the void,
When God hath made the pile complete;

That not a worm is cloven in vain;
  That not a moth with vain desire
  Is shrivelled in a fruitless fire,
Or but subserves another's gain.

Behold, we know not anything;
    I can but trust that good shall fall
    At last—far off—at last, to all,
And every winter change to spring.

So runs my dream: but what am I?
    An infant crying in the night:
    An infant crying for the light:
And with no language but a cry.

The wish, that of the living whole
    No life may fail beyond the grave,
    Derives it not from what we have
The likest God within the soul?

Are God and Nature then at strife,
    That Nature lends such evil dreams?
    So careful of the type she seems,
So careless of the single life;

That I, considering everywhere
    Her secret meaning in her deeds,
    And finding that of fifty seeds
She often brings but one to bear,

I falter where I firmly trod,
    And falling with my weight of cares
    Upon the great world's altar-stairs
That slope through darkness up to God,

I stretch lame hands of faith, and grope,
    And gather dust and chaff, and call
    To what I feel is Lord of all,
And faintly trust the larger hope.

'So careful of the type?' but no.
    From scarpèd cliff and quarried stone
    She cries, 'A thousand types are gone:
I care for nothing, all shall go.

'Thou makest thine appeal to me:
    I bring to life, I bring to death:
    The spirit does but mean the breath:
I know no more.' And he, shall he,

Man, her last work, who seemed so fair,
    Such splendid purpose in his eyes,
    Who rolled the psalm to wintry skies,
Who built him fanes of fruitless prayer,

Who trusted God was love indeed
    And love Creation's final law–
    Though Nature, red in tooth and claw
With ravine, shrieked against his creed–

Who loved, who suffered countless ills,
    Who battled for the True, the Just,
    Be blown about the desert dust,
Or sealed within the iron hills?

No more? A monster then, a dream,
    A discord. Dragons of the prime,
    That tare each other in their slime,
Were mellow music matched with him.

O life as futile, then, as frail!
    O for thy voice to soothe and bless!
    What hope of answer, or redress?
Behind the veil, behind the veil.

147   'There rolls the deep'

There rolls the deep where grew the tree.
    O earth, what changes hast thou seen!
    There where the long street roars, hath been
The stillness of the central sea.

The hills are shadows, and they flow
    From form to form, and nothing stands;
    They melt like mist, the solid lands,
Like clouds they shape themselves and go.

But in my spirit will I dwell,
    And dream my dream, and hold it true;
    For though my lips may breathe adieu,
I cannot think the thing farewell.

That which we dare invoke to bless;
    Our dearest faith; our ghastliest doubt;
    He, They, One, All; within, without;
The Power in darkness whom we guess;

I found Him not in world or sun,
    Or eagle's wing, or insect's eye;
    Nor through the questions men may try,
The petty cobwebs we have spun:

If e'er when faith had fall'n asleep,
    I heard a voice 'believe no more'
    And heard an ever-breaking shore
That tumbled in the Godless deep;

A warmth within the breast would melt
 The freezing reason's colder part,
 And like a man in wrath the heart
Stood up and answered 'I have felt.'

No, like a child in doubt and fear:
 But that blind clamour made me wise;
 Then was I as a child that cries,
But, crying, knows his father near;

And what I am beheld again
 What is, and no man understands;
 And out of darkness came the hands
That reach through nature, moulding men.

ROBERT BROWNING
(1812–1889)

[Unfaith and Faith]

Why first, you don't believe, you don't and can't,
(Not statedly, that is, and fixedly
And absolutely and exclusively)
In any revelation called divine.
No dogmas nail your faith; and what remains
But say so, like the honest man you are?
First, therefore, overhaul theology!
Nay, I too, not a fool, you please to think,
Must find believing every whit as hard:
And if I do not frankly say as much,
The ugly consequence is clear enough.

Now wait, my friend: well, I do not believe–
If you'll accept no faith that is not fixed,
Absolute and exclusive, as you say.
You're wrong–I mean to prove it in due time.
Meanwhile, I know where difficulties lie
I could not, cannot solve, nor ever shall,
So give up hope accordingly to solve–
(To you, and over the wine). Our dogmas then
With both of us, though in unlike degree,
Missing full credence–overboard with them!
I mean to meet you on your own premise:
Good, there go mine in company with yours!

And now what are we? unbelievers both,
Calm and complete, determinately fixed
Today, to-morrow and for ever, pray?
You'll guarantee me that? Not so, I think!
In no wise! all we've gained is, that belief,
As unbelief before, shakes us by fits,
Confounds us like its predecessor. Where's

The gain? how can we guard our unbelief,
Make it bear fruit to us–the problem here.
Just when we are safest, there's a sunset-touch,
A fancy from a flower-bell, someone's death,
A chorus-ending from Euripides,–
And that's enough for fifty hopes and fears
As old and new at once as nature's self,
To rap and knock and enter in our soul,
Take hands and dance there, a fantastic ring,
Round the ancient idol, on his base again,–
The grand Perhaps! We look on helplessly.
There the old misgivings, crooked questions are–
This good God,–what he could do, if he would,
Would, if he could–then must have done long since:
If so, when, where and how? some way must be,–
Once feel about, and soon or late you hit
Some sense, in which it might be, after all.
Why not, 'The Way, the Truth, the Life'?

149   Abt Vogler

(After he has been extemporizing upon the
musical instrument of his invention.)

I

Would that the structure brave, the manifold music I build,
  Bidding my organ obey, calling its keys to their work,
Claiming each slave of the sound, at a touch, as when Solomon
    willed
  Armies of angels that soar, legions of demons that lurk,
Man, brute, reptile, fly,—alien of end and of aim,
  Adverse, each from the other heaven-high, hell-deep removed,–
Should rush into sight at once as he named the ineffable Name,
  And pile him a palace straight, to pleasure the princess he loved!

II

Would it might tarry like his, the beautiful building of mine,
  This which my keys in a crowd pressed and importuned to
    raise!
Ah, one and all, how they helped, would dispart now and now
    combine,
  Zealous to hasten the work, heighten their master his praise!
And one would bury his brow with a blind plunge down to hell,
  Burrow awhile and build, broad on the roots of things,
Then up again swim into sight, having based me my palace well,
  Founded it, fearless of flame, flat on the nether springs.

III

And another would mount and march, like the excellent minion
    he was,
  Ay, another and yet another, one crowd but with many a crest,
Raising my rampired walls of gold as transparent as glass,
  Eager to do and die, yield each his place to the rest:
For higher still and higher (as a runner tips with fire,
  When a great illumination surprises a festal night—
Outlining round and round Rome's dome from space to spire)
  Up, the pinnacled glory reached, and the pride of my soul was
    in sight.

IV

In sight? Not half! for it seemed, it was certain, to match man's
    birth,
  Nature in turn conceived, obeying an impulse as I;
And the emulous heaven yearned down, made effort to reach the
    earth,
  As the earth had done her best, in my passion, to scale the sky:
Novel splendours burst forth, grew familiar and dwelt with mine,
  Not a point nor peak but found and fixed its wandering star;
Meteor-moons, balls of blaze: and they did not pale nor pine,
  For earth had attained to heaven, there was no more near nor
    far.

V

Nay more; for there wanted not who walked in the glare and
  glow,
  Presences plain in the place; or, fresh from the Protoplast,
Furnished for ages to come, when a kindlier wind should blow,
  Lured now to begin and live, in a house to their liking at last;
Or else the wonderful Dead who have passed through the body
  and gone,
  But were back once more to breathe in an old world worth
  their new:
What never had been, was now; what was, as it shall be anon;
  And what is,—shall I say, matched both? for I was made perfect
  too.

VI

All through my keys that gave their sounds to a wish of my soul,
  All through my soul that praised as its wish flowed visibly forth,
All through music and me! For think, had I painted the whole,
  Why, there it had stood, to see, nor the process so wonder-
  worth:
Had I written the same, made verse—still, effect proceeds from
  cause,
  Ye know why the forms are fair, ye hear how the tale is told;
It is all triumphant art, but art in obedience to laws,
  Painter and poet are proud in the artist-list enrolled:—

VII

But here is the finger of God, a flash of the will that can,
  Existent behind all laws, that made them and, lo, they are!
And I know not if, save in this, such gift be allowed to man,
  That out of three sounds he frame, not a fourth sound, but a
  star.
Consider it well: each tone of our scale in itself is nought;
  It is everywhere in the world—loud, soft, and all is said:
Give it to me to use! I mix it with two in my thought:
  And, there! Ye have heard and seen: consider and bow the head!

VIII

Well, it is gone at last, the palace of music I reared;
  Gone! and the good tears start, the praises that come too slow;
For one is assured at first, one scarce can say that he feared,
  That he even gave it a thought, the gone thing was to go.
Never to be again! But many more of the kind
  As good, nay, better perchance: is this your comfort to me?
To me, who must be saved because I cling with my mind
  To the same, same self, same love, same God: ay, what was,
    shall be.

IX

Therefore to whom turn I but to thee, the ineffable Name?
  Builder and maker, thou, of houses not made with hands!
What, have fear of change from thee who art ever the same?
  Doubt that thy power can fill the heart that thy power expands?
There shall never be one lost good! What was, shall live as before;
  The evil is null, is nought, is silence implying sound;
What was good shall be good, with, for evil, so much good more;
  On the earth the broken arcs; in the heaven, a perfect round.

X

All we have willed or hoped or dreamed of good shall exist;
  Not its semblance, but itself; no beauty, nor good, nor power
Whose voice has gone forth, but each survives for the melodist
  When eternity affirms the conception of an hour.
The high that proved too high, the heroic for earth too hard,
  The passion that left the ground to lose itself in the sky,
Are music sent up to God by the lover and the bard;
  Enough that he heard it once: we shall hear it by-and-by.

XI

And what is our failure here but a triumph's evidence
  For the fulness of the days? Have we withered or agonized?

Why else was the pause prolonged but that singing might issue
    thence?
  Why rushed the discords in but that harmony should be
    prized?
Sorrow is hard to bear, and doubt is slow to clear,
  Each sufferer says his say, his scheme of the weal and woe:
But God has a few of us whom he whispers in the ear;
  The rest may reason and welcome: 'tis we musicians know.

XII

Well, it is earth with me; silence resumes her reign:
  I will be patient and proud, and soberly acquiesce.
Give me the keys. I feel for the common chord again,
  Sliding by semitones, till I sink to the minor,—yes,
And I blunt it into a ninth, and I stand on alien ground,
  Surveying awhile the heights I rolled from into the deep;
Which, hark, I have dared and done, for my resting-place is
    found,
  The C Major of this life: so, now I will try to sleep.

EMILY BRONTË
(1818–1848)

150

The Visionary*

SILENT is the house: all are laid asleep:
One alone looks out o'er the snow-wreaths deep,
Watching every cloud, dreading every breeze
That whirls the wildering drift, and bends the groaning trees.

Cheerful is the hearth, soft the matted floor;
Not one shivering gust creeps through pane or door;
The little lamp burns straight, its rays shoot strong and far:
I trim it well, to be the wanderer's guiding-star.

Frown, my haughty sire! chide, my angry dame;
Set your slaves to spy; threaten me with shame:
But neither sire nor dame, nor prying serf shall know,
What angel nightly tracks that waste of frozen snow.

What I love shall come like visitant of air,
Safe in secret power from lurking human snare;
Who loves me, no word of mine shall e'er betray,
Though for faith unstained my life must forfeit pay.

Burn, then, little lamp; glimmer straight and clear—
Hush! a rustling wing stirs, methinks, the air:
He for whom I wait, thus ever comes to me;
Strange Power! I trust thy might; trust thou my constancy.

151

The Prisoner*

'STILL, let my tyrants know, I am not doomed to wear
Year after year in gloom, and desolate despair;
A messenger of Hope comes every night to me,
And offers for short life, eternal liberty.

* For note, see p. 348

'He comes with western winds, with evening's wandering airs,
With that clear dusk of heaven that brings the thickest stars.
Winds take a pensive tone, and stars a tender fire,
And visions rise, and change, that kill me with desire.

'Desire for nothing known in my maturer years,
When Joy grew mad with awe, at counting future tears.
When, if my spirit's sky was full of flashes warm,
I knew not whence they came, from sun or thunder-storm.

'But, first, a hush of peace—a soundless calm descends;
The struggle of distress, and fierce impatience ends;
Mute music soothes my breast—unuttered harmony,
That I could never dream, till Earth was lost to me.

'Then dawns the Invisible; the Unseen its truth reveals;
My outward sense is gone, my inward essence feels:
Its wings are almost free—its home, its harbour found,
Measuring the gulf, it stoops and dares the final bound.

'O! dreadful is the check- intense the agony—
When the ear begins to hear, and the eye begins to see;
When the pulse begins to throb, the brain to think again;
The soul to feel the flesh, and the flesh to feel the chain.

'Yet I would lose no sting, would wish no torture less;
The more that anguish racks, the earlier it will bless;
And robed in fires of hell, or bright with heavenly shine,
If it but herald death, the vision is divine!'

152   [Last Lines][1]

    No coward soul is mine,
    No trembler in the world's storm-troubled sphere:

[1] 'The following are the last lines my sister Emily ever wrote.' (Note by Charlotte Brontë)

I see Heaven's glories shine,
And faith shines equal, arming me from fear.

O God within my breast,
Almighty, ever-present Deity!
Life—that in me has rest,
As I—undying Life—have power in Thee!

Vain are the thousand creeds
That move men's hearts: unutterably vain;
Worthless as withered weeds,
Or idlest froth amid the boundless main,

To waken doubt in one
Holding so fast by Thine infinity;
So surely anchored on
The steadfast rock of immortality.

With wide-embracing love
Thy spirit animates eternal years,
Pervades and broods above,
Changes, sustains, dissolves, creates, and rears.

Though earth and man were gone,
And suns and universes ceased to be,
And Thou were left alone,
Every existence would exist in Thee.

There is not room for Death,
Nor atom that his might could render void:
Thou—THOU art Being and Breath,
And what THOU art may never be destroyed.

ARTHUR HUGH CLOUGH
(1819–1861)

153   The Latest Decalogue

Thou shalt have one God only; who
Would be at the expense of two?
No graven images may be
Worshipped, except the currency:
Swear not at all; for, for thy curse
Thine enemy is none the worse:
At church on Sunday to attend
Will serve to keep the world thy friend:
Honour thy parents; that is, all
From whom advancement may befall:
Thou shalt not kill; but needst not strive
Officiously to keep alive:
Do not adultery commit;
Advantage rarely comes of it:
Thou shalt not steal; an empty feat,
When it's so lucrative to cheat:
Bear not false witness; let the lie
Have time on its own wings to fly:
Thou shalt not covet; but tradition
Approves all forms of competition.

The sum of all is, thou shalt love,
If any body, God above:
At any rate shall never labour
More than thyself to love thy neighbour.

COVENTRY PATMORE
(1823–1896)

154   The Toys

My little Son, who looked from thoughtful eyes
And moved and spoke in quiet grown-up wise,
Having my law the seventh time disobeyed,
I struck him, and dismissed
With hard words and unkissed,
His Mother, who was patient, being dead.
Then, fearing lest his grief should hinder sleep,
I visited his bed,
But found him slumbering deep,
With darkened eyelids, and their lashes yet
From his late sobbing wet.
And I, with moan,
Kissing away his tears, left others of my own;
For, on a table drawn beside his head,
He had put, within his reach,
A box of counters and a red-veined stone,
A piece of glass abraded by the beach
And six or seven shells,
A bottle with bluebells
And two French copper coins, ranged there with careful art,
To comfort his sad heart.
So when that night I prayed
To God, I wept, and said:
Ah, when at last we lie with trancèd breath,
Not vexing thee in death,
And thou rememberest of what toys
We made our joys,
How weakly understood,
Thy great commanded good,
Then, fatherly not less
Than I whom thou hast moulded from the clay,
Thou'lt leave thy wrath, and say,
'I will be sorry for their childishness.'

CHRISTINA ROSSETTI
(1830–1894)

155   'Marvel of marvels'

Marvel of marvels, if I myself shall behold
With mine own eyes my King in his city of gold;
Where the least of lambs is spotless white in the fold,
Where the least and last of saints in spotless white is stoled,
Where the dimmest head beyond a moon is aureoled.
O saints, my beloved, now mouldering to mould in the mould,
Shall I see you lift your heads, see your cerements unrolled,
See with these very eyes? who now in darkness and cold
Tremble for the midnight cry, the rapture, the tale untold,
'The Bridegroom cometh, cometh, his Bride to enfold.'

Cold it is, my beloved, since your funeral bell was tolled:
Cold it is, O my King, how cold alone on the wold.

156   Twice

I took my heart in my hand
    (O my love, O my love),
I said: Let me fall or stand,
    Let me live or die,
But this once hear me speak—
    (O my love, O my love)—
Yet a woman's words are weak;
    You should speak, not I.

You took my heart in your hand
    With a friendly smile,
With a critical eye you scanned,
    Then set it down.

And said: It is still unripe,
   Better wait awhile;
Wait while the skylarks pipe,
   Till the corn grows brown.

As you set it down it broke—
   Broke, but I did not wince;
I smiled at the speech you spoke,
   At your judgement that I heard:
But I have not often smiled
   Since then, nor questioned since,
Nor cared for corn-flowers wild,
   Nor sung with the singing bird.

I take my heart in my hand,
   O my God, O my God,
My broken heart in my hand:
   Thou hast seen, judge thou.
My hope was written on sand,
   O my God, O my God:
Now let thy judgement stand—
   Yea, judge me now.

This contemned of a man,
   This marred one heedless day,
This heart take thou to scan
   Both within and without:
Refine with fire its gold,
   Purge thou its dross away—
Yea, hold it in thy hold,
   Whence none can pluck it out.

I take my heart in my hand—
   I shall not die, but live—
Before thy face I stand;
   I, for thou callest such:

All that I have I bring,
   All that I am I give,
Smile thou and I shall sing,
   But shall not question much.

157   'Safe where I cannot lie yet'

Safe where I cannot lie yet,
   Safe where I hope to lie too,
Safe from the fume and the fret;
   You, and you,
Whom I never forget.

Safe from the frost and the snow,
   Safe from the storm and the sun,
Safe where the seeds wait to grow
   One by one
And to come back in blow.

158   Who shall Deliver me?

God strengthen me to bear myself,
That heaviest weight of all to bear,
Inalienable weight of care.

All others are outside myself;
I lock my door and bar them out,
The turmoil, tedium, gad-about.

I lock my door upon myself,
And bar them out; but who shall wall
Self from myself, most loathed of all?

If I could once lay down myself,
And start self-purged upon the race
That all must run! Death runs apace.

If I could set aside myself,
And start with lightened heart upon
The road by all men overgone!

God harden me against myself,
This coward with pathetic voice
Who craves for ease, and rest, and joys:

Myself, arch-traitor to myself;
My hollowest friend, my deadliest foe,
My clog whatever road I go.

Yet One there is can curb myself,
Can roll the strangling load from me,
Break off the yoke and set me free.

159   A Christmas Carol

In the bleak mid-winter
    Frosty wind made moan,
Earth stood hard as iron,
    Water like a stone;
Snow had fallen, snow on snow,
    Snow on snow,
In the bleak mid-winter
    Long ago.

Our God, Heaven cannot hold him,
    Nor earth sustain;
Heaven and earth shall flee away
    When he comes to reign:

In the bleak mid-winter
  A stable-place sufficed
The Lord God Almighty
  Jesus Christ.

Enough for him whom cherubim
  Worship night and day,
A breastful of milk
  And a mangerful of hay;
Enough for him whom angels
  Fall down before,
The ox and ass and camel
  Which adore.

Angels and archangels
  May have gathered there,
Cherubim and seraphim
  Thronged the air,
But only his mother
  In her maiden bliss
Worshipped the Beloved
  With a kiss.

What can I give him,
  Poor as I am?
If I were a shepherd
  I would bring a lamb,
If I were a wise man
  I would do my part,—
Yet what I can I give him,
  Give my heart.

THOMAS HARDY
(1840–1928)

The Darkling Thrush

I leant upon a coppice gate
  When Frost was spectre-gray,
And Winter's dregs made desolate
  The weakening eye of day.
The tangled bine-stems scored the sky
  Like strings of broken lyres,
And all mankind that haunted nigh
  Had sought their household fires.

The land's sharp features seemed to be
  The Century's corpse outleant,
His crypt the cloudy canopy,
  The wind his death-lament.
The ancient pulse of germ and birth
  Was shrunken hard and dry,
And every spirit upon earth
  Seemed fervourless as I.

At once a voice arose among
  The bleak twigs overhead
In a full-hearted evensong
  Of joy illimited;
An aged thrush, frail, gaunt, and small,
  In blast-beruffled plume,
Had chosen thus to fling his soul
  Upon the growing gloom.

So little cause for carollings
  Of such ecstatic sound
Was written on terrestrial things
  Afar or nigh around,

That I could think there trembled through
   His happy good-night air
Some blessed Hope, whereof he knew
   And I was unaware.

ROBERT BRIDGES
(1844–1930)

161   *Johannes Milton, Senex*

Since I believe in God the Father Almighty,
Man's Maker and Judge, Overruler of Fortune,
'Twere strange should I praise anything and refuse him praise,
Should love the creature forgetting the Creator,
Nor unto him in suff'ring and sorrow turn me:
Nay how could I withdraw me from his embracing?

But since that I have seen not, and cannot know him,
Nor in my earthly temple apprehend rightly
His wisdom and the heavenly purpose eternal;
Therefore will I be bound to no studied system
Nor argument, nor with delusion enslave me,
Nor seek to please him in any foolish invention,
Which my spirit within me, that loveth beauty
And hateth evil, hath reproved as unworthy:

But I cherish my freedom in loving service,
Gratefully adoring for delight beyond asking
Or thinking, and in hours of anguish and darkness
Confiding always on his excellent greatness.

GERARD MANLEY HOPKINS
(1844–1889)

162   The Wreck of the Deutschland*

*To the
happy memory of five Franciscan nuns
exiles by the Falck Laws
drowned between midnight and morning of
Dec. 7th, 1875*

PART THE FIRST

1

Thou mastering me
God! giver of breath and bread;
World's strand, sway of the sea;
Lord of living and dead;
Thou hast bound bones and veins in me, fastened me flesh,
And after it almost unmade, what with dread,
Thy doing: and dost thou touch me afresh?
Over again I feel thy finger and find thee.

2

I did say yes
O at lightning and lashed rod;
Thou heardst me truer than tongue confess
Thy terror, O Christ, O God;
Thou knowest the walls, altar and hour and night:
The swoon of a heart that the sweep and the hurl of thee trod
Hard down with a horror of height:
And the midriff astrain with leaning of, laced with fire of stress.

3

The frown of his face
Before me, the hurtle of hell

* See notes, p. 349

277

Behind, where, where was a, where was a place?
    I whirled out wings that spell[1]
And fled with a fling of the heart to the heart of the Host.
My heart, but you were dovewinged, I can tell,
    Carrier-witted,[2] I am bold to boast,
To flash from the flame to the flame then, tower from the grace
    to the grace.

4

    I am soft sift[3]
    In an hourglass – at the wall
Fast, but mined[4] with a motion, a drift,
    And it crowds and it combs[5] to the fall;
I steady as a water in a well, to a poise, to a pane,
But roped with, always, all the way down from the tall
    Fells or flanks of the voel,[6] a vein
Of the gospel proffer, a pressure, a principle, Christ's gift.

5

    I kiss my hand
    To the stars, lovely-asunder
Starlight, wafting him out of it; and
    Glow, glory in thunder;
Kiss my hand to the dappled-with-damson west:
Since, tho' he is under the world's splendour and wonder,
    His mystery must be instressed, stressed;
For I greet him the days I meet him, and bless when I understand.

6

    Not out of his bliss
    Springs the stress felt[7]
Nor first from heaven (and few know this)
    Swings the stroke dealt –

[1] *that spell*: *either*, that time, *or*, which climb   [2] *carrier-witted*: with the instinct of a carrier pigeon   [3] *sift*: sand   [4] *mined*: undermined   [5] *combs*: rolls over like a wave   [6] *voel*: hillside   [7] *stress felt*: the inner intuition of God's presence

Stroke and a stress that stars and storms deliver,
That guilt is hushed by, hearts are flushed by and melt –
    But it rides time like riding a river
(And here the faithful waver, the faithless fable and miss).

7

    It dates from day
        Of his going in Galilee;
    Warm-laid grave of a womb-life grey;
        Manger, maiden's knee;
    The dense and the driven Passion, and frightful sweat:
    Thence the discharge of it, there its swelling to be,
        Though felt before, though in high flood yet –
What none would have known of it, only the heart, being hard at
    bay,

8

    Is out with it! Oh,
        We lash with the best or worst
    Word last! How a lush-kept plush-capped sloe
        Will, mouthed to flesh-burst,
    Gush! – flush the man, the being with it, sour or sweet,
    Brim, in a flash, full! – Hither then, last or first,
        To hero of Calvary, Christ's feet –
Never ask if meaning it, wanting it, warned of it – men go.

9

    Be adored among men,
        God, three-numberèd form;
    Wring thy rebel, dogged in den,
        Man's malice, with wrecking and storm.
    Beyond saying sweet, past telling of tongue,
    Thou art lightning and love, I found it, a winter and warm;
        Father and fondler of heart thou hast wrung:
Hast thy dark descending and most art merciful then.

10

With an anvil-ding
And with fire in him forge thy will
Or rather, rather then, stealing as Spring
Through him, melt him but master him still:
Whether at once, as once at a crash Paul,
Or as Austin, a lingering-out swéet skíll,
Make mercy in all of us, out of us all
Mastery, but be adored, but be adored King.

PART THE SECOND

11

'Some find me a sword; some
The flange and the rail;[1] flame,
Fang, or flood' goes Death on drum,
And storms bugle his fame.   –
But wé dream we are rooted in earth – Dust!
Flesh falls within sight of us, we, though our flower the same,
Wave with the meadow, forget that there must
The sour scythe cringe,[2] and the blear share come.

12

On Saturday sailed from Bremen,
American-outward-bound,
Take settler and seamen, tell men with women,
Two hundred souls in the round—
O Father, not under thy feathers nor ever as guessing
The goal was a shoal, of a fourth the doom to be drowned;
Yet did the dark side of the bay of thy blessing
Not vault them, the million of rounds of thy mercy not reeve[3]
even them in?

[1] *The flange and the rail*: railway disasters   [2] *cringe*: probably the obsolete sense
'make us cower'   [3] *reeve:* rope together (nautical)

13

Into the snows she sweeps,
   Hurling the haven behind,
  The Deutschland, on Sunday; and so the sky keeps,
    For the infinite air is unkind,
 And the sea flint-flake, black-backed in the regular blow,
Sitting Eastnortheast, in cursed quarter, the wind;
  Wiry and white-fiery and whirlwind-swivellèd snow
Spins to the widow-making unchilding unfathering deeps.

14

She drove in the dark to leeward,
   She struck—not a reef or a rock
  But the combs[1] of a smother of sand: night drew her
    Dead to the Kentish Knock;[2]
And she beat the bank down with her bows and the ride
   of her keel:
The breakers rolled on her beam with ruinous shock;
  And canvas and compass, the whorl[3] and the wheel
Idle for ever to waft her or wind[4] her with, these she endured.

15

Hope had grown grey hairs,
   Hope had mourning on,
  Trenched with tears, carved with cares,
    Hope was twelve hours gone;
 And frightful a nightfall folded rueful a day
Nor rescue, only rocket and lightship, shone,
  And lives at last were washing away:
To the shrouds they took,—they shook in the hurling and
   horrible airs.

[1] *combs*: crests or ridges   [2] A sandbank in the Thames estuary   [3] *whorl*: propeller
[4] *wind*: steer

16

One stirred from the rigging to save
The wild woman-kind below,
  With a rope's end round the man, handy and brave–
  He was pitched to his death at a blow,
For all his dreadnought breast and braids of thew:
They could tell him for hours, dandled the to and fro
  Through the cobbled foam-fleece. What could he do
With the burl[1] of the fountains of air, buck[2] and the flood of the
wave?

17

They fought with God's cold–
And they could not and fell to the deck
  (Crushed them) or water (and drowned them) or rolled
  With the sea-romp over the wreck.
Night roared, with the heart-break hearing a heart-broke
rabble,
The woman's wailing, the crying of child without check–
  Till a lioness arose breasting the babble,
A prophetess towered in the tumult, a virginal tongue told.

18

Ah, touched in your bower of bone,
Are you! turned for an exquisite smart,
  Have you! make words break from me here all alone,
  Do you!–mother of being in me, heart.
O unteachably after[3] evil, but uttering truth,
Why, tears! is it? tears; such a melting, a madrigal start!
  Never-eldering revel and river of youth,
What can it be, this glee? the good you have there of your own?

19

Sister, a sister calling
A master, her master and mine!–

[1] *burl*: vortex [2] *buck*: toss [3] *after*: bent on

And the inboard seas run swirling and hawling;
    The rash smart sloggering brine
Blinds her; but she that weather sees one thing, one;
Has one fetch[1] in her: she rears herself to divine
    Ears, and the call of the tall nun
To the men in the tops and the tackle rode over the storm's
    brawling.

20

    She was first of a five and came
    Of a coifèd sisterhood.
  (O Deutschland, double a desperate name![2]
    O world wide of its good!
But Gertrude,[3] lily, and Luther, are two of a town,
Christ's lily and beast of the waste wood:
    From life's dawn it is drawn down,
Abel is Cain's brother and breasts they have sucked the same.)

21

    Loathed for a love men knew in them,
    Banned by the land of their birth,
  Rhine refused them, Thames would ruin them;
    Surf, snow, river and earth
Gnashed: but thou art above, thou Orion of light;
Thy unchancelling poising palms were weighing the worth,
    Thou martyr-master: in thy sight
Storm flakes were scroll-leaved flowers, lily showers- sweet
    heaven was astrew in them.

22

    Five! the finding and sake[4]
    And cipher of suffering Christ.
    Mark, the mark is of man's make
    And the word of it Sacrificed.

[1] *fetch*: device   [2] Germany is doubly a desperate name, as home of the Reformation and expeller of the nuns   [3] Gertrude the Great, mystic of the thirteenth century, lived near Eisleben, Luther's birthplace   [4] *sake*: sign

But he scores it in scarlet himself on his own bespoken,
Before-time-taken, dearest prizèd and priced—
    Stigma, signal, cinquefoil token
For lettering of the lamb's fleece, ruddying of the rose-flake.

23

    Joy fall to thee, father Francis,
    Drawn to the Life that died;
  With the gnarls of the nails in thee, niche of the lance, his
    Lovescape crucified
And seal of his seraph-arrival! and these thy daughters
And five-livèd and leavèd favour and pride,
    Are sisterly sealed in wild waters,
To bathe in his fall-gold mercies, to breathe in his all-fire glances.

24

    Away in the loveable west,
    On a pastoral forehead of Wales,
  I was under a roof here, I was at rest,
    And they the prey of the gales;
She to the black-about air, to the breaker, the thickly
Falling flakes, to the throng that catches and quails
    Was calling 'O Christ, Christ, come quickly':
The cross to her she calls Christ to her, christens her wild-worst
  Best.

25

    The majesty! what did she mean?
    Breathe, arch and original Breath.
  Is it love in her of the being as her lover had been?
    Breathe, body of lovely Death.
They were else-minded then, altogether, the men
Woke thee with a *We are perishing* in the weather of Gennesa-
  reth.
    Or is it that she cried for the crown then,
The keener to come at the comfort for feeling the combating
  keen?

26

    For how to the heart's cheering
      The down-dugged ground-hugged grey
  Hovers off, the jay-blue heavens appearing
      Of pied and peeled May!
Blue-beating and hoary-glow height; or night, still higher,
With belled fire and the moth-soft Milky Way,
    What by your measure is the heaven of desire,
The treasure never eyesight got, nor was ever guessed what for
  the hearing?

27

    No, but it was not these.
      The jading and jar of the cart,
  Time's tasking, it is fathers that asking for ease
      Of the sodden-with-its-sorrowing heart,
  Not danger, electrical horror; then further it finds
  The appealing of the Passion is tenderer in prayer apart:
    Other, I gather, in measure her mind's
Burden, in wind's burly and beat of endragonèd seas.

28

    But how shall I . . . make me room there:
      Reach me a . . . Fancy, come faster–
  Strike you the sight of it? look at it loom there
      Thing that she . . . There then! the Master,
Ipse, the only one, Christ, King, Head:
He was to cure the extremity where he had cast her;
    Do, deal, lord it with living and dead;
Let him ride, her pride, in his triumph, despatch and have done
  with his doom there.

29

    Ah! there was a heart right!
    There was single eye!

Read the unshapeable shock night
　　And knew the who and the why;
　Wording it how but by him that present and past,
　Heaven and earth are word of, worded by?–
　　The Simon Peter of a soul! to the blast
Tarpeïan-fast,[1] but a blown beacon of light.

30

　　Jesu, heart's light,
　　Jesu, maid's son,
　What was the feast followed the night
　　Thou hadst glory of this nun?[2]
Feast of the one woman without stain.
For so conceivèd, so to conceive thee is done;
　But here was heart-throe, birth of a brain,
Word, that heard and kept thee and uttered thee outright.

31

　　Well, she has thee for the pain, for the
　　Patience; but pity of the rest of them!
　Heart, go and bleed at a bitterer vein for the
　　Comfortless unconfessed of them–
No not uncomforted: lovely-felicitous Providence
Finger of a tender of, O of a feathery delicacy, the breast of the
　Maiden could obey so, be a bell to, ring of it, and
Startle the poor sheep back! is the shipwrack then a harvest,
　does tempest carry the grain for thee?

32

　　I admire thee, master of the tides,
　　Of the Yore-flood, of the year's fall;
　The recurb and the recovery of the gulf's sides,
　　The girth of it and the wharf of it and the wall;

[1] Bound to the blast as if to the Tarpeïan-rock, from which traitors were thrown in ancient Rome　[2] Dec. 8 is the Feast of the Immaculate Conception

Stanching, quenching ocean of a motionable mind;
Ground of being, and granite of it: past all
Grasp God, throned behind
Death with a sovereignty that heeds but hides, bodes but abides;

33

With a mercy that outrides
The all of water, an ark
For the listener; for the lingerer with a love glides
Lower than death and the dark;
A vein for the visiting of the past-prayer, pent in prison,
The-last-breath penitent spirits—the uttermost mark
Our passion-plungèd giant risen,
The Christ of the Father compassionate, fetched in the storm
of his strides.

34

Now burn, new born to the world,
Double-naturèd name,
The heaven-flung, heart-fleshed, maiden-furled
Miracle-in-Mary-of-flame,
Mid-numberèd he in three of the thunder-throne!
Not a dooms-day dazzle in his coming nor dark as he came;
Kind, but royally reclaiming his own;
A released shower, let flash to the shire, not a lightning of fire
hard-hurled.

35

Dame, at our door
Drowned, and among our shoals,
Remember us in the roads, the heaven-haven of the reward:
Our King back, Oh, upon English souls!
Let him easter in us, be a dayspring to the dimness of us,
be a crimson-cresseted east,
More brightening her, rare-dear Britain, as his reign rolls,
Pride, rose, prince, hero of us, high-priest,
Our hearts' charity's hearth's fire, our thoughts' chivalry's
throng's Lord.

163   God's Grandeur

The world is charged with the grandeur of God.
　It will flame out, like shining from shook foil;
　It gathers to a greatness, like the ooze of oil
Crushed. Why do men then now not reck his rod?
Generations have trod, have trod, have trod;
　And all is seared with trade; bleared, smeared with toil;
　And wears man's smudge and shares man's smell: the soil
Is bare now, nor can foot feel, being shod.

And for all this, nature is never spent;
　There lives the dearest freshness deep down things;
And though the last lights off the black West went
　Oh, morning, at the brown brink eastward, springs–
Because the Holy Ghost over the bent
　World broods with warm breast and with ah! bright wings.

164   The Windhover

                    To Christ our Lord

　I caught this morning morning's minion, king–
　　dom of daylight's dauphin, dapple-dawn-drawn Falcon, in
　　　his riding
　　Of the rolling level underneath him steady air, and
　　　striding
　High there, how he rung upon the rein of a wimpling wing
　In his ecstasy! then off, off forth on swing,
　　As a skate's heel sweeps smooth on a bow-bend! the hurl
　　　and gliding
　　Rebuffed the big wind. My heart in hiding
　Stirred for a bird,–the achieve of, the mastery of the thing!

Brute beauty and valour and act, oh, air, pride, plume, here
    Buckle! AND the fire that breaks from thee then, a billion
Times told lovelier, more dangerous, O my chevalier!

    No wonder of it: shéer plód makes plough down sillion
Shine, and blue-bleak embers, ah my dear,
    Fall, gall themselves, and gash gold-vermilion.

165   Pied Beauty

Glory be to God for dappled things—
    For skies of couple-colour as a brinded cow;
        For rose-moles all in stipple upon trout that swim;
Fresh firecoal chestnut-falls; finches' wings;
    Landscapes plotted and pieced—fold, fallow, and plough;
        And áll trádes, their gear and tackle and trim.

All things counter, original, spare, strange;
    Whatever is fickle, freckled (who knows how?)
        With swift, slow; sweet, sour; adazzle, dim;
He fathers-forth whose beauty is past change:
                            Praise him.

166   Felix Randal

Felix Randal the farrier, O is he dead then? my duty all ended,
Who have watched his mould of man, big-boned and hardy-
    handsome
Pining, pining, till time when reason rambled in it and some
Fatal four disorders, fleshed there, all contended?

Sickness broke him. Impatient, he cursed at first, but mended
Being anointed and all; though a heavenlier heart began some

Months earlier, since I had our sweet reprieve and ransom
Tendered to him. Ah well, God rest him all road ever he offended!

This seeing the sick endears them to us, us too it endears.
My tongue had taught thee comfort, touch had quenched thy tears,
Thy tears that touched my heart, child, Felix, poor Felix Randal;

How far from then forethought of, all thy more boisterous years,
When thou at the random grim forge, powerful amidst peers,
Didst fettle for the great grey drayhorse his bright and battering
sandal!

167   [Carrion Comfort]

Not, I'll not, carrion comfort, Despair, not feast on thee;
Not untwist—slack they may be—these last strands of man
In me ór, most weary, cry *I can no more*. I can;
Can something, hope, wish day come, not choose not to be.
But ah, but O thou terrible, why wouldst thou rude on me
Thy wring-world right foot rock? lay a lionlimb against me? scan
With darksome devouring eyes my bruisèd bones? and fan,
O in turns of tempest, me heaped there; me frantic to avoid
thee and flee?
Why? That my chaff might fly; my grain lie, sheer and clear.
Nay in all that toil, that coil, since (seems) I kissed the rod,
Hand rather, my heart lo! lapped strength, stole joy, would
laugh, chéer.
Cheer whom though? The hero whose heaven-handling
flung me, fóot tród
Me? or me that fought him? O which one? is it each one?
That night, that year
Of now done darkness I wretch lay wrestling with (my God!)
my God.

168   'No worst'

No worst, there is none. Pitched past pitch of grief,
More pangs will, schooled at forepangs, wilder wring.
Comforter, where, where is your comforting?
Mary, mother of us, where is your relief?
My cries heave, herds-long; huddle in a main, a chief-
woe, world-sorrow; on an age-old anvil wince and sing—
Then lull, then leave off. Fury had shrieked 'No ling-
ering! Let me be fell: force I must be brief'.
O the mind, mind has mountains; cliffs of fall
Frightful, sheer, no-man-fathomed. Hold them cheap
May who ne'er hung there. Nor does long our small
Durance deal with that steep or deep. Here! creep,
Wretch, under a comfort serves in a whirlwind; all
Life death does end and each day dies with sleep.

169   'I wake and feel the fell of dark'

I wake and feel the fell of dark, not day.
What hours, O what black hoürs we have spent
This night! what sights you, heart, saw; ways you went!
And more must, in yet longer light's delay.

With witness I speak this. But where I say
Hours I mean years, mean life. And my lament
Is cries countless, cries like dead letters sent
To dearest him that lives alas! away.

I am gall, I am heartburn. God's most deep decree
Bitter would have me taste: my taste was me;
Bones built in me, flesh filled, blood brimmed the curse.

Selfyeast of spirit a dull dough sours. I see
The lost are like this, and their scourge to be
As I am mine, their sweating selves; but worse.

ALICE MEYNELL
(1847–1922)

Christ in the Universe

With this ambiguous earth
His dealings have been told us. These abide:
The signal to a maid, the human birth,
The lesson, and the young Man crucified.

But not a star of all
The innumerable host of stars has heard
How he administered this terrestrial ball.
Our race have kept their Lord's entrusted Word....

No planet knows that this
Our wayside planet, carrying land and wave,
Love and life multipled, and pain and bliss,
Bears, as chief treasure, one forsaken grave.

Nor, in our little day,
May his devices with the heavens be guessed,
His pilgrimage to thread the Milky Way,
Or his bestowals there be manifest.

But, in the eternities,
Doubtless we shall compare together, hear
A million alien Gospels, in what guise
He trod the Pleiades, the Lyre, the Bear.

O be prepared, my soul!
To read the inconceivable, to scan
The million forms of God those stars unroll
When, in our turn, we show to them a Man.

171   Easter Night

All night had shout of men and cry
    Of woeful women filled his way;
Until that noon of sombre sky
    On Friday, clamour and display
Smote him; no solitude had he,
No silence, since Gethsemane.

Public was Death; but Power, but Might,
    But Life again, but Victory,
Were hushed within the dead of night,
    The shuttered dark, the secrecy.
And all alone, alone, alone,
He rose again behind the stone.

A. E. HOUSMAN
(1859–1936)

Easter Hymn

If in that Syrian garden, ages slain,
You sleep, and know not you are dead in vain,
Nor even in dreams behold how dark and bright
Ascends in smoke and fire by day and night
The hate you died to quench and could but fan,
Sleep well and see no morning, son of man.

But if, the grave rent and the stone rolled by,
At the right hand of majesty on high
You sit, and sitting so remember yet
Your tears, your agony and bloody sweat,
Your cross and passion and the life you gave,
Bow hither out of heaven and see and save.

For my Funeral

O thou that from thy mansion
   Through time and place to roam,
Dost send abroad thy children,
   And then dost call them home,

That men and tribes and nations
   And all thy hand hath made
May shelter them from sunshine
   In thine eternal shade:

We now to peace and darkness
   And earth and thee restore
Thy creature that thou madest
   And wilt cast forth no more.

MARY COLERIDGE
(1861–1907)

174 There

There, in that other world, what waits for me?
What shall I find after that other birth?
No stormy, tossing, foaming, smiling sea,
    But a new earth.

No sun to mark the changing of the days,
No slow, soft falling of the alternate night,
No moon, no star, no light upon my ways,
    Only the Light.

No gray cathedral, wide and wondrous fair,
That I may tread where all my fathers trod.
Nay, nay, my soul, no house of God is there,
    But only God.

175 [*Salus Mundi*]

I saw a stable, low and very bare,
    A little child in a manger.
The oxen knew Him, had Him in their care,
    To men He was a stranger.
The safety of the world was lying there,
    And the world's danger.

W. B. YEATS
(1865–1939)

Vacillation[1]

(i)

My fiftieth year had come and gone,
I sat, a solitary man,
In a crowded London shop,
An open book and empty cup
On the marble table-top.

While on the shop and street I gazed
My body of a sudden blazed;
And twenty minutes more or less
It seemed, so great my happiness,
That I was blessèd and could bless.

(ii)

Although the summer sunlight gild
Cloudy leafage of the sky,
Or wintry moonlight sink the field
In storm-scattered intricacy,
I cannot look thereon,
Responsibility so weighs me down.

Things said or done long years ago,
Or things I did not do or say
But thought that I might say or do,
Weigh me down, and not a day
But something is recalled,
My conscience or my vanity appalled.

(iii)

The Soul. Seek out reality, leave things that seem.
The Heart. What, be a singer born and lack a theme?

[1] Nos. iv, v, vii, and viii of the short lyrics collected under this title

The Soul. Isaiah's coal, what more can man desire?
The Heart. Struck dumb in the simplicity of fire!
The Soul. Look on that fire, salvation walks within.
The Heart. What theme had Homer but original sin?

(iv)

Must we part, Von Hügel,[1] though much alike, for we
Accept the miracles of the saints and honour sanctity?
The body of Saint Teresa lies undecayed in tomb,
Bathed in miraculous oil, sweet odours from it come,
Healing from its lettered slab. Those self-same hands
    perchance
Eternalised the body of a modern saint that once
Had scooped out Pharaoh's mummy. I–though heart
    might find relief
Did I become a Christian man and choose for my belief
What seems most welcome in the tomb–play a pre-
    destined part.
Homer is my example and his unchristened heart.
The lion and the honeycomb, what has Scripture said?
So get you gone, Von Hügel, though with blessings on
    your head.

177   Supernatural Songs[2]

(i) Ribh[3] considers Christian Love insufficient

Why should I seek for love or study it?
It is of God and passes human wit.
I study hatred with great diligence,
For that's a passion in my own control,
A sort of besom that can clear the soul
Of everything that is not mind or sense.

[1] Baron Friedrich von Hügel (1852–1925), Roman Catholic theologian, and author of *The Mystical Element of Religion* [2] Nos. v and ix [3] An imaginary ancient Irish hermit, a critic of St. Patrick

Why do I hate man, woman or event?
That is a light my jealous soul has sent.
From terror and deception freed it can
Discover impurities, can show at last
How soul may walk when all such things are past,
How soul could walk before such things began.

Then my delivered soul herself shall learn
A darker knowledge and in hatred turn
From every thought of God mankind has had.
Thought is a garment and the soul's a bride
That cannot in that trash and tinsel hide:
Hatred of God may bring the soul to God.

At stroke of midnight soul cannot endure
A bodily or mental furniture.
What can she take until her Master give!
Where can she look until He make the show!
What can she know until He bid her know!
How can she live till in her blood He live!

(ii) The Four Ages of Man

He with body waged a fight,
But body won; it walks upright.

Then he struggled with the heart;
Innocence and peace depart.

Then he struggled with the mind;
His proud heart he left behind.

Now his wars on God begin;
At stroke of midnight God shall win.

178   The Black Tower*

SAY that the men of the old black tower,
Though they but feed as the goatherd feeds,
Their money spent, their wine gone sour,
Lack nothing that a soldier needs,
That all are oath-bound men:
Those banners come not in.

*There in the tomb stand the dead upright,
But winds come up from the shore:
They shake when the winds roar,
Old bones upon the mountain shake.*

Those banners come to bribe or threaten,
Or whisper that a man's a fool
Who, when his own right king's forgotten,
Cares what king sets up his rule.
If he died long ago
Why do you dread us so?

*There in the tomb drops the faint moonlight,
But wind comes up from the shore:
They shake when the winds roar,
Old bones upon the mountain shake.*

The tower's old cook that must climb and clamber
Catching small birds in the dew of the morn
When we hale men lie stretched in slumber
Swears that he hears the king's great horn.
But he's a lying hound:
Stand we on guard oath-bound!

* See note, p. 349

There in the tomb the dark grows blacker,
But wind comes up from the shore:
They shake when the winds roar,
Old bones upon the mountain shake.

January 21, 1939

ERNEST DOWSON
(1867–1900)

Extreme Unction

Upon the eyes, the lips, the feet,
  On all the passages of sense,
The atoning oil is spread with sweet
  Renewal of lost innocence.

The feet, that lately ran so fast
  To meet desire, are soothly sealed;
The eyes, that were so often cast
  On vanity, are touched and healed.

From troublous sights and sounds set free;
  In such a twilight hour of breath,
Shall one retrace his life, or see,
  Through shadows, the true face of death?

Vials of mercy! Sacring oils!
  I know not where nor when I come,
Nor through what wanderings and toils,
  To crave of you Viaticum.

Yet, when the walls of flesh grow weak,
  In such an hour, it well may be,
Through mist and darkness, light will break,
  And each anointed sense will see.

LIONEL JOHNSON
(1867–1902)

The Dark Angel

DARK Angel, with thine aching lust
To rid the world of penitence:
Malicious Angel, who still dost
My soul such subtile violence!

Because of thee, no thought, no thing,
Abides for me undesecrate:
Dark Angel, ever on the wing,
Who never reachest me too late!

When music sounds, then chang:st thou
Its silvery to a sultry fire:
Nor will thine envious heart allow
Delight untortured by desire.

Through thee, the gracious Muses turn
To Furies, O mine Enemy!
And all the things of beauty burn
With flames of evil ecstasy.

Because of thee, the land of dreams
Becomes a gathering place of fears:
Until tormented slumber seems
One vehemence of useless tears.

When sunlight glows upon the flowers,
Or ripples down the dancing sea:
Thou, with thy troop of passionate powers,
Beleaguerest, bewilderest, me.

Within the breath of autumn woods,
Within the winter silences:
Thy venomous spirit stirs and broods,
O Master of impieties!

The ardour of red flame is thine,
And thine the steely soul of ice:
Thou poisonest the fair design
Of nature, with unfair device.

Apples of ashes, golden bright;
Waters of bitterness, how sweet!
O banquet of a foul delight,
Prepared by thee, dark Paraclete!

Thou art the whisper in the gloom,
The hinting tone, the haunting laugh:
Thou art the adorner of my tomb,
The minstrel of mine epitaph.

I fight thee, in the Holy Name!
Yet, what thou dost, is what God saith:
Tempter! should I escape thy flame,
Thou wilt have helped my soul from Death:

The second Death, that never dies,
That cannot die, when time is dead:
Live Death, wherein the lost soul cries,
Eternally uncomforted.

Dark Angel, with thine aching lust!
Of two defeats, of two despairs:
Less dread, a change to drifting dust,
Than thine eternity of cares.

Do what thou wilt, thou shalt not so,
Dark Angel! triumph over me:
Lonely, unto the Lone I go:
Divine, to the Divinity.[1]

[1] 'This, therefore, is the life of the Gods, and of divine and happy men, a liberation from all terrene concerns, a life unaccompanied with human pleasures, and a flight of the alone to the alone' (Plotinus, *Enneads* VI.ix)

D. H. LAWRENCE
(1885–1930)

Pax

All that matters is to be at one with the living God
to be a creature in the house of the God of Life.

Like a cat asleep on a chair
at peace, in peace
and at one with the master of the house, with the mistress,
at home, at home in the house of the living,
sleeping on the hearth, and yawning before the fire.

Sleeping on the hearth of the living world,
yawning at home before the fire of life
feeling the presence of the living God
like a great reassurance
a deep calm in the heart
a presence
as of a master sitting at the board
in his own and greater being,
in the house of life.

182   Shadows

And if tonight my soul may find her peace
in sleep, and sink in good oblivion,
and in the morning wake like a new-opened flower
then I have been dipped again in God, and new-created.

And if, as weeks go round, in the dark of the moon
my spirit darkens and goes out, and soft strange gloom
pervades my movements and my thoughts and words
then I shall know that I am walking still
with God, we are close together now the moon's in shadow.

And if, as autumn deepens and darkens
I feel the pain of falling leaves, and stems that break in storms
and trouble and dissolution and distress
and then the softness of deep shadows folding, folding
around my soul and spirit, around my lips
so sweet, like a swoon, or more like the drowse of a low, sad song
singing darker than the nightingale, on, on to the solstice
and the silence of short days, the silence of the year, the shadow,

then I shall know that my life is moving still
with the dark earth, and drenched
with the deep oblivion of earth's lapse and renewal.

And if, in the changing phases of man's life
I fall in sickness and in misery
my wrists seem broken and my heart seems dead
and strength is gone, and my life
is only the leavings of a life:

and still, among it all, snatches of lovely oblivion, and snatches of
renewal
odd, wintry flowers upon the withered stem, yet new, strange
flowers
such as my life has not brought forth before, new blossoms of me—

then I must know that still
I am in the hands of the unknown God,
he is breaking me down to his own oblivion
to send me forth on a new morning, a new man.

SIEGFRIED SASSOON
(1886–1967)

183   Faith Unfaithful

Mute, with signs I speak:
Blind, by groping seek:
Heed; yet nothing hear:
Feel; find no one near.

Deaf, eclipsed, and dumb,
Through this gloom I come
On the time-path trod
Toward ungranted God.

Carnal, I can claim
Only his known name
Dying, can but be
One with him in me.

EDWIN MUIR
(1887–1959)

184

The Border*

What shall avail me
When I reach the border?
This staff will fail me,
This pass all in order.

These words I have learned
Will not help me then,
These honours hard earned,
And applause of men.

My harp truly set
Will break string by string;
I shall quite forget
That once I could sing.

Absence pure and cold
Of sense and memory
Lightly will hold
All that is me.

All, all will fail me,
Tongue, foot and hand.
Strange I shall hale me
To that strange land.

185

The Annunciation

The angel and the girl are met.
Earth was the only meeting place.
For the embodied never yet

* For note, see p. 350

Travelled beyond the shore of space.
The eternal spirits in freedom go.

See, they have come together, see,
While the destroying minutes flow,
Each reflects the other's face
Till heaven in hers and earth in his
Shine steady there. He's come to her
From far beyond the farthest star,
Feathered through time. Immediacy
Of strangest strangeness is the bliss
That from their limbs all movement takes.
Yet the increasing rapture brings
So great a wonder that it makes
Each feather tremble on his wings.

Outside the window footsteps fall
Into the ordinary day
And with the sun along the wall
Pursue their unreturning way.
Sound's perpetual roundabout
Rolls its numbered octaves out
And hoarsely grinds its battered tune.

But through the endless afternoon
These neither speak nor movement make,
But stare into their deepening trance
As if their gaze would never break.

186   One Foot in Eden

One foot in Eden still, I stand
And look across the other land.
The world's great day is growing late,

Yet strange these fields that we have planted
So long with crops of love and hate.
Time's handiworks by time are haunted,
And nothing now can separate
The corn and tares compactly grown.
The armorial weed in stillness bound
About the stalk; these are our own.
Evil and good stand thick around
In the fields of charity and sin
Where we shall lead our harvest in.

Yet still from Eden springs the root
As clean as on the starting day.
Time takes the foliage and the fruit
And burns the archetypal leaf
To shapes of terror and of grief
Scattered along the winter way.
But famished field and blackened tree
Bear flowers in Eden never known.
Blossoms of grief and charity
Bloom in these darkened fields alone.
What had Eden ever to say
Of hope and faith and pity and love
Until was buried all its day
And memory found its treasure trove?
Strange blessings never in Paradise
Fall from these beclouded skies.

EDITH SITWELL
(1887-1964)

Still Falls the Rain
(The Raids, 1940. Night and Dawn)

STILL falls the Rain–
Dark as the world of man, black as our loss–
Blind as the nineteen hundred and forty nails
Upon the Cross.

Still falls the Rain
With a sound like the pulse of the heart that is changed to the
    hammer-beat
In the Potter's Field, and the sound of the impious feet

On the Tomb:
                     Still falls the Rain
In the Field of Blood where the small hopes breed and the human
    brain
Nurtures its greed, that worm with the brow of Cain.

Still falls the Rain
At the feet of the Starved Man hung upon the Cross.
Christ that each day, each night, nails there,
                        have mercy on us–
On Dives and on Lazarus:
Under the Rain the sore and the gold are as one.

Still falls the Rain–
Still falls the Blood from the Starved Man's wounded Side:
He bears in his Heart all wounds,–those of the light
                        that died,
The last faint spark
In the self-murdered heart, the wounds of the sad
                    uncomprehending dark,

The wounds of the baited bear,—
The blind and weeping bear whom the keepers beat
On his helpless flesh . . . the tears of the hunted hare.

Still falls the Rain—
Then— O Ile leape up to my God: who pulles me doune—
See, see where Christ's blood streames in the firmament:
It flows from the Brow we nailed upon the tree
Deep to the dying, to the thirsting heart
That holds the fires of the world,—dark-smirched with pain
As Caesar's laurel crown.

Then sounds the voice of One who like the heart of man
Was once a child who among beasts has lain—
'Still do I love, still shed my innocent light, my Blood, for thee.'

T. S. ELIOT
(1888–1965)

The Hippopotamus

*And when this epistle is read among you, cause that
it be read also in the church of the Laodiceans.*[1]

The broad-backed hippopotamus
Rests on his belly in the mud;
Although he seems so firm to us
He is merely flesh and blood.

Flesh and blood is weak and frail,
Susceptible to nervous shock;
While the True Church can never fail
For it is based upon a rock.

The hippo's feeble steps may err
In compassing material ends,
While the True Church need never stir
To gather in its dividends.

The 'potamus can never reach
The mango on the mango-tree;
But fruits of pomegranate and peach
Refresh the Church from over sea.

At mating time the hippo's voice
Betrays inflexions hoarse and odd,
But every week we hear rejoice
The Church, at being one with God.

The hippopotamus's day
Is passed in sleep; at night he hunts;
God works in a mysterious way—
The Church can sleep and feed at once.

[1] For the Church of Laodicea, a byword for 'lukewarmness', see Revelation,
3. 14–22.

I saw the 'potamus take wing
Ascending from the damp savannas,
And quiring angels round him sing
The praise of God, in loud hosannas.

Blood of the Lamb shall wash him clean
And him shall heavenly arms enfold,
Among the saints he shall be seen
Performing on a harp of gold.

He shall be washed as white as snow,
By all the martyred virgins kist,
While the True Church remains below
Wrapt in the old miasmal mist.

189   The Journey of the Magi

'A cold coming we had of it,
Just the worst time of the year
For a journey, and such a long journey:
The ways deep and the weather sharp,
The very dead of winter.'
And the camels galled, sore-footed, refractory,
Lying down in the melting snow.
There were times we regretted
The summer palaces on slopes, the terraces,
And the silken girls bringing sherbet.
Then the camel men cursing and grumbling
And running away, and wanting their liquor and women,
And the night-fires going out, and the lack of shelters,
And the cities hostile and the towns unfriendly
And the villages dirty and charging high prices:
A hard time we had of it.
At the end we preferred to travel all night,
Sleeping in snatches,

With the voices singing in our ears, saying
That this was all folly.

    Then at dawn we came down to a temperate valley,
Wet, below the snow line, smelling of vegetation,
With a running stream and a water-mill beating the darkness,
And three trees on the low sky.
And an old white horse galloped away in the meadow.
Then we came to a tavern with vine-leaves over the lintel,
Six hands at an open door dicing for pieces of silver,
And feet kicking the empty wine-skins.
But there was no information, and so we continued
And arrived at evening, not a moment too soon
Finding the place; it was (you may say) satisfactory.

    All this was a long time ago, I remember,
And I would do it again, but set down
This set down
This: were we led all that way for
Birth or Death? There was a Birth, certainly,
We had evidence and no doubt. I had seen birth and death,
But had thought they were different; this Birth was
Hard and bitter agony for us, like Death, our death.
We returned to our places, these Kingdoms,
But no longer at ease here, in the old dispensation,
With an alien people clutching their gods.
I should be glad of another death.

190   Ash-Wednesday[1]

(i)

Because I do not hope to turn again
Because I do not hope
Because I do not hope to turn

[1] Parts I and VI

Desiring this man's gift and that man's scope
I no longer strive to strive towards such things
(Why should the aged eagle stretch its wings?)
Why should I mourn
The vanished power of the usual reign?

Because I do not hope to know again
The infirm glory of the positive hour
Because I do not think
Because I know I shall not know
The one veritable transitory power
Because I cannot drink
There, where trees flower, and springs flow, for there is nothing
    again

Because I know that time is always time
And place is always and only place
And what is actual is actual only for one time
And only for one place
I rejoice that things are as they are and
I renounce the blessed face
And renounce the voice
Because I cannot hope to turn again
Consequently I rejoice, having to construct something
Upon which to rejoice

And pray to God to have mercy upon us
And I pray that I may forget
These matters that with myself I too much discuss
Too much explain
Because I do not hope to turn again
Let these words answer
For what is done, not to be done again
May the judgement not be too heavy upon us
Because these wings are no longer wings to fly
But merely vans to beat the air
The air which is now thoroughly small and dry

Smaller and dryer than the will
Teach us to care and not to care
Teach us to sit still.

Pray for us sinners now and at the hour of our death
Pray for us now and at the hour of our death.

(ii)

Although I do not hope to turn again
Although I do not hope
Although I do not hope to turn

Wavering between the profit and the loss
In this brief transit where the dreams cross
The dreamcrossed twilight between birth and dying
(Bless me father) though I do not wish to wish these things
From the wide window towards the granite shore
The white sails still fly seaward, seaward flying
Unbroken wings

And the lost heart stiffens and rejoices
In the lost lilac and the lost sea voices
And the weak spirit quickens to rebel
For the bent golden-rod and the lost sea smell
Quickens to recover
The cry of quail and the whirling plover
And the blind eye creates
The empty forms between the ivory gates
And smell renews the salt savour of the sandy earth

This is the time of tension between dying and birth
The place of solitude where three dreams cross
Between blue rocks
But when the voices shaken from the yew-tree drift away
Let the other yew be shaken and reply.
Blessed sister, holy mother, spirit of the fountain, spirit of the
    garden,

Suffer us not to mock ourselves with falsehood
Teach us to care and not to care
Teach us to sit still
Even among these rocks,
Our peace in His will
And even among these rocks
Sister, mother
And spirit of the river, spirit of the sea,
Suffer me not to be separated

And let my cry come unto Thee.

191   Marina

Quis hic locus, quae
regio, quae mundi plaga?

What seas what shores what grey rocks and what islands
What water lapping the bow
And scent of pine and the woodthrush singing through the fog
What images return
O my daughter.
Those who sharpen the tooth of the dog, meaning
Death
Those who glitter with the glory of the hummingbird, meaning
Death
Those who sit in the sty of contentment, meaning
Death
Those who suffer the ecstasy of the animals, meaning
Death

Are become unsubstantial, reduced by a wind,
A breath of pine, and the woodsong fog
By this grace dissolved in place

What is this face, less clear and clearer
The pulse in the arm, less strong and stronger—

Given or lent? more distant than stars and nearer than the eye

    Whispers and small laughter between leaves and hurrying
       feet
Under sleep, where all the waters meet.

    Bowsprit cracked with ice and paint cracked with heat.
I made this, I have forgotten
And remember.
The rigging weak and the canvas rotten
Between one June and another September.
Made this unknowing, half conscious, unknown, my own.
The garboard strake leaks, the seams need caulking.
This form, this face, this life
Living to live in a world of time beyond me; let me
Resign my life for this life, my speech for that unspoken,
The awakened, lips parted, the hope, the new ships.

    What seas what shores what granite islands towards my
       timbers
And woodthrush calling through the fog
My daughter.

192   Little Gidding*

I

Midwinter spring is its own season
Sempiternal though sodden towards sundown,
Suspended in time, between pole and tropic.
When the short day is brightest, with frost and fire,
The brief sun flames the ice, on pond and ditches,
In windless cold that is the heart's heat,
Reflecting in a watery mirror
A glare that is blindness in the early afternoon.

* For note, see p. 350

And glow more intense than blaze of branch, or brazier,
Stirs the dumb spirit: no wind, but pentecostal fire
In the dark time of the year. Between melting and freezing
The soul's sap quivers. There is no earth smell
Or smell of living thing. This is the spring time
But not in time's covenant. Now the hedgerow
Is blanched for an hour with transitory blossom
Of snow, a bloom more sudden
Than that of summer, neither budding nor fading,
Not in the scheme of generation.
Where is the summer, the unimaginable
Zero summer?

           If you came this way,
Taking the route you would be likely to take
From the place you would be likely to come from,
If you came this way in may time, you would find the hedges
White again, in May, with voluptuary sweetness.
It would be the same at the end of the journey,
If you came at night like a broken king,
If you came by day not knowing what you came for,
It would be the same, when you leave the rough road
And turn behind the pig-sty to the dull façade
And the tombstone. And what you thought you came for
Is only a shell, a husk of meaning
From which the purpose breaks only when it is fulfilled
If at all. Either you had no purpose
Or the purpose is beyond the end you figured
And is altered in fulfilment. There are other places
Which also are the world's end, some at the sea jaws,
Or over a dark lake, in a desert or a city—
But this is the nearest, in place and time,
Now and in England.

           If you came this way,
Taking any route, starting from anywhere,
At any time or at any season,

It would always be the same: you would have to put off
Sense and notion. You are not here to verify,
Instruct yourself, or inform curiosity
Or carry report. You are here to kneel
Where prayer has been valid. And prayer is more
Than an order of words, the conscious occupation
Of the praying mind, or the sound of the voice praying.
And what the dead had no speech for, when living,
They can tell you, being dead: the communication
Of the dead is tongued with fire beyond the language of the
      living.
Here, the intersection of the timeless moment
Is England and nowhere. Never and always.

II

Ash on an old man's sleeve
Is all the ash the burnt roses leave.
Dust in the air suspended
Marks the place where a story ended.
Dust inbreathed was a house–
The wall, the wainscot and the mouse.
The death of hope and despair,
      This is the death of air.

There are flood and drouth
Over the eyes and in the mouth,
Dead water and dead sand
Contending for the upper hand.
The parched eviscerate soil
Gapes at the vanity of toil,
Laughs without mirth.
      This is the death of earth.

Water and fire succeed
The town, the pasture and the weed.
Water and fire deride
The sacrifice that we denied.

Water and fire shall rot
   The marred foundations we forgot,
Of sanctuary and choir.
      This is the death of water and fire.

In the uncertain hour before the morning
   Near the ending of interminable night
   At the recurrent end of the unending
After the dark dove with the flickering tongue
   Had passed below the horizon of his homing
   While the dead leaves still rattled on like tin
Over the asphalt where no other sound was
   Between three districts whence the smoke arose
   I met one walking, loitering and hurried
As if blown towards me like the metal leaves
   Before the urban dawn wind unresisting.
   And as I fixed upon the down-turned face
That pointed scrutiny with which we challenge
   The first-met stranger in the waning dusk
   I caught the sudden look of some dead master
Whom I had known, forgotten, half recalled
   Both one and many; in the brown baked features
   The eyes of a familiar compound ghost
Both intimate and unidentifiable.
   So I assumed a double part, and cried
   And heard another's voice cry: 'What ! are *you* here?'
Although we were not. I was still the same,
   Knowing myself yet being someone other—
   And he a face still forming; yet the words sufficed
To compel the recognition they preceded.
   And so, compliant to the common wind,
   Too strange to each other for misunderstanding,
In concord at this intersection time
   Of meeting nowhere, no before and after,
   We trod the pavement in a dead patrol.
I said: 'The wonder that I feel is easy,
   Yet ease is cause of wonder. Therefore speak:

I may not comprehend, may not remember.'
And he: 'I am not eager to rehearse
  My thought and theory which you have forgotten.
  These things have served their purpose: let them be.
So with your own, and pray they be forgiven
  By others, as I pray you to forgive
  Both bad and good. Last season's fruit is eaten
And the fullfed beast shall kick the empty pail.
  For last year's words belong to last year's language
  And next year's words await another voice.
But, as the passage now presents no hindrance
  To the spirit unappeased and peregrine
  Between two worlds become much like each other,
So I find words I never thought to speak
  In streets I never thought I should revisit
  When I left my body on a distant shore.
Since our concern was speech, and speech impelled us
  To purify the dialect of the tribe
  And urge the mind to aftersight and foresight,
Let me disclose the gifts reserved for age
  To set a crown upon your lifetime's effort.
  First, the cold friction of expiring sense
Without enchantment, offering no promise
  But bitter tastelessness of shadow fruit
  As body and soul begin to fall asunder.
Second, the conscious impotence of rage
  At human folly, and the laceration
  Of laughter at what ceases to amuse.
And last, the rending pain of re-enactment
  Of all that you have done, and been; the shame
  Of motives late revealed, and the awareness
Of things ill done and done to others' harm
  Which once you took for exercise of virtue.
  Then fools' approval stings, and honour stains.
From wrong to wrong the exasperated spirit
  Proceeds, unless restored by that refining fire
  Where you must move in measure, like a dancer.'

The day was breaking. In the disfigured street
  He left me, with a kind of valediction,
  And faded on the blowing of the horn.

III

There are three conditions which often look alike
Yet differ completely, flourish in the same hedgerow:
Attachment to self and to things and to persons, detachment
From self and from things and from persons; and, growing
    between them, indifference
Which resembles the others as death resembles life,
Being between two lives—unflowering, between
The live and the dead nettle. This is the use of memory:
For liberation—not less of love but expanding
Of love beyond desire, and so liberation
From the future as well as the past. Thus, love of a country
Begins as attachment to our own field of action
And comes to find that action of little importance
Though never indifferent. History may be servitude,
History may be freedom. See, now they vanish,
The faces and places, with the self which, as it could, loved
    them,
To become renewed, transfigured, in another pattern.
Sin is Behovely, but
All shall be well, and
All manner of thing shall be well.
If I think, again, of this place,
And of people, not wholly commendable,
Of no immediate kin or kindness,
But some of peculiar genius,
All touched by a common genius,
United in the strife which divided them;
If I think of a king at nightfall,
Of three men, and more, on the scaffold
And a few who died forgotten
In other places, here and abroad,
And of one who died blind and quiet,

Why should we celebrate
These dead men more than the dying?
It is not to ring the bell backward
Nor is it an incantation
To summon the spectre of a Rose.
We cannot revive old factions
We cannot restore old policies
Or follow an antique drum.
These men, and those who opposed them
And those whom they opposed
Accept the constitution of silence
And are folded in a single party.
Whatever we inherit from the fortunate
We have taken from the defeated
What they had to leave us—a symbol:
A symbol perfected in death.
And all shall be well and
All mannner of thing shall be well
By the purification of the motive
In the ground of our beseeching.

IV

The dove descending breaks the air
With flame of incandescent terror
Of which the tongues declare
The one discharge from sin and error.
The only hope, or else despair
   Lies in the choice of pyre or pyre—
   To be redeemed from fire by fire.

Who then devised the torment? Love.
Love is the unfamiliar Name
Behind the hands that wove
The intolerable shirt of flame
Which human power cannot remove.
   We only live, only suspire
   Consumed by either fire or fire.

V

What we call the beginning is often the end
And to make an end is to make a beginning.
The end is where we start from. And every phrase
And sentence that is right (where every word is at home,
Taking its place to support the others,
The word neither diffident nor ostentatious,
An easy commerce of the old and the new,
The common word exact without vulgarity,
The formal word precise but not pedantic,
The complete consort dancing together)
Every phrase and every sentence is an end and a beginning,
Every poem an epitaph. And any action
Is a step to the block, to the fire, down the sea's throat
Or to an illegible stone: and that is where we start.
We die with the dying:
See, they depart, and we go with them.
We are born with the dead:
See, they return, and bring us with them.
The moment of the rose and the moment of the yew-tree
Are of equal duration. A people without history
Is not redeemed from time, for history is a pattern
Of timeless moments. So, while the light fails
On a winter's afternoon, in a secluded chapel
History is now and England.

With the drawing of this Love and the voice of this Calling

We shall not cease from exploration
And the end of all our exploring
Will be to arrive where we started
And know the place for the first time.
Through the unknown, remembered gate
When the last of earth left to discover
Is that which was the beginning;
At the source of the longest river

The voice of the hidden waterfall
And the children in the apple-tree
Not known, because not looked for
But heard, half-heard, in the stillness
Between two waves of the sea.
Quick now, here, now, always–
A condition of complete simplicity
(Costing not less than everything)
And shall be well and
All manner of thing shall be well
When the tongues of flame are in-folded
Into the crowned knot of fire
And the fire and the rose are one.

JOHN BETJEMAN
(1906–   )

193   In Westminster Abbey

LET me take this other glove off
　　As the *vox humana* swells,
And the beauteous fields of Eden
　　Bask beneath the Abbey bells.
Here, where England's statesmen lie,
Listen to a lady's cry.

Gracious Lord, oh bomb the Germans.
　　Spare their women for Thy Sake,
And if that is not too easy
　　We will pardon Thy Mistake.
But, gracious Lord, whate'er shall be,
Don't let anyone bomb me.

Keep our Empire undismembered
　　Guide our Forces by Thy Hand,
Gallant blacks from far Jamaica,
　　Honduras and Togoland;
Protect them Lord in all their fights,
And, even more, protect the whites.

Think of what our Nation stands for,
　　Books from Boots' and country lanes,
Free speech, free passes, class distinction,
　　Democracy and proper drains.
Lord, put beneath Thy special care
One-eighty-nine Cadogan Square.

Although dear Lord I am a sinner,
　　I have done no major crime;
Now I'll come to Evening Service
　　Whensoever I have the time.

So, Lord, reserve for me a crown,
And do not let my shares go down.

I will labour for Thy Kingdom,
    Help our lads to win the war,
Send white feathers to the cowards
    Join the Women's Army Corps,
Then wash the Steps around Thy Throne
In the Eternal Safety Zone.

Now I feel a little better,
    What a treat to hear Thy Word,
Where the bones of leading statesmen,
    Have so often been interr'd.
And now, dear Lord, I cannot wait
Because I have a luncheon date.

194   Christmas

The bells of waiting Advent ring,
    The Tortoise stove is lit again
And lamp-oil light across the night
    Has caught the streaks of winter rain
In many a stained-glass window sheen
From Crimson Lake to Hooker's Green.

The holly in the windy hedge
    And round the Manor House the yew
Will soon be stripped to deck the ledge,
    The altar, font and arch and pew,
So that the villagers can say
'The church looks nice' on Christmas Day.

Provincial public houses blaze
    And Corporation tramcars clang,

On lighted tenements I gaze
   Where paper decorations hang,
And bunting in the red Town Hall
Says 'Merry Christmas to you all.'

And London shops on Christmas Eve
   Are strung with silver bells and flowers
As hurrying clerks the City leave
   To pigeon-haunted classic towers,
And marbled clouds go scudding by
The many-steepled London sky.

And girls in slacks remember Dad,
   And oafish louts remember Mum,
And sleepless children's hearts are glad,
   And Christmas-morning bells say 'Come!'
Even to shining ones who dwell
Safe in the Dorchester Hotel.

And is it true? And is it true,
   This most tremendous tale of all,
Seen in a stained-glass window's hue,
   A Baby in an ox's stall?
The Maker of the stars and sea
Become a Child on earth for me?

And is it true? For if it is,
   No loving fingers tying strings
Around those tissued fripperies,
   The sweet and silly Christmas things,
Bath salts and inexpensive scent
And hideous tie so kindly meant,

No love that in a family dwells,
   No carolling in frosty air,
Nor all the steeple-shaking bells
   Can with this single Truth compare—
That God was Man in Palestine
And lives to-day in Bread and Wine.

W. H. AUDEN
(1907–   )

[*'O da quod jubes, Domine'*][1]

O Unicorn among the cedars
To whom no magic charm can lead us,
White childhood moving like a sigh
Through the green woods unharmed in thy
Sophisticated innocence
To call thy true love to the dance;
O Dove of science and of light
Upon the branches of the night;
O Icthus playful in the deep
Sea-lodges that for ever keep
Their secret of excitement hidden;
O sudden Wind that blows unbidden
Parting the quiet reeds; O Voice
Within the labyrinth of choice
Only the passive listener hears;
O Clock and Keeper of the years;
O Source of equity and rest,
Quando non fuerit, non est,
It without image, paradigm
Of matter, motion, number, time,
The grinning gap of Hell, the hill
Of Venus and the stairs of Will,
Disturb our negligence and chill,
Convict our pride of its offence
In all things, even penitence,
Instruct us in the civil art
Of making from the muddled heart
A desert and a city where
The thoughts that have to labour there
May find locality and peace,

[1] 'Lord, give what thou commandest.' Augustine, *Confessions*, X. xxix. From
New Year Letter (ll. 1651–84)

And pent-up feelings their release.
Send strength sufficient for our day,
And point our knowledge on its way,
O da quod jubes, Domine.

196   At the Manger
                        Mary sings

O shut your bright eyes that mine must endanger
With their watchfulness; protected by its shade
Escape from my care: what can you discover
From my tender look but how to be afraid?
Love can but confirm the more it would deny.
    Close your bright eye.

Sleep. What have you learned from the womb that bore you
But an anxiety your Father cannot feel?
Sleep. What will the flesh that I gave do for you,
Or my mother love, but tempt you from His will?
Why was I chosen to teach His Son to weep?
    Little One, sleep.

Dream. In human dreams earth ascends to Heaven
Where no one need pray nor ever feel alone.
In your first few hours of life here, O have you
Chosen already what death must be your own?
How soon will you start on the Sorrowful Way?
    Dream while you may.

LOUIS MACNEICE
(1907–1963)

Prayer in Mid-Passage

O Thou my monster, Thou my guide,
Be with me where the bluffs divide
Nor let me contemplate return
To where my backward chattels burn
In haunts of friendship and untruth–
The Cities of the Plain of Youth.

O pattern of inhuman good,
Hard critic of our thought and blood,
By whose decree there is no zone
Where man can live by men alone,
Unveil Thyself that all may see
Thy fierce impersonality.

We were the past–and doomed because
We were a past that never was;
Yet grant to men that they may climb
This time-bound ladder out of time
And by our human organs we
Shall thus transcend humanity.

Take therefore, though Thou disregard,
This prayer, this hymn, this feckless word,
O Thou my silence, Thou my song,
To whom all focal doubts belong
And but for whom this breath were breath–
Thou my meaning, Thou my death.

DAVID GASCOYNE
(1916–   )

Ecce Homo

WHOSE is this horrifying face,
This putrid flesh, discoloured, flayed,
Fed on by flies, scorched by the sun?
Whose are these hollow red-filmed eyes
And thorn-spiked head and spear-struck side?
Behold the Man: He is Man's Son.

Forget the legend, tear the decent veil
That cowardice or interest devised
To make their mortal enemy a friend,
To hide the bitter truth all His wounds tell,
Lest the great scandal be no more disguised:
He is in agony till the world's end,

And we must never sleep during that time!
He is suspended on the cross-tree now
And we are onlookers at the crime,
Callous contemporaries of the slow
Torture of God. Here is the hill
Made ghastly by His spattered blood

Whereon He hangs and suffers still:
See, the centurions wear riding-boots,
Black shirts and badges and peaked caps,
Greet one another with raised-arm salutes;
They have cold eyes, unsmiling lips;
Yet these His brothers know not what they do.

And on his either side hang dead
A labourer and a factory hand,
Or one is maybe a lynched Jew
And one a Negro or a Red,

Coolie or Ethiopian, Irishman,
Spaniard or German democrat.

Behind His rolling head the sky
Glares like a fiery cataract
Red with the murders of two thousand years
Committed in His name and by
Crusaders, Christian warriors
Defending faith and property.

Amid the plain beneath His transfixed hands,
Exuding darkness as indelible
As guilty stains, fanned by funereal
And lurid airs, besieged by drifting sands
And clefted landslides our about-to-be
Bombed and abandoned cities stand.

He who wept for Jerusalem
Now sees His prophecy extend
Across the greatest cities of the world,
A guilty panic reason cannot stem
Rising to raze them all as He foretold;
And He must watch this drama to the end.

Though often named, He is unknown
To the dark kingdoms at His feet
Where everything disparages His words,
And each man bears the common guilt alone
And goes blindfolded to his fate,
And fear and greed are sovereign lords.

The turning point of history
Must come. Yet the complacent and the proud
And who exploit and kill, may be denied—
Christ of Revolution and of Poetry—
The resurrection and the life
Wrought by your spirit's blood.

Involved in their own sophistry
The black priest and the upright man
Faced by subversive truth shall be struck dumb,
Christ of Revolution and of Poetry,
While the rejected and condemned become
Agents of the divine.

Not from a monstrance silver-wrought
But from the tree of human pain
Redeem our sterile misery,
Christ of Revolution and of Poetry,
That man's long journey through the night
May not have been in vain.

R. S. THOMAS
(1913–   )

199

The Country Clergy

I see them working in old rectories
By the sun's light, by candlelight,
Venerable men, their black cloth
A little dusty, a little green
With holy mildew. And yet their skulls,
Ripening over so many prayers,
Toppled into the same grave
With oafs and yokels. They left no books,
Memorial to their lonely thought
In grey parishes; rather they wrote
On men's hearts and in the minds
Of young children sublime words
Too soon forgotten. God in his time
Or out of time will correct this.

200

The Musician

A memory of Kreisler once:
At some recital in this same city,
The seats all taken, I found myself pushed
On to the stage with a few others,
So near that I could see the toil
Of his face muscles, a pulse like a moth
Fluttering under the fine skin,
And the indelible veins of his smooth brow.

I could see, too, the twitching of the fingers,
Caught temporarily in art's neurosis,
As we sat there or warmly applauded
This player who so beautifully suffered
For each of us upon his instrument.

So it must have been on Calvary
In the fiercer light of the thorns' halo:
The men standing by and that one figure,
The hands bleeding, the mind bruised but calm,
Making such music as lives still.
And no one daring to interrupt
Because it was himself that he played
And closer than all of them the God listened.

TEXTUAL SOURCES

The ultimate source of the text is given here. Standard editions and collected works are given after the biographical notes (pp. 352–71).

Most of the medieval poems (Nos. 2–27) are modernized from the normalized texts in the *Oxford Book of Medieval English Verse* (OBMV), with the permission of the editors and the Clarendon Press. Texts preserving the manuscript spelling can be found in Carleton Brown's three anthologies: *Religious Lyrics of the Thirteenth Century* (1932), *Religious Lyrics of the Fourteenth Century* (1924), *Religious Lyrics of the Fifteenth Century* (1939), referred to as CB XIII, XIV and XV.

After the introduction of printing, the source given is normally the first appearance of a poem in book form. Previous publication in periodicals is noted only when there is a significant gap between the appearance of a poem in a periodical and its publication in a volume, or when the date of periodical publication has special significance. Similarly, date of composition has only occasionally been supplied, when publication was posthumous or much delayed.

1. Vercelli MS. Translation by Helen Gardner from text in Sweet's *Anglo-Saxon Reader* (revised edn. 1967)

2. Durham Cathedral MS. A III 12 (*c.* 1225–50): *OBMV* 4, *CB XIV* 1a

3. Bodl. MS. Selden Supra 74 (*c.* 1275–1300): *OBMV* 269, *CB XIII* 1

4. B.M. MS. Egerton 613 (*c.* 1250): *OBMV* 13, *CB XIII* 17b

5. New Coll. MS. F 88 (*c.* 1275–1300): *OBMV* 21, *CB XIV* 5

6. Lambeth MS. 577 (*c.* 1275): *OBMV* 20

7 and 8. B.M. MS. Add. 46919 (*c.* 1330, probably Herebert's autograph): *OBMV* 74, *CB XIV* 25; *CB XIV* 16

9. Merton Coll. MS. 248 (*c.* 1350): *OBMV* 75, *CB XIV* 36

10. B.M. MS. Harl. 7322 (*c.* 1375): *OBMV* 87, *CB XIV* 75

11 and 12. Advocates Library MS. 18 7 21 (Commonplace Book of Friar John Grimeston, copied 1372): *CB XIV* 59; *OBMV* 84, *CB XIV* 66

13 and 14. *Piers Plowman*, ed. W. W. Skeat, 2 vols. (1896): C Text, ii. 149–56; B Text xviii, 1–69; 110–79; 258–269; C Text xxi, 283–296; B Text xviii, 313–337; 359–375; 391–431. Some readings from the C Text have been adopted into the B Text, and I have substituted modern forms and occasionally a modern word more freely than in other medieval texts.

15–18. *Complete Works of Geoffrey Chaucer*, ed. F. N. Robinson (2nd edn. 1957): *Short Poems*; *Troilus and Criseyde*, V. 1835–48; *Cant. Tales*, General Prologue, 208–68 and 478–528

19. *Meditations on the Life and Passion of Christ* (c. 1375), ed. C. D'Evelyn (1921), 218–50: *OBMV* 135

20. Camb. U.L. MS. Hh 4 12, with some readings from Lambeth MS. 853: *OBMV* 136

21. Bodl. MS. Douce 302: *OBMV* 160

22 and 23. B.M. MS. Sloane 2593 (c. 1450): *OBMV* 188, 191, *CB XV* 81, 83

24. B.M. MS. Harl. 4012: *CB XV* 103

25. Bodl. MS. Rawl. B 332: *CB XV* 120

26 and 27. Ball. Coll. MS. 354 (c. 1530): *OBMV* 255, 247

28 and 29. Nat. Lib. Scotland MS. Bannatyne

30 and 31. More, *Works* (1557): written 1504–5

32 and 33. Spenser, *Faerie Queene* (1590), II. viii. 1–2; *Amoretti* (1595), No. 68

34 and 35. Ralegh: A. Skoloker, *Daiphantus* (1604); *The Prerogative of Parliaments in England* (1608)

36 and 37. Greville, 'Caelica', sonnets 87 and 88 (written probably between 1600 and 1610), *Certain Learned and Elegant Works* (1633)

38. Sidney, 'Certain Sonnets', printed with *Arcadia* (1598)

39–42. Southwell: 39 *St. Peter's Complaint* (1595); 40 and 41 *St. Peter's Complaint* (1602); 42 *Maeoniae* (1595)

43. B.M. MS. Add. 15225

44. Alabaster, Bodl. MS. Eng. Poet. e 57

45–47. Campion, *Two Books of Airs* (n.d. ?1613)

48. Wotton, *Reliquiae Wottonianae* (1651)

49–54. Donne: 49 'Satire III', 72–110 (written probably c. 1595) *Poems* (1633); 50 'A Litany' stanzas xv–xvii, xxi (written probably c. 1608), *Poems* (1633); 51 'Holy Sonnets' (i–v written probably 1609; vi written after 1617), i *Poems* (1635) ii–v *Poems* (1633), vi Westmoreland MS.; 52 *The Second Anniversary* (1612), 85–120, 157–219, 251–300; 53 and 54 *Poems* (1633)

55. Jonson, *Underwoods* (1641)

56 and 57. Phineas Fletcher, *The Purple Island* etc. (1633); *A Father's Testament* (1670)

58–60. Giles Fletcher, *Christ's Victory and Triumph* (1610), I. lxxvi–ix, III. xxxii–iv, IV. xxxix–xlii

61–63. Herrick, *Noble Numbers*, printed with *Hesperides* (1648)

64–65. Quarles, *Divine Fancies* (1632); *Emblems* (1635)

66–77. Herbert, *The Temple* (1633)

78–82. Milton: 78–80 *Poems* (1645); 81 *Poems* (1673); 82 *Samson Agonistes* (1671), 667–704, 1268–1296

83. Godolphin, Bodl. MS. Malone 13

84–88. Crashaw: 84 and 85 *Steps to the Temple* (1648), revised and expanded versions of poems from *Steps to the Temple* (1646); 86 From the conclusion added in *Carmen Deo Nostro* (Paris 1652) to 'The Flaming Heart' in *Steps to the Temple* (1648); 87 *Steps to the Temple* (1648); 88 *A Letter* etc. (1653), revised version of poem printed in *Carmen Deo Nostro* (Paris 1652)

89–92. Marvell, *Miscellaneous Poems* (1681), probably written in the 1650's

93–102. Vaughan: 93–101 *Silex Scintillans* (second edn. in two books, 1655); *Thalia Rediviva* (1678)

103–105. Dryden, *Religio Laici* (1682), 1–41; *The Hind and the Panther* (1687), 61–149; *Examum Poeticum* (1693)

106. Wanley, B.M. MS. Add. 22472

107–109. Traherne, Bodl. MS. Eng. Poet c 42; 'Poems of Felicity', B.M. MS. Burney 392; *Centuries of Meditation*, Bodl. MS. Eng. Th. e 50

110 and 111. Addison, *Spectator*, 23 Aug. 1712, 18 Oct. 1712

112–115. Watts: 112 and 113 *Hymns and Spiritual Songs* (1707); 114 *The Psalms of David Imitated* (1719); 115 *Horae Lyricae* (1709)

116. Young, 'Satire VI', *Love of Fame* (1727)

117. Pope, *Of the Use of Riches* (1733), revised in *Epistles* (1744), 339–402

118 and 119. Byrom, *Miscellaneous Poems* (1773); 119, written c. 1750

120–122. Wesley: *Hymns and Sacred Poems* (1742); *Hymns and Sacred Poems* (1739); *Hymns and Sacred Poems* (1740)

123 and 124. Johnson, *The Vanity of Human Wishes* (1749), 343–68; *Gentleman's Magazine*, 1783

125 and 126. Smart, *A Song to David* (1763), stanzas 1–3, 49–86; *The Psalms of David* etc. (1765), Hymn xxxii

127. Newton, *Olney Hymns* (1779)

128–130. Cowper, *Olney Hymns* (1779)

131–136. Blake: 131 and 132 *Songs of Innocence* (1789); 133 and 134 *Songs of Experience* (1794); 135 and 136 Rossetti MS.

137. Burns, *Poems*, ed. Stewart (1801), written 1785

138–141. Wordsworth, *The Prelude*, 1805 text (ed. de Selincourt, 1926), i. 372–427; ii. 415–34; iv. 315–45; vi. 494–572

142. Coleridge, *Morning Post*, 11 Sept. 1802; *Sibylline Leaves* (1817)

143 and 144. Shelley, *Rosalind and Helen* (1819); *Adonais* (1821), stanzas, xxxix–xliv, lii–lv

Textual Sources

145–147. Tennyson, *In Memoriam* (1850), prologue; liv–lvi; cxxiii–iv

148 and 149. Browning, 'Bishop Blougram's Apology', 150–97, *Men and Women* (1855); *Dramatis Personae* (1864)

150–152. Emily Brontë, *Wuthering Heights* (new edn., 1850); *Poems* (1846); *Wuthering Heights, 1850*

153. Clough, *Poems* (1862)

154. Patmore, *The Unknown Eros* (1877)

155–159. Christina Rossetti: 155 *The Face of the Deep* (1892); 156 *The Prince's Progress* (1866); 157 *The Face of the Deep* (1892); 158 and 159 *Poems* (1875)

160. Hardy, *Poems of Past and Present* (1901)

161. Bridges, *Poems in Classical Prosody* (1913)

162–169. Hopkins, *Poems*, ed. Bridges (1918): 162 written 1875; 163–165 written 1877; 166 written 1880; 167–169 written 1885

170 and 171. Alice Meynell, *Collected Poems* (1913); *A Father of Women* (1917)

172 and 173. Housman, *More Poems* (1936)

174 and 175. Mary Coleridge, *Poems* (1908)

176–178. Yeats: *The Winding Stair* (1933); *A Full Moon in March* (1935); *Last Poems* (1939)

179. Dowson, *The Second Book of the Rhymers' Club* (1894)

180. Johnson, *The Second Book of the Rhymers' Club* (1894)

181 and 182. Lawrence, *Last Poems* (1932)

183. Sassoon, *The Tasking* (1954)

184–186. Muir: *The Labyrinth* (1949); *One Foot in Eden* (1956); *Collected Poems* (1952)

187. Edith Sitwell, *Street Songs* (1942)

188–192. Eliot: *Poems* (1919); *Ariel Poems*, No. 8 (1927); *Ash-Wednesday* (1930), I and VI; *Ariel Poems*, No. 29 (1930); *Little Gidding* (1942), reprinted *Four Quartets* (1943)

193 and 194. Betjeman, *New Statesman*, 30 Sept. 1939; and *Old Lights for New Chancels* (1940); *A Few Late Chrysanthemums* (1954)

195 and 196. Auden: *New Year Letter* (1941), 1651–84; *For the Time Being* (1945)

197. MacNeice, *Springboard* (1944)

198. Gascoyne, *Poems 1937–42* (1943)

199 and 200. Thomas, *Poetry for Supper* (1958); *Tares* (1961)

NOTES

1. The Dream of the Rood (p. 25)

The poem survives in a single manuscript (the Vercelli Book), preserved in a monastery in North Italy, dating from the tenth century; but quotations from the speech of the Cross are found engraved in runes on the Ruthwell Cross in Dumfriesshire, usually dated at the end of the seventh or beginning of the eighth century. Two lines that echo the poem are engraved on a reliquary at Brussels (considerably later in date than the manuscript) which once contained a fragment of the True Cross. I have put them above my translation to give a taste of the simple paratactic syntax and powerful rhythms of Anglo-Saxon verse and to set as it were the tune.

Anglo-Saxon verse is not syllabic and does not employ rhyme. Its basic constituents are stress and alliteration. I have attempted to combine a literal translation with an approximation to the verse-form and poetic conventions of the original, preserving formulaic phrases and attempting to respect the poet's choice among various synonyms for the Cross or for Christ.

The poem strikingly blends the Germanic heroic ideal with the ancient doctrine of the Atonement, familiar from such hymns as 'Ye choirs of New Jerusalem', which saw Christ's death as the rescue of humanity from the power of the Devil. Christ is a warrior, the champion who 'in sight of many' fights sin and death. The basic heroic virtues are courage, endurance, and loyalty. By a tragic paradox, the Cross, in obedience to its Lord, is the 'slayer' of its Lord, and the disciples, his faithful thanes, cannot fulfil the thane's duty, to avenge his lord, since the Cross acted in obedience to his Lord's will. The poet most strikingly ignores the Gospel narrative of the Passion in his picture of Christ the Hero hastening to the hill on which the Cross is set up. His theme is Christ coming to the rescue of mankind. The poem closes, not with the Resurrection, but with the Harrowing of Hell, the return of a King to his Kingdom followed by the captives he has redeemed. This is in accordance with Byzantine tradition for the decoration of churches, in which the last episode of the cycle of Christ's life is always the Anastasis, or Harrowing of Hell.

For a commentary on my translation and on the poem, see *Essays and Poems presented to Lord David Cecil* (Constable, 1970), pp. 24–36.

11. 'Lullay, lullay, little child' (p. 37)

This is unique among lullaby carols in being sung to the infant Christ not by his Mother but by a spokesman for sinful mankind. It has the same burden as a melancholy lullaby in the Kildare manuscript in which a human mother soothing her weeping child envisages the woes of human life.

13 and 14. William Langland (p. 39)
[*Et Incarnatus Est*]
and [The Jousting of Jesus]

Out of Langland's immense visionary poem I have selected a short passage, from the C text, illustrative of his power to render theological conceptions in poetic imagery, and a shortened version of the climax of the central section of the poem: the dreamer's vision of the Trial and Crucifixion of Jesus and his Harrowing of Hell. I have reduced the theological arguments between the Four Daughters of God and between Christ and Satan.

The vision opens on Palm Sunday and closes with the bells ringing for the first Mass of Easter Sunday. The interspersed Latin phrases and sentences from the offices continually remind us that this is more than a narrative of past events. We are sharing the dreamer's experience of the most solemn week in the Christian year. I have, therefore, quoted texts from the Authorized Version or the Prayer Book Psalter rather than translated the Vulgate texts literally, since the point of the poet's use of these Latin phrases was their familiarity. The ultimate source for the narrative of Christ's descent into Hell is the apocryphal Gospel of Nicodemus, but this was one of the most vivid and popular episodes in the contemporary Craft Cycle Plays. Langland blends liturgical, theological, and dramatic traditions in his vision of the Crucifixion as a joust with Sin and Death.

Langland's poem represents the survival in the West Midlands of the old alliterative metre, and a translation into chivalric terms of the old conception of Christ the Hero and Champion, rescuing mankind from the devil's power. The persistence of the popularity of the theme of the Harrowing of Hell in English poetry is remarkable. As late as the sixteenth century Dunbar, in his Easter Hymn (No. 29), is still celebrating Christ as 'our Champion'.

ll. 1–70. *The Entry into Jerusalem, Trial and Crucifixion.*

ll. 6–7. On Palm Sunday (*Dominica in ramis palmarum* in the Breviary) a procession of children sang the hymn 'All glory, laud, and honour'.

l. 9. Christ entering on his Passion appears somewhat like the Good Samaritan, type of Charity, the highest Christian virtue, whom the Dreamer has met earlier, and like Piers Plowman, the object of his search throughout the poem. Piers, the good life, in this middle section of the poem displays the virtues of a true priest: to teach, to heal, and to suffer. Jesus will fight in his armour, that is 'human nature', deceiving the devil who will not recognize him as 'the most high God'; but he will be unhurt since he will fight 'in the Godhead of the Father'.

l. 36. 'O death I will be thy death' (Hos. 13;14), an antiphon in the Offices for Holy Saturday.

ll. 36–70. The narrative combines phrases from the Passion according to Matthew, sung on Palm Sunday, with the Passion according to John, sung on

Good Friday. Pilate is 'sitting on the judgement-seat'. The Jews cry 'Crucify him' and 'Away with him, away'. The salutation of Judas, 'Hail, Rabbi', at the betrayal is confused with the 'Hail, King of the Jews' of the Mocking. The 'It is finished' of John is followed by the 'Truly this was the Son of God' of the centurion in Matthew.

Some forty lines are omitted here. They relate an incident from the apocryphal Gospel of Nicodemus, telling how a blind centurion, Longinus, wounded Christ's body with his spear, and how the blood that gushed out restored his sight.

ll. 71–142. *The Four Daughters of God.*

With the clause of the Creed 'He descended into Hell', the dreamer passes to Holy Saturday. In a No-Man's-Land outside the gates of Hell he learns how God's Justice is reconciled with his Mercy. The debate between the Four Daughters of God, based on the text 'Mercy and Truth are met together; Righteousness and Peace have kissed each other' (Ps. 85:10), originated in the twelfth century and reflects the development of a legalistic doctrine of the Atonement. The text is quoted at l.250.

l. 110. 'Because there is no redemption in Hell.' This is a sentence, loosely based on Job 7:9, from the Sarum Offices for the Dead.

l. 122. 'That art might deceive art', that is, that the beguiler might be beguiled. This is a line from the third stanza of the Passion Hymn *'Pange lingua'* ('Sing my tongue the glorious battle'). Mercy's analogy is a 'scientific' commonplace of the day: that the cure for a scorpion's sting is to lay a dead scorpion on the wound.

l. 142. 'Heaviness may endure for a night but joy cometh in the morning' (Ps. 30:5).

Some sixty lines containing the debate of the Four Daughters and their instruction by Book are omitted.

ll. 143–262. *The Harrowing of Hell.* I have included from the C text one of Langland's most lively additions, Satan's instructions for the defence of Hell (ll. 157–170); but I have omitted his conversation with Lucifer and the latter part of Christ's speech (some 40 lines), which expand the theme of the justice by which the 'guiler is guiled', and by which he claims men's souls as lawfully his.

l. 145. 'Lift up your heads, O ye gates, and be ye lift up, ye everlasting doors' (Ps. 24:9).

ll. 179–80. 'The people in darkness' sing 'Behold the Lamb of God', the salutation of the Baptist. Cf. Isaiah 9:2: 'The people that walked in darkness have seen a great light; they that dwell in the land of the shadow of death, upon them hath the light shined.'

l. 196. 'A tooth for a tooth and an eye for an eye' (Ex. 21:34 and Matt. 5:38).

ll. 205–6. The valley of Jehoshaphat was traditionally the place of the last judgement and the 'Resurrection of the Dead'; cf. Joel 3:2, 12, 13.

l. 218. 'I have heard unspeakable words, which it is not lawful for a man to utter' (2 Cor. 12:4).

l. 223. 'Enter not into judgement with thy servant, O Lord' (Ps. 143:2) These two last Latin phrases are comments by the Dreamer.

l. 233. 'The flesh sins, the flesh purges from sin and the flesh reigns as God of God.' These are lines from the fourth stanza of the Ascension Office Hymn 'Eternal Monarch, King most High', translated by Neale as

> Flesh hath purged what flesh had stained,
> And God, the Flesh of God, hath reigned.

ll. 234–5. 'The sun shines more brightly than usual after heavy mists, and love also is brighter after dissension.' The idea is proverbial; no exact source has been found.

l. 254. 'Behold, how good and joyful a thing it is: brethren to dwell together in unity' (Ps. 133:1).

20. ['Quia Amore Langueo'] (p. 56)

There are two distinct poems with this refrain in the same stanza form. Both date from the end of the fourteenth century and both are *chansons d'aventure*, poems in which the poet overhears a love-complaint. In this one, the finer to my judgement, the speaker is Christ, the Knight-Lover. The poem blends the traditional appeal of Christ to man with the imagery of the Song of Songs, from which the refrain is taken. In the other poem the speaker is the Virgin. She appeals to man as Mother of God and Mother of Man, pleading with him as his mother and his sister, and finally offering herself as his wife. It is an original handling of the complaint of Mary from the foot of the Cross. The fact that the refrain is a more integral part of the conception makes me regard this poem in which Christ is the speaker as the original, providing a formal model for a second poem in which the erotic refrain 'For I am sick of love' seems less suitable.

24. 'Woefully arrayed' (p. 64)

This complaint of Christ has been ascribed to John Skelton on the grounds that in a list of his own compositions in 'A Garland of Laurel' he mentions, among pious works, 'Woefully arayd and shamefully betrayd', and that a copy of the poem with a variant version of the last stanza and a unique additional final stanza, written on the fly-leaf of a book, is ascribed to him. But the three manuscript versions make no attribution and it seems likely that the poem Skelton claims he wrote was a different poem based on the same burden.

27. Corpus Christi Carol (p. 67)

There has been much debate over this most magical of all carols. The original version, given here, is preserved in a manuscript of the sixteenth century, which there is some reason to connect with the Abbey of Glastonbury. There are three traditional versions, all taken down in the nineteenth century. Two of them substitute for the falcon burden internal refrains: 'The bells of Paradise I heard them ring' and 'And I love my Lord Jesus above anything'. Both of these have references to the famous blossoming thorn of Glastonbury. A third (Scottish) version has neither burden nor refrains but has preserved, with a difference, the bird of the original burden: 'The heron flew east, the heron flew west, the heron flew to the fair forest'. (See R. L. Greene, *A Selection of English Carols*, Clarendon Press 1962, Nos. 67 a, b, c, d.)

Many scholars think the original carol is inspired by the Grail legend. Professor Greene has suggested it was written to arouse sympathy with the unhappy lot of Catherine of Aragon. He points out that the much exploited badge of Anne Boleyn was a white falcon and that the weeping and praying maiden, contemplating the dead knight (Christ), and the final reference to 'Corpus Christi' reflect descriptions of the devotions of the deserted wife of Henry VIII in her exile from the court. I find it difficult to accept this suggestion. The falcon who bears the 'make' away bears him to the orchard in which is found the mysterious hall with its dead knight and weeping maiden, and it seems highly inappropriate to refer to a deserted wife as a 'may'. The poem is inspired by the urge to Christianize chivalric romance which led to the creation of the Arthurian Grail story, and the strange bird recalls the bird or beast guides common in medieval love-visions.

30 and 31. Sir Thomas More (p. 72)
[The Measure of Love]
and [A Prayer]

These stanzas are taken from More's expansion into rhyme royal stanzas of Pico della Mirandola's 'Twelve properties or conditions of a lover', and the two concluding stanzas of the 'Prayer of Pico' with which More ended his *Life of Pico*. In the contents list of the *Works* (1557) More's translation of the *Life of Pico* is dated 1510; but this date probably refers to an edition published in that year. The work itself, dedicated to Joyce Leigh, a Minoress of Aldgate, was probably written 1504–5, when More, after a period in the London Charterhouse where he lived austerely to test his vocation to the religious life, had decided on secular life and was about to marry. Pico was to him the type of the devout layman.

35. Sir Walter Ralegh (p. 78)
Epitaph

Manuscripts and printed texts unanimously ascribe this poem to Ralegh, many adding that he wrote it the night before he died, and some that he wrote it in his Bible. The first six lines are the final stanza of a love poem ascribed to him, 'Nature that washed her hands in milk', with the first three words altered from 'O cruel Time'. It is moving to think of him recalling a poem written in happier times and adding to an old stanza the concluding expression of faith. As Miss Latham says, it is 'characteristic of his sombre temper that even his love songs could at will supply an epitaph'.

42. Robert Southwell (p. 85)
Upon the Image of Death

Although published with Southwell's poems and now, by its frequent appearance under his name in anthologies, usually accepted as his, this poem, in the judgement of Southwell's latest editor, is probably not by him. Both its simple vocabulary and its rather monotonous stanza seem to belong to the mid-sixteenth century and look back to late medieval treatments of the theme *memento mori*. It is in the tradition of the hymn *'Cur Mundus Militat'*, attributed to St. Bernard, a much translated and imitated poem.

43. 'Hierusalem, my happy home' (p. 87)

This famous poem exists in many versions, with variants and omissions or additions, one late broadsheet even attempting to turn it into a Puritan ballad. The version excerpted from here (twenty six stanzas) from a Catholic Common-place Book dated 1616, is headed 'A song Mad by I. B. P. To the Tune of Diana'. Earlier in the manuscript there is a longer, inferior version (fifty-five stanzas). A shorter version (nineteen stanzas) is printed in *The Song of Mary the Mother of Christ*, 1601. It seems likely that the initials stand for 'J. B. Priest'. The author, whoever he was, was inspired both by the hymn of Peter Damien *'Ad perennis vitae fontem'* and the native ballad traditions.

49. John Donne (p. 94)
['Seek True Religion!']

According to Walton, Donne, who came of a family notable for loyalty to the Roman Church, began when he was a young law-student 'seriously to survey and consider' the points 'controverted betwixt the Reformed and the Roman Church'. By the time he was twenty-five and had taken service with the Lord Keeper he must have conformed to the Established Church. He said later that he 'used no inordinate haste, nor precipitation in binding his conscience to any local Religion' or, in Walton's words, he for a while 'bethrothed himself to no Religion that might give him any other denomination than a Christian'. The third Satire, of which this is the concluding section, belongs to this period of enquiry. Donne's noble defence of the rights of conscience rests on an unsceptical conviction that Truth exists and that the human mind can attain it, as well as on the view he often expressed that 'in all Christian professions there is way to salvation'. The central section of the poem attacks the trivial and insufficient reasons for which men adhere to one Church rather than another.

52. John Donne (p. 99)
[The Progress of the Soul]

Donne's two *Anniversaries*, the only poems he published, celebrated the virtue of Elizabeth Drury, a young girl he had never seen. He defended his extravagant praises of her by saying that in her he 'described the Idea of a Woman and not as she was'. In *The Anatomy of the World* (1611), the *First Anniversary*, he attempted to link the traditional theme of the progressive decay of the world with the death of Miss Drury. *The Second Anniversary* (1612), or 'The Progress of the Soul', from which these passages are excerpted, is more unified. It alternates between a meditation on death, the soul's enfranchisement by death, and the joys of heaven, and the praise of Elizabeth Drury, who now, after a life of virtue, experiences those joys. I have printed the first three meditations, omitting the interspersed eulogies and the two final meditations: on 'our company in this life and the next' and on 'essential joy in this life and the next'.

125. Christopher Smart (p. 215)
A Song to David

Considerations of space forbid printing all eighty-six stanzas of Smart's stupendous paean of praise to the Creator. I was tempted to present a shortened version, by omitting the weaker stanzas; but I have preferred to print the opening address to the Psalmist and then give the last sequence without omission, since it moves with such power to the final grand climax.

150 and 151. Emily Brontë (p. 264)
The Visionary
and The Prisoner

It is now known that both these poems originated in a long poem extant in Emily Brontë's transcription of poems dealing with the history of the imaginary land of Gondal and its inhabitants. Charlotte published the first three stanzas of this poem, with two additional stanzas, under the title 'The Visionary', in the handful of Emily's poems added to the second edition of *Wuthering Heights*. Whether the additional stanzas are her own or Emily's does not affect the beauty of the poem as printed. Emily herself had earlier extracted fifteen stanzas which she published, with an additional concluding stanza, in *Poems* (1846) as 'The Prisoner. A Fragment'. The origin of these two poems (and, we are told, of 'Last Lines' also) in the rather tawdry and infantile romanticism of the Gondal stories should not hinder response to them as expressions of an intense faith and of the communion of the devoted soul with the divine. As with many other poems, what they have become is more important than how they began.

162. Gerard Manley Hopkins (p. 277)
The Wreck of the Deutschland

On his entry into the Jesuit Order Hopkins burned his poems and resolved to write no more. Seven years later he read in *The Times* of the death by shipwreck of the five Franciscan nuns: 'Five German nuns ... clasped hands and were drowned together, the chief sister, a gaunt woman 6ft. high, calling out loudly and often "O Christ, come quickly!" till the end came.' On a hint from his Rector, who said that he wished someone would write a poem on the event, Hopkins composed the poem 'in a new rhythm' that had been haunting his ear. It was sent to the Jesuit periodical *The Month*, but the editors withdrew it before publication as too 'daring'.

In the first part Hopkins writes of his own spiritual crisis and conversion, meditating on the paradox that, since the Incarnation and Passion, God's mastery and mercy is known not only in beauty and joy but more profoundly in terror and loss. 'What refers to myself in the poem', he wrote to Bridges, 'is all strictly and literally true and did all occur; nothing is added for poetical padding.' In the second part the nun's faith and her vision of Christ at the heart of the storm, re-enacting the Passion, is seen as redemptive. Remembering his own conversion, the poet appeals to her to intercede for the conversion of England.

178. W. B. Yeats (p. 299)
The Black Tower

The poem is dated 21 January 1939, that is, seven days before Yeats died. Mrs. Yeats stated that it was a poem 'on the subject of political propaganda'; but it seems to transcend this theme and to embody Yeats's life-long commitment to belief in some supernatural reality while rejecting commitment to any historic creed. A garrison is waiting, bound by oath to a rightful king who, according to their assailants, died long ago. They are surrounded by the graves of ancient warriors, buried upright with their arms beside them as in ancient Ireland. The bones of the dead are shaken by great winds, and to Irish country folk the Sidhe, or Fairy folk, journey on whirling winds. The old cook ('old

Tom' in some drafts of the poem) climbs the hill in the early morning while the garrison sleeps. He swears he 'hears the king's great horn' but they refuse to believe him. Yet they remain, against all reason, 'oath-bound'. Jon Stallworthy believes that the cook represents the Christian in Yeats' 'whom he could never entirely suppress, and struggled with particularly, Mrs. Yeats told me, when he was ill'. See *Between the Lines*, Clarendon Press 1963, pp. 202–244, for drafts and discussion. Although I would not press my own reading of this poem as a religious poem, I have myself always read it as such and hope some others may think it rightly included in this volume.

184. Edwin Muir (p. 307)
The Border

This poem is included as a striking modern treatment of a classic religious theme: the contemplation of death as the stripping away of all the goods of this life.

192. T. S. Eliot (p. 318)
Little Gidding

Little Gidding is a village in Huntingdonshire to which Nicholas Ferrar retired with his family in 1626 to lead an ordered life of prayer and good works. The community was visited by King Charles in 1633 and again in 1642, and legend, familiar to readers of *John Inglesant*, says that he came there at night, as 'a broken king', after the final defeat of Naseby. The community was scattered in 1647, the chapel left to go to ruin, and Nicholas Ferrar's ideal of a religious community based on the family was never revived. Little Gidding, whose chapel was restored for worship in the nineteenth century, remains a 'symbol perfected in death'.

Eliot visited Little Gidding in May 1936. He recalls his visit in an aside: 'If you came this way in may-time.' The first draft of the poem, the last and culminating poem of *Four Quartets*, summing Eliot's meditation on time and eternity, and the meaning of history, was finished by August 1941. It was extensively revised for its publication in October 1942. Eliot's experience as a fire-watcher on the roof of Faber's, and as a warden patrolling the streets in Kensington, provided him with his second and fourth movements. The colloquy after the air-raid, in a verse-form that approximates to Italian terza rima, is soaked in Dantean reminiscence. Although the 'dead master' is 'both one and many' and a 'compound familiar ghost' it seems that it was mainly the greatest of his contemporaries, Yeats, who had died in 1939 and been buried 'on a distant shore', that Eliot had in mind.

At the turn of the third movement Eliot quotes from the *Revelations of Divine Love*, written by Dame Julian of Norwich, an anchoress of the fourteenth century: 'Sin is behovely but all shall be well, and all shall be well, and all manner of thing shall be well.' He quotes from her again at the close of the third movement. In her revelation concerning prayer she heard the words 'I am Ground of thy Beseeching.' Another quotation from a fourteenth-century mystic, the unknown author of *The Cloud of Unknowing*, divides the two sections of the last movement, which returns to Dante with its final image of the infolded rose.

BIOGRAPHICAL NOTES

JOSEPH ADDISON (1672–1719), educated at Charterhouse and Queen's College, Oxford, became Demy and later Fellow of Magdalen. Political patronage deflected him from following his father in taking Orders; but he was not unjustly described as 'a parson in a tye-wig'. He contributed to Steele's *The Tatler*, and on its demise began *The Spectator*, published daily from March 1711 to December 1712. His religious and ethical papers were widely popular, and in them he took up the question of divine poetry, supplying a paraphrase of Psalm 23, an original hymn ('When all thy mercies, O my God') at the end of an essay on 'Gratitude', and the 'Ode', based on Psalm 19, at the close of an essay on the impressions of 'divine power and wisdom in the universe'. 'How are thy Servants blest' he printed from 'a correspondent' and the hymn 'When rising from the bed of death' he ascribed to an 'Excellent Man in Holy Orders'. There seems a genuine humility in his thus not claiming credit for poems designed to edify.

The Spectator, ed. Donald F. Bond, 5 vols., Clarendon Press, Oxford, 1965.

WILLIAM ALABASTER (1567–1640), educated at Westminster and Trinity, College, Cambridge, where he was a Fellow, went as chaplain to Essex on the Cadiz Expedition in 1596. On his return he declared himself a Catholic. His divine sonnets, surviving in manuscripts, were probably written when in prison and under pressure to recant. After some years abroad, having got into trouble with the Inquisition at Rome, he returned to England and declared himself once more a Protestant. He ended an adventurous life as a country parson, absorbed in recondite speculation on the Book of Revelation, and published several cabbalistic works.

Sonnets, ed. G. M. Story and Helen Gardner, Clarendon Press, Oxford, 1959.

JOHN AUDELAY (fl. 1426), in the manuscript in which his verses are preserved, describes himself as a *capellanus*, adding he is blind and deaf and is living in Haghmond Abbey. The note is dated 1426. At the end of the last poem in the book he tells us that he was 'first priest to the Lord Strange of this chantry here in this place', and that he made his book 'by God's grace, deaf, sick, and blind as he lay'.

Poems, ed. E. K. Whiting, *E.E.T.S.*, Clarendon Press, Oxford, 1931.

WYSTAN HUGH AUDEN (1907–), educated at Gresham's School, Holt, and Christ Church, Oxford, published his first volume of poems in 1930. In January 1939 he migrated to the United States with his friend and collaborator

Christopher Isherwood, and in 1946 took out American citizenship. Professor of Poetry at Oxford from 1956–1961.

Collected Longer Poems, Faber and Faber, London, 1968.
Collected Shorter Poems 1927–1957, Faber and Faber, London, 1966.

SIR JOHN BETJEMAN (1906–), educated at Marlborough and Magdalen College, Oxford, combines strongly held religious beliefs (he is a devoted Anglican), a passionate interest in ecclesiology, and an acute sense of place, with a vein of satire. His poetry appealed at first mainly to sophisticated readers, who appreciated his impulse to 'love the lovely that is not beloved'; but with the publication of his verse autobiography, *Summoned by Bells* (1960), he became a best-seller. He was knighted in 1969.

Collected Poems, third edition, John Murray, London, 1970.

WILLIAM BLAKE (1757–1827), poet, artist and mystic, was apprenticed to Basire to learn engraving, and then studied for a short time at the Royal Academy school. He earned a modest income as an engraver. To Blake the spiritual alone was real; he looked 'through, not with the eye'. The imagination was for him the way to truth. From Swedenborg, Boehme, neo-Platonism and Christianity he took what his imagination required to create his own system.

Complete Writings, ed. G. Keynes, second edition, Oxford University Press, London, 1966.

ROBERT BRIDGES (1844–1930), educated at Eton, Corpus Christi College, Oxford, and St. Bartholomew's Hospital, practised as a doctor from 1874–1881, when illness cut short his medical career. He settled at Yattendon, Berkshire, moving to Boar's Hill, near Oxford, in 1907. Founder of the Society for Pure English, prosodist, amateur musician, Bridges remained all his life an experimenter in metrics. He was made Poet Laureate in 1913 and received the Order of Merit in 1929. He published his *magnum opus*, *The Testament of Beauty*, on his eighty-fifth birthday.

Poems, including *The Testament of Beauty*, Oxford University Press, London, 1953.

EMILY BRONTË (1818–1848), daughter of the Rev. Patrick Brontë, perpetual curate of Haworth, Yorkshire, went like her sisters to the school for the daughters of the clergy described by Charlotte in *Jane Eyre*. Apart from a few, unhappy, and brief attempts to earn her living as a teacher, she spent her short life at Haworth. Many of her poems were originally written as part of the chronicles of the imaginary kingdom of Gondal which she wrote with her sisters; but they outsoar their origin in these romantic fictions to express her dedication to her 'God of Visions'.

Complete Poems, ed. C. W. Hatfield, Oxford University Press, London, 1941.

Biographical Notes

ROBERT BROWNING (1812–1889) was privately educated and relieved by devoted parents from the necessity of following a profession. After his romantic marriage to Elizabeth Barrett in 1846 he lived, until her death in 1861, mainly in Italy. In *Christmas Eve and Easter Day* Browning attempted to come to terms directly with the crisis of faith. But both his apologetic and the expression of his personal faith are more impressive when put into the mouth of historic or imaginary personages.

Poetical Works, 1833–1864, ed. Ian Jack, Oxford University Press, London, 1970.

ROBERT BURNS (1759–1796), was the son of a small Ayrshire farmer whose piety he commemorated in his poem 'The Cotter's Saturday Night'. After short periods at various small local schools he educated himself by wide reading. Theological controversy raged in the Scotland of his day between the stricter Calvinists, the 'Auld Licht', and the more liberal 'New Licht'. Burns wrote a series of pungent satires on the 'stricter sort'. The most famous, 'Holy Willie's Prayer', attacked William Fisher, elder of Mauchline. Written in the 'language of the saints' it exposes not only Fisher's hypocrisy and uncharitableness but also the corruption of the old orthodox doctrine of 'effectual calling'.

Poems and Songs, ed. James Kinsley, 3 vols., Clarendon Press, Oxford, 1968.

JOHN BYROM (1692–1763), educated at Chester, at the Merchant Taylors' School, and Trinity College, Cambridge, of which he became a Fellow, as a non-juror was unable to take Orders and had to relinquish his Fellowship. He studied medicine at Montpellier, but subsequently made his living teaching shorthand. His journals and letters reveal his passionate interest in religious speculation. He had a predilection for mystical writers and was a disciple of William Law. His most famous poem 'Christians Awake!' he wrote as a present for his daughter.

Poems, ed. A. W. Ward, 2 vols., Chetham Society, Manchester, 1894–5.

THOMAS CAMPION (1567–1620), poet, musician, and physician, was educated at Peterhouse, Cambridge, which he left in 1584 without a degree, and admitted to Gray's Inn in 1586, but was never called to the Bar. He was almost certainly fighting as a gentleman volunteer in France in 1591. He published his *First Book of Airs* in 1601. Some time between 1602 and 1606 he studied medicine, probably on the Continent. *Two Books of Airs*, of which the first contained 'Divine and Moral Songs', the second 'Light Conceits of Lovers', were followed by a third and fourth book. A composer-poet, his avowed aim was 'to couple my Words and Notes lovingly together'.

Works, ed. W. R. Davis, Faber and Faber, London, 1967.

Biographical Notes

GEOFFREY CHAUCER (?1343–1400). Born in London, his father a prosperous vintner, Chaucer served as a page to Lionel, Duke of Clarence, fought in France, and was taken prisoner in 1359. By 1367 he was in the King's service, and involved in a series of diplomatic missions (the most momentous being his first journey to Italy in 1373) and professional and business appointments. His competence in great affairs, his relations with a sophisticated court and prosperous city, and his travels abroad are reflected in the range of his poetry and its broad humanity. Chaucer's earliest poems were 'love-visions', a courtly French form; his first major work, the 'tragedy' of *Troilus*, was probably written about 1385; the immensely ambitious plan of the *Canterbury Tales* he left unfinished at his death.

Works, ed. F. N. Robinson, second edition, Oxford University Press, London, 1957.

ARTHUR HUGH CLOUGH (1819–1861), educated at Rugby and Balliol College, Oxford, elected Tutor and Fellow of Oriel in 1842, resigned his Fellowship in 1848 on account of religious scruples, having come to regard the dogmas of the Church of England as untenable. He never found permanent occupation equal to his abilities. Arnold commemorated him and their friendship in 'Thyrsis'.

Poems, ed. A. L. P. Norrington, Oxford University Press, London, 1968.

MARY COLERIDGE (1861–1907), daughter of a great-nephew of Coleridge, pupil of William Cory, who taught her Greek, and friend of Henry Newbolt, published little poetry in her life-time and that under a pseudonym. Newbolt published a collection made from her manuscripts after her death.

Collected Poems, ed. Theresa Whistler, Hart-Davis, London, 1954.

SAMUEL TAYLOR COLERIDGE (1772–1834), son of the Vicar of Ottery St. Mary, educated at Christ's Hospital and Jesus College, Cambridge, moved, like Wordsworth, from revolutionary enthusiasm to conservatism. His speculative and metaphysical mind led him in youth to Unitarianism, but he returned to Christian orthodoxy. His conception of the Church of England as a religious organism was to be highly influential in the nineteenth century. All his great poetry belongs to the years of his close association with Wordsworth, his *annus mirabilis* being 1797. After 1802 he wrote little that was not mediocre.

Poems, ed. E. H. Coleridge, Oxford University Press, London, 1912.

WILLIAM COWPER (1731–1800), was educated at Westminster and as a law-student. Though he suffered from a serious depression as a young man, his first attack of madness was in 1763, after an attempt at suicide. He laboured under the terrible illusion that he was damned. As a young man he had not

Biographical Notes

been notably religious; but on his recovery and after boarding with the Unwins, he experienced conversion. On the death of Mr. Unwin, Mrs. Unwin moved with Cowper to Olney, where John Newton was curate. From 1773 to 1774 Cowper suffered another attack of mania. It was when he felt the onset of this illness that he wrote 'Light Shining out of Darkness'. In 1787 he had a fresh relapse into insanity, and after a short period of partial recovery, he declined into a state of melancholy stupor.

Poetical Works, ed. H. S. Milford, revised Norma Russell, Oxford University Press, London, 1967.

RICHARD CRASHAW (1612–1649), son of a noted Puritan divine, was educated at Charterhouse and Pembroke College, Cambridge, and in 1635 elected to 'the little contented kingdom' of a Fellowship at Peterhouse, the centre of Laudian High Churchmanship at Cambridge. In 1643, after the visitation of the Parliamentary Commissioners had stripped the chapel at Peterhouse and broken down 'Superstitious Pictures' in Little St. Mary's, he left Cambridge, and is next heard of at Leyden. He seems to have returned to England and to have been for a while at Oxford; but in 1646 he was in Paris and had by then entered the Roman Church. From Paris he went to Rome, where, in spite of a recommendation from Henrietta Maria, he found himself neglected, until he was appointed to a post at Loreto where he died in 1649.

Poems, ed. L. C. Martin, second edition, Clarendon Press, Oxford, 1957.

JOHN DONNE (1572–1631), poet and divine, was educated by his widowed mother, a staunch Catholic (daughter of John Heywood, the interlude writer, and sister of Ellis and Jasper Heywood, both Jesuits), and went when very young to Hart Hall, Oxford. In 1591 he entered the Inns of Court. He sailed with Essex to Cadiz and to the Azores in 1596 and 1597, and on his return became secretary to Sir Thomas Egerton, the Lord Keeper. He had by then broken with his family tradition and conformed to the Established Church. At the close of 1601 he wrecked his career by a clandestine marriage with the young niece of his employer's wife, Ann More, and found himself without employment and his wife without a dowry. Long years of poverty and insecurity came to an end in January 1615, when, under pressure from King James, he took Orders. From 1621 to his death he was Dean of St. Paul's and the greatest preacher of his day.

Poems, ed. H. J. C. Grierson, 2 vols., Clarendon Press, Oxford, 1912; *Divine Poems*, ed. Helen Gardner, Clarendon Press, Oxford, 1952.

ERNEST DOWSON (1867–1900), a member of the Rhymers' Club, was the most gifted of Yeats's 'Companions of the Cheshire Cheese' commemorated by him as 'The Tragic Generation' in *The Trembling of the Veil*. Educated

356

irregularly abroad, he left Queen's College, Oxford, after only one year, and after his father's death in 1894 lived mainly in France. He was for long painfully in love with a London restaurant-keeper's daughter, whose marriage to a waiter destroyed him, and he died of tuberculosis and drink. Yeats said his religion was 'a desire for a condition of virginal ecstasy'. Unlike his fellow Rhymer and friend, Lionel Johnson, he was tormented by sexual desire.

Poetical Works, ed. Desmond Flower, Cassell and Co., London, 1934.

JOHN DRYDEN (1631–1700), educated at Westminster and Trinity College, Cambridge, established himself as a man of letters soon after the Restoration. In 1668 he was made Poet Laureate and in 1670 Historiographer Royal. After *Annus Mirabilis* (1667), he was almost wholly occupied in writing for the stage, until public events turned him to political satire, and he produced his two masterpieces, *Absalom and Achitophel* (1681) and *The Medal* (1682). At the close of 1682 he appeared in a new role with *Religio Laici*, at once the confession of faith of a lively, sceptical, enquiring mind, and a discussion of the problem of religious authority, solved by acceptance of the *via media* of the Church of England. Some time in 1685 he was converted to Roman Catholicism, and defended his new-found security by writing *The Hind and the Panther*. At the Revolution in 1688, he lost both his appointments, and turned largely to verse-translation for his living.

Poems, ed. James Kinsley, 4 vols., Clarendon Press, Oxford, 1958; an annotated edition in one volume is edited by George R. Noyes, Houghton Mifflin Co., Boston, second edition, 1950.

WILLIAM DUNBAR (?1460–?1520). Very little is known of Dunbar's life. He *may* have been the William Dunbar who took his B.A. in 1477 and M.A. in 1479 at St. Andrews. He *may* have been a Franciscan novice. He had certainly taken priest's orders by 1504. From 1500 to 1513 he received a royal pension and in 1501 he was probably in London on an embassy connected with the marriage of James IV to Margaret Tudor. As his pension stops in 1513 he perhaps then obtained his long-sought benefice.

Complete Poems, ed. W. M. Mackenzie, The Porpoise Press, Edinburgh, 1932; *Selected Poems*, ed. James Kinsley, Clarendon Press, Oxford, 1958.

THOMAS STEARNS ELIOT (1888–1965) was born at St. Louis, Missouri, of a New England family, whose religious tradition was Unitarian, and educated at Smith Academy, St. Louis, and Harvard. Caught in Europe in 1914, he came to England where he remained for the rest of his life, becoming a British citizen. With *The Waste Land* (1922), he established himself as the leader of the modern movement in poetry; and, from *The Sacred Wood* (1920) onwards, as the most influential modern critic. In 1927 he was baptized and confirmed in the Church of England. In his poetry and his verse plays, from *The Journey of the Magi* (1927) to *The Elder Statesman* (1959), he attempted to present his acceptance of orthodox belief in a modern idiom. He was awarded the Nobel Prize for Literature and received the Order of Merit in 1948.

Complete Poetry and Plays, Faber and Faber, London, 1969.

GILES FLETCHER (1586–1623), brother of Phineas Fletcher and cousin to John Fletcher, the dramatist, was a Fellow of Trinity College, Cambridge, where he had been an undergraduate, from 1605 to 1618, and reader in Greek. While at Trinity he published his most famous poem, *Christ's Victory and Triumph in Heaven and Earth, over and after Death* (1610). He took a country living in 1618, but according to Fuller his 'clownish low-parted parishioners . . . valued not their pastor, according to his worth, which disposed him to melancholy and hastened his dissolution.'

Giles and Phineas Fletcher: Poetical Works, ed. F. S. Boas, 2 vols., Cambridge University Press, Cambridge, 1908.

PHINEAS FLETCHER (1582–1650), elder brother of Giles Fletcher, educated at Eton and King's College, Cambridge, where he held a Fellowship, was Rector of Hilgay in Norfolk from 1621 until his death. *The Purple Island*, a long allegorical poem describing the human body, assailed by vices and defended by virtues, was printed in 1633, with other poems attached. In his youth he wrote an erotic poem, *Venus and Anchises*, which was printed in 1628 as Spenser's under the title *Britain's Idea. A Father's Testament*, published posthumously in 1670, was written for the edification of his family, with poems at the conclusion of its chapters.

DAVID GASCOYNE (1916–), educated at Salisbury Cathedral Choir School and the Regent Street Polytechnic, published his first book of poems when he was sixteen, and his first novel in the following year. He spent some years in France where he came in contact with Surrealist artists and poets. His collection *Poems 1937–42* was illustrated by Graham Sutherland.

Collected Poems, Oxford University Press, London, 1965.

SIDNEY GODOLPHIN (1610–1643), a Cornishman, was educated at Exeter College, Oxford, and the Inns of Court. He was a friend of Falkland and the circle around Jonson, and wrote a fine elegy on Donne, praising his powers as a preacher, as well as contributing to *Jonsonus Virbius*. He was Member for Helston in 1628 and sat in both the Short and Long Parliaments of 1640. In spite of delicacy and a pacific temper, he joined the King's forces under Hopton and was killed in a skirmish at Chagford in Devonshire. He figures in Suckling's

Biographical Notes

'Sessions of the Poets' as 'little *Cid*', and Clarendon said of him that 'there was never so great a Mind and Spirit contained in so little Room'. Hobbes described him as 'hating no man, nor hated of any'.

Poems, ed. W. Deighton, Clarendon Press, Oxford, 1931.

FULKE GREVILLE, first LORD BROOKE (1554–1628), son of a great Warwick-shire landowner of that name, was born at Beauchamp Castle in that county and is buried in St. Mary's Warwick, where his epitaph records he was 'the Friend of Sir Philip Sidney'. They knew each other from their schooldays at Shrewsbury. After Sidney's death, Greville was active in politics, without reaching great eminence, and was also a patron of younger writers. He was knighted in 1603, given a peerage in 1621, and, having been given by James the abandoned and half-ruined castle at Warwick, he rebuilt it. He died at the hands of a servant whose expectations under his will he had disappointed. Apart from the unauthorized edition of *Mustapha* in 1609, his works were published posthumously.

Poems and Dramas, ed. G. Bullough, 2 vols., Oliver and Boyd, Edinburgh, 1939; *The Remains*, ed. G. A. Wilkes, Clarendon Press, Oxford, 1965 (containing his 'Treatise on Religion').

THOMAS HARDY (1840–1928), born near Stinsford, Dorset, went at sixteen to be the pupil of an ecclesiastical architect, and practised as an architect and church-restorer in Dorset and for a while in London. Poetry was his first love, and after the publication of his last novel, *Jude the Obscure*, in 1895, he devoted himself to it. The finest of his lyrical poems are the product of his old age. Moving from the orthodoxy of his youth to the determinist belief in the 'Immanent Will' to which he gave grand expression in *The Dynasts* (its three parts published together in 1910) his pitiful heart and profoundly pious spirit warred with his intellectual convictions.

Collected Poems, Macmillan, London, 1930.

GEORGE HERBERT (1593–1633), fifth son of Richard and Magdalen Herbert, was only three years old when his father died. He was brought up wholly by his pious mother (the friend of Donne), who sent him to Westminster and Trinity College, Cambridge, where he was elected Fellow in 1616. He was made Reader in Rhetoric in 1618 and was Public Orator from 1620–1627. Like Donne, Herbert looked towards the Court, and it was only with the death of his 'Court hopes' that he decided 'to lose himself *in an humble way*' and take Orders, an unusual step for a man of family at this period. He was ordained deacon some time in 1626 and spent the next years in retirement. In April 1630, he was presented with the living of Bemerton, near Salisbury, and ordained priestthe following September. Less than three years after he died. Herbert wrote no secular verse. *The Temple* was published a few months after his death and was constantly reprinted through the century. Walton's *Life of Herbert* (1670) was not based on personal acquaintance, but on good hearsay.

Works, ed F. E. Hutchinson, Clarendon Press, Oxford, 1941.

FRIAR WILLIAM HEREBERT (d. 1333). Except for the date of his death, given by Bale, who adds that he was buried in the Convent of his Order at Hereford, nothing is known of Herebert. Seventeen of his poems, translations and expansions of Latin Hymns and Antiphons, survive in a manuscript in his own hand. His poems were almost certainly designed for use in the pulpit.

ROBERT HERRICK (1591–1674), son of a London goldsmith, was apprenticed to his uncle, also a goldsmith, but went, at a late age, to Cambridge in 1613, and was ordained in 1623. Between 1617 and 1629 he seems to have been in London and by 1625 had a reputation as a poet, although he had published nothing. In 1627 he went on the expedition to the Isle of Rhé, as chaplain to Buckingham, and in 1629 became vicar of Dean Prior in Devonshire. He was ejected in 1647, but returned in 1660. A volume of his poems was entered for publication in 1640, but *Hesperides*, with *Noble Numbers*, his only volume of verse, did not appear until 1648.

Poetical Works, ed. L. C. Martin, Clarendon Press, Oxford, 1956.

GERARD MANLEY HOPKINS (1844–1889), educated at Highgate School and Balliol College, Oxford, came of a cultivated High Anglican family. He was converted to Rome in 1866 and received into the Roman Church by Newman. Two years later he decided to become a priest, to enter the Jesuit Order, and to burn his poems, thinking the practice of poetry incompatible with dedication to the religious life. Two years before his ordination, he was moved to write his greatest poem, *The Wreck of the Deutschland*, and from then to his death he continued to write, showing his poems to his friends, Robert Bridges and Canon Dixon in particular, and corresponding with them on problems of prosody. Eleven of his poems were published by Bridges in 1893 and six in his anthology *The Spirit of Man* (1915). The first collected edition, edited by Bridges, appeared in 1918; its 750 copies took ten years to sell out. It was not until some forty years after his death that Hopkins's genius was recognized.

Poems, ed. W. H. Gardner and N. H. Mackenzie, Oxford University Press, London, 1967.

ALFRED EDWARD HOUSMAN (1859–1936), educated at Bromsgrove School and St. John's College, Oxford, after a first class in Classical Moderations, failed to obtain a class in Greats. As a clerk in the Patent Office, he published a series of powerful articles in classical journals, and was elected to the Chair of Latin at University College, London, in 1892. He moved to Cambridge in 1911. Probably the finest Latinist in Europe in his generation, his quite appalling acerbity as a scholar contrasts strikingly with the moods of his lyrics, although a vein of bitterness runs beneath their nostalgic sentiment. The sixty-three lyrics of *A Shropshire Lad* (1896) were largely written he said 'in continuous excitement' in the early months of 1895. *Last Poems* (1922) were followed by the posthumous *More Poems* (1936), edited by his brother Laurence. He refused all honours, including the Order of Merit.

Collected Poems, Jonathan Cape, London, 1939.

LIONEL JOHNSON (1867–1902), educated at Winchester and New College, Oxford, was received into the Church of Rome in 1891. A member, like Dowson, of the Rhymers' Club, commemorated by Yeats in 'The Tragic Generation' in *The Trembling of the Veil*, he destroyed himself by drink. He 'came first to mind' when Yeats thought of the companions of his youth, as one

> That loved his learning better than mankind,
> Though courteous to the worst; much falling he
> Brooded upon sanctity
> Till all his Greek and Latin learning seemed
> A long blast upon the horn that brought
> A little nearer to his thought
> A measureless consummation that he dreamed.

Complete Poems, ed. Iain Fletcher, The Unicorn Press, London, 1953.

SAMUEL JOHNSON (1709–1784), was educated at Lichfield and Stourbridge Schools and Pembroke College, Oxford, which he left without taking a degree. His extraordinary achievements as a man of letters, author of the *Dictionary* (1755), editor of Shakespeare (1765), periodical essayist (*The Rambler*, 1750–1752; *The Idler*, 1758–1760), and a biographer and critic in the *Lives of the Poets* (1779 and 1781), to name only his major enterprises, were carried through in spite of early poverty, constant ill health, and constitutional melancholy. At the end of his second imitation of Juvenal, *The Vanity of Human Wishes* (1749), he supplemented the stoicism of his original with a noble passage on prayer. His own *Prayers and Meditations* appeared posthumously in 1785.

Poems, ed. D. Nichol Smith and E. L. McAdam, Clarendon Press, Oxford, 1941.

BEN JONSON (1572–1637), posthumous son of a 'grave minister of the gospel', was educated, at a friend's expense, under William Camden at Westminster. Here he laid the foundations of a learning that makes him the most erudite of our poets before Milton. Both Oxford and Cambridge gave him honorary degrees. He ran away from his step-father's trade of brick-laying to fight in the Low Countries, and is first heard of as a player and playwright in 1597. In the following year, having killed a fellow-actor, he escaped execution by claiming Benefit of Clergy. While in prison he became a Roman Catholic, but reverted twelve years later to the Church of England. From 1616 he received a court pension of £100 and was virtually 'poet Laureate'.

Works, ed. C. H. Herford and Percy and Evelyn Simpson, 11 vols., Clarendon Press, Oxford, 1925–52. The text of the Poems is in vol. viii and the commentary on them in vol. xi.

WILLIAM LANGLAND (?1330–?1400). Tradition, going back to the fifteenth century, ascribes *Piers Plowman* to William Langland. Nothing is known for certain about him, except what can be deduced from his poem. Its three texts can be dated by contemporary allusions: the first version (A Text) c. 1362, the greatly expanded and extended B Text, c. 1377, and the final revision (C Text) after 1394. It has been suggested he was the bastard son of a peasant bond-woman and of a certain Eustace de Rokayle, named as his father in one manuscript. He ascribes his schooling to 'my father and his friends'. He cannot have proceeded beyond Minor Orders since, after he came to London where he lived in a hovel in Cornhill, he married and had a daughter. Earlier generations saw Langland as the 'poet of the suffering poor'; in this century he has come to be seen as a great visionary and theological poet, speaking in the poem that occupied his life, 'for all Christendom, though with an English accent'.

Piers Plowman, ed. W. W. Skeat, 2 vols., Clarendon Press, Oxford, 1886, prints parallel texts. A modern translation by Henry W. Wells, Sheed and Ward, London, 1938, conflates the three texts.

DAVID HERBERT LAWRENCE (1885–1930), son of a Nottinghamshire miner who had married a woman socially and culturally his superior, worked as a shop-assistant, and for five years, as a schoolmaster. In 1912 he left England with the wife of a Professor at Nottingham, whom he married two years later. Apart from the war years, when they were in England, they lived abroad, mainly in Italy, but visiting Australia and New Mexico, until his death of consumption in France. Brought up a Congregationalist, Lawrence revolted against the restraints Christianity imposes on man's instinctual nature. In his last poems, when this lover of life had come to terms with the imminence of his own death, he displays as J. I. M. Stewart has said, 'a mind at last revealed to itself as innately religious and glimpsing truth beyond the reach of conceptual statement'; but it would be wrong to see in them any submission to the ethic he had rejected.

Complete Poems, ed. V. de Sola Pinto and W. Roberts, 2 vols., Heinemann, London, 1964.

Biographical Notes

LOUIS MACNEICE (1907–1963), educated at Marlborough and Merton College, Oxford, was the son of a Bishop of the Church of Ireland. A fine classical scholar, he was for some years a university lecturer in Classics; but left the academic world in 1941 for the B.B.C.

Collected Poems, ed. E. R. Dodds, Faber and Faber, London, 1966.

ANDREW MARVELL (1621–1678), son of a Calvinist clergyman, preacher and master of the Almhouse at Hull, was educated at Hull Grammar School and Trinity College, Cambridge. From 1642–46 he was abroad, tutoring for part of the time in France. In 1651 he became tutor to the daughter of Lord Fairfax at Nun Appleton House in Yorkshire. Fairfax, the victor of Naseby, had retired to his estate owing to disagreement with Cromwell's policy. The career and friendships of Marvell up to this time suggest that his sympathies were with moderate men, even with Royalists; but he came to accept Cromwell's 'forced power' and finally to admire him. In 1653 he became tutor to one of Cromwell's wards at Eton, and in the same year Milton recommended him to be his assistant as Latin Secretary, although he was not appointed until 1657. As Member for Hull from 1659 to his death, Marvell was a staunch defender of constitutional liberties and his patriotism found expression in political satires. His *Miscellaneous Poems* (1681) were published ostensibly by his widow, Mary Marvell. This was some kind of legal fiction, as Marvell never married.

Poems and Letters, ed. H. M. Margoliouth, second edition, Clarendon Press, Oxford, 1952.

ALICE MEYNELL (1847–1922), poet, essayist, and journalist, became a Roman Catholic in 1870 and in 1877 married Wilfrid Meynell, by whom she had eight children. She and her husband led a busy professional literary life of editing, reviewing, and lecturing. She was a friend of Coventry Patmore, and she and her husband discovered and protected Francis Thompson.

Collected Poems, Burns, Oates and Washbourne, London, 1923.

JOHN MILTON (1608–1674), educated at St. Paul's and Christ's College, Cambridge, after a period of study in the country, visited Italy, returning to England on the outbreak of the Civil War. Appointed Latin Secretary to the Commonwealth in 1649, he defended before Europe the King's execution, in spite of failing sight. By 1652 he was totally blind. Milton was a poet by vocation, dedicated from his youth to the achievement of something of 'highest hope and hardest attempting'. He published his early Poems in 1645. From 1642, apart from the composition of a handful of sonnets, he gave himself up to what he conceived to be a more pressing call: the defence of liberty, religious, domestic, and political. He was spared to produce, in his blind old age, the great religious epic he had planned years before. *Paradise Lost* was published in 1667; *Paradise Regained* and *Samson Agonistes* in 1671. There is dispute over the date of composition of the latter; but the majority of scholars accept the traditional view that it was Milton's last work.

Poetical Works, ed., with masterly, economical annotation, by Douglas Bush, Oxford University Press, London, 1966.

SIR THOMAS MORE (1478–1535), humanist, author of *Utopia*, and statesman, rose in the King's service to be Lord High Chancellor in 1529, the first layman to hold the office. He resigned his office and attempted to retire into private life rather than consent to the King's divorce and breach with Rome. He was committed to the Tower in 1534, and executed on Tower Hill on 6 July 1535 for refusing to take the Oath of Supremacy. He was beatified in 1886 and canonised in 1935. His poetry belongs to his youth. After a period in the London Charterhouse, where he lived austerely to test his vocation, he decided on secular life and married in 1505.

English Works, vol. i, Eyre and Spottiswoode, London, 1931.

EDWIN MUIR (1887–1959), was born on a farm in Orkney, where he spent his first fourteen years, until his family moved to Glasgow. He was self-educated. His *Autobiography*, a classic in a genre in which this century is peculiarly rich, first published under the title *The Story and the Fable* in 1940 and much enlarged for its publication in 1954, tells how he came, late in life, to accept the Christian Faith. He was thirty-five before he began to write poetry.

Collected Poems, Faber and Faber, London, 1960.

JOHN NEWTON (1725–1807) went to sea at eleven with his father, a commander in the merchant service, and later worked as a slave-trader. In a dangerous storm in March 1748 he experienced conversion. He educated himself in his years at sea, even teaching himself Greek and a smattering of Hebrew and Syriac, and finally secured ordination in 1764. As curate of Olney he became the friend of William Cowper, who added sixty-eight poems to the two-hundred-and-eight of Newton's in *Olney Hymns* (1779). In 1780 he moved to London to St. Mary Woolnoth, and in 1788 he assisted Wilberforce by publishing his own experiences of the slave-trade. His *Authentic Narrative* (1764) is a prime document in the history of the evangelical movement.

COVENTRY PATMORE (1823–1896) was educated privately. After his father's bankruptcy in 1845 he made a living by working in the printed books department of the British Museum and by literary journalism. His first wife died in 1862, leaving him with six young children. Two years later he became a

Roman Catholic and remarried. His most famous poem, *The Angel in the House*, designed to celebrate married love and domestic felicities, is in striking contrast to his later poems, *The Unknown Eros and Other Odes*.

Poems, ed. F. Page, Oxford University Press, London, 1949.

ALEXANDER POPE (1688–1744), son of devoutly Catholic parents, was educated privately at his father's home at Binfield in Windsor Forest. Puny and deformed, he suffered all his life from ill-health, but nevertheless became the first English poet to earn not merely a living but literary independence by his pen. He remained loyal to the religion of his parents, in spite of the inducement that conformity would make him eligible for a pension. In his personal religion he leaned towards the rationalism of his friend Bolingbroke, and in his *Essay on Man* (1733 and 1734) attempted a defence of religion on natural grounds. He had not Dryden's gift for arguing in verse, but excelled him in the range of his satire. His story of Sir Balaam illustrates nicely the scorn of Pope's proud and independent spirit for those who make use of and then discard religion.

Poems, ed. J. Butt, 1 vol., Methuen, London, 1963.

FRANCIS QUARLES (1592–1644), son of a surveyor-general of victualling for the Navy, was born in Essex, educated at a country school, Christ's College, Cambridge, and Lincoln's Inn, and published his first poem, a gloomy Biblical paraphrase, *A Feast for Worms*, in 1620. From 1623 to 1630 he was in Ireland as secretary to Archbishop Usher. In 1633 he retired to Essex; but in 1640 he was appointed chronologer to the City of London, and combined his duties with the composition of manuals of piety in prose. He married in 1618 and had eighteen children. He was equally prolific as a poet. His *Emblems* (first published in 1635) was far the most popular book of the century. A devoted member of the Church of England and a staunch Royalist, Quarles took many of the plates for his *Emblems* from Jesuit Emblem Books, and yet was rightly called by Wood 'an old puritanical poet'.

Poems, ed. A. B. Grosart, 3 vols., Edinburgh University Press, Manchester, 1880–1.

SIR WALTER RALEGH (c. 1552–1618), son of a Devonshire gentleman, came to Court in 1582, after fighting in the Irish wars. He rose rapidly in the Queen's favour, though he lost it when his secret marriage came to light. He explored Guiana in 1595, distinguished himself in the attack on Cadiz in 1596, and was strongly anti-Spanish in his policies. His pride and arrogance made him enemies, who found their opportunity on the Queen's death. He was charged with treason and sentenced to death in 1603. Reprieved, he spent twelve years in the Tower, where he wrote his *History of the World*. Released in 1616 to make his last voyage, he returned from it having found no treasure, embroiled himself with the Spaniards, and lost his son in the fighting. He was executed on 29 October 1618.

Poems, ed. Agnes Latham, revised edition, Routledge and Kegan Paul, London, 1951 (Muses' Library).

CHRISTINA ROSSETTI (1830–1894), daughter of a distinguished Italian political exile who became Professor of Italian at King's College, and younger sister of Dante Gabriel Rossetti, wrote verse all her life. Her first published volume was *Goblin Market* (1862). She was a devoted High Anglican and occupied herself in works of charity as well as in composing works of edification. For much of her life she was an invalid. Her unpublished poems were collected after her death by her brother William.

Collected Poems, ed. W. M. Rossetti, Macmillan, London, 1904.

SIEGFRIED SASSOON (1886–1967), poet of the First World War, and author of *Memoirs of a Fox-Hunting Man* and *Memoirs of an Infantry Officer*, decorated with the M.C. for gallantry, followed up his war poems with an official protest in 1917 against the appalling slaughter on the Western Front. Towards the end of his life he became a Roman Catholic.

Collected Poems 1908–1956, Faber and Faber, London, 1961.

PERCY BYSSHE SHELLEY (1792–1822), educated at Eton and University College, Oxford, was sent down for circulating a pamphlet on *The Necessity of Atheism*. Shelley's Radicalism embraced politics, the social morality of his day, and Christianity. His object was 'to break through the crust of those outworn opinions on which established institutions depend'. The 'passion for reforming the world', which he confessed to, went with an equally passionate belief that 'the great secret of morals is Love', a devotion to 'Intellectual Beauty', that is to a Beauty that is beyond the apprehension of the senses, and a faith in the One, the ultimate reality and absolute perfection, which he thought of as a transcendent Power.

Poetical Works, ed. T. Hutchinson, Oxford University Press, London, 1943.

SIR PHILIP SIDNEY (1554–1586), educated at Shrewsbury and Christ Church, Oxford, was courtier, soldier, scholar and poet. Nephew to Leicester, he went abroad in his train in 1572 and remained for two years in Europe acquainting himself with courts and cities, returning to Europe later as ambassador to the Emperor. Author of the first and one of the finest of sonnet sequences, *Astrophil and Stella*, of *Arcadia*, which blends the worlds of pastoral, romance and epic, and of the finest sustained piece of critical writing in the Elizabethan age, *The Defence of Poetry*, Sidney is herald of our Golden Age.

Poems, ed. W. A. Ringler, Clarendon Press, Oxford, 1962.

EDITH SITWELL (1887–1964), daughter of Sir George Sitwell, was educated privately. She and her brothers, Osbert and Sacheverell, led a gay campaign in the twenties, as patrons of modern artists and musicians, and writers of fantastic and satiric verse. Her delightful *Façade*, set to music by William Walton, which she recited, or rather intoned, herself, retains its period charm and wit. In late life she became a Roman Catholic. In her later poetry she became obsessed with the agonies of the world and, perhaps, over-strained her talent.

Collected Poems, Macmillan, London, 1957.

CHRISTOPHER SMART (1722–1771) was enabled by a patronage to enter Pembroke College, Cambridge, and was elected a Fellow in 1745. His university career was darkened by his predilection for taverns and for amassing debts, and by a mental breakdown that led to his first incarceration in Bedlam in 1751. His illness took the form of taking over-literally the injunction to 'pray without ceasing'. He left Cambridge for Grub Street in 1755 and in 1763 he was again in Bedlam, where the story goes that he wrote the 'Song to David'. Overwhelmed by debt he ended by being confined by his creditors to the King's Bench and died in its rules. His long dithyramb 'Rejoice in the Lamb' was not published until 1939.

Collected Poems, ed. N. Callan, 2 vols., Routledge and Kegan Paul, London, 1949 (Muses' Library).

ROBERT SOUTHWELL (1561–1595) was born in Norfolk and sent abroad in 1576 to study at Douai. Inspired by Jesuit teachers there and in Paris he determined to enter the Order and became a novice at Rome in 1578. Ordained priest in 1584 he was, at his own wish, nominated to the dangerous English mission. He landed in May 1586 with Fr. Henry Garnet, later implicated in the Gunpowder Plot. Only one Jesuit had preceded them. Southwell was closely watched, but for some time evaded arrest. His literary activity was a part of his pastoral work and reflects his single-minded and ardent temperament. He was arrested in June 1592 and from then to his death was imprisoned and constantly racked and tortured. He suffered martyrdom at Tyburn on 21 February 1595. His poems were published almost immediately and went into edition after edition.

Poems, ed. J. H. McDonald and Nancy P. Brown, Clarendon Press, Oxford, 1967.

EDMUND SPENSER (1552–1599). Educated at Merchant Taylors' School and Pembroke College, Cambridge, Spenser by 1578 was at Leicester House, familiar with Sidney and Dyer. In the following year he appeared as the 'new poet' with his *Shepherd's Calendar*, dedicated to Sidney. In 1580 he went to Ireland, as secretary to the Lord Deputy, and spent his working life in various forms of public employment there. In 1589 Ralegh visited him, and he returned with Ralegh to London to be presented to the Queen and publish, in the following year, the first three books of *The Faerie Queene*. Disappointed in his hopes of preferment at Court, he returned to Ireland, revisiting London in 1595 to publish a further three books of his poem, and again in 1598 after the sack of his Irish home by Tyrone's men. He died in London and was buried in the Abbey near to Chaucer.

Poetical Works, ed. J. C. Smith and E. de Selincourt, 1 vol., Oxford University Press, London, 1912.

ALFRED, LORD TENNYSON (1809–1892), born in a Lincolnshire Rectory at Somersby, was educated at Louth Grammar School and Trinity College, Cambridge. His *Poems* (1833) were badly reviewed, and in the same year he suffered the crushing blow of the death of his dearest friend, Arthur Hallam. After years of poverty and melancholy he established himself as the greatest living poet of his day with the two volume *Poems* of 1842, and three years later was awarded a Civil List pension. By 1850 he found himself, after an engagement of ten years, at last able to marry; and, in the same year, was made Poet Laureate. The years of Tennyson's prosperity and fame have masked in popular imagination the long years of poverty, melancholy, and emotional insecurity out of which his greatest poetry sprang. *In Memoriam* (1850), published without the author's name, is remarkable for its reflection of the depth of the religious crisis of the nineteenth century, and what T.S. Eliot called 'the quality of the doubt'.

Poems, ed. Christopher Ricks, Longmans, London, 1969.

RONALD STUART THOMAS (1913–). Educated at the University of Wales and St. Michael's College, Llandaff, ordained deacon 1936 and priest 1937, vicar of a rural Welsh parish, Mr. Thomas is distinguished among the honourable company of parson-poets for the poetry he has made out of his vocation as a parish priest. He was awarded the Queen's Medal for Poetry in 1965.

Song at the Year's Turning, Poetry for Supper, Tares, Rupert Hart Davis, London, 1955, 1958, 1961.

THOMAS TRAHERNE (1637–1674), son of a Hereford shoemaker, was sent at the expense of a relative to Brasenose College, Oxford, and presented in 1657 to the living of Credenhill, Herefordshire, which he held until his death. He was ordained in 1660. He spent most of his time at Oxford, with only occasional visits to his parish, until 1667 when he went to London as chaplain to Sir Orlando Bridgeman, the Lord Keeper. On Bridgeman's retirement he accompanied him to Teddington, where he died. The only work he published in his lifetime was the polemical *Roman Forgeries*; his *Christian Ethics* was published after his death. His fame dates from Bertram Dobell's discovery in 1896 and 1897 of manuscripts containing both the prose *Centuries of Meditation* and poems, and his identification of the author as the forgotten Restoration divine.

Centuries, Poems etc., ed. H. M. Margoliouth, 2 vols., Clarendon Press, Oxford, 1958.

HENRY VAUGHAN, the Silurist (1622–1695), was educated, with his twin brother Thomas, at the local school in Brecknockshire, a county once inhabited by the Silures, and at Jesus College, Oxford. He left without a degree to study law in London. He was an ardent Royalist, a devoted member of the Church of England, and fought on the King's side. It is not known where he studied medicine; but he practised as a doctor at Brecknock and at Newton by Usk. He was twice married. His secular verse is unremarkable. Grief at the death of friends, particularly of a brother, the defeat of his cause, and the virtual destruction of his Church are the circumstances, if not the explanation, of his conversion to the poet of *Silex Scintillans*. 'Certain Divine Raies', he wrote, 'breake out of the Soul in adversity, like sparks of fire out of the afflicted flint.'

Works, ed. L. C. Martin, second edition, Clarendon Press, Oxford, 1957.

NATHANIEL WANLEY (1634–1680), educated at Trinity College, Cambridge, was the father of Humphrey Wanley, librarian and bibliographer. He held a living in Leicestershire before becoming Vicar of Holy Trinity, Coventry. His encyclopedic *The Wonders of the Little World* (1678) provided Browning with the story of the Pied Piper. His poems remained in manuscript until this century. Widely read in the metaphysical poets, he was most strongly influenced by Vaughan. His portrait is in the Bodleian.

Poems, ed. L. C. Martin, Clarendon Press, Oxford, 1928.

ISAAC WATTS (1674–1748), educated at Edward VI Grammar School, Southampton, and Stoke Newington Dissenting Academy, was for many years Pastor of the Independent Congregation in Mark Lane, which removed to Pinners Hall. His *Hymns and Spiritual Songs* (1707), corrected and enlarged from *Horae Lyricae* (1706), and further revised and enlarged in 1709, may be said to have established the hymn as a permanent and essential element in English worship. Watts's purpose was 'to promote the pious entertainment of souls truly serious, even of the meanest capacity', and he thus eschewed, on his own confession, 'some of the Beauties of Poesy'. If, at times, his concern for the simple, here, and in his *Divine Songs for Children* (1715), lands him in doggerel, it is also the source of the unmatched intensity of feeling and directness of phrase in his greatest hymns.

Works, ed. G. Burder, 6 vols., John Barfield, London, 1810–11.

Biographical Notes

CHARLES WESLEY (1707–1788), younger brother of John Wesley, educated at Westminster and Christ Church Oxford, was a fine scholar. He and his friends earned the name of 'methodists' from their regular life of study and religious exercises at Oxford. He did not take Orders until 1735, when he went with his brother on the mission to Georgia. He dated his conversion from Whit-Sunday 1738, and in the following year joined his brother as an itinerant missionary. Differences of opinion on the relation of Methodism to the Church of England did not weaken their mutual affection. Wesley is said to have written over six thousand hymns; some five hundred or so being in use. John Wesley reports that 'Dr. Watts did not scruple to say that that single poem "Wrestling Jacob", was worth all the verses he himself had written'. Some authorities have held that 'Free Grace' is the poem Wesley wrote two days after his conversion.

Representative Verse, ed. Frank Baker, Epworth Press, London, 1962.

WILLIAM WORDSWORTH (1770–1850), educated at Hawkshead School and St. John's College, Cambridge, spent a year in France (1791–2) and, after a period of distress and unsettlement owing to the course of the Revolution, settled with his sister Dorothy in the West Country where he met Coleridge. They published the *Lyrical Ballads* in 1798. In 1799 he moved, with his sister, to Grasmere. In later life Wordsworth became an orthodox Christian, but at the period when he wrote his greatest poetry he was inspired by a profoundly personal sense of spiritual reality that owes nothing to Christian doctrine or Christian feeling. The original version of *The Prelude*, the 'Orphic Song' read to Coleridge in 1805, records the moments of illumination that made him a 'dedicated Spirit'.

Poetical Works, ed. T. Hutchinson, revised by E. de Selincourt, Oxford University Press, London, 1936.

SIR HENRY WOTTON (1568–1639), educated at Winchester and New College, Oxford, was abroad for seven years, supplying intelligence to the Earl of Essex. On his return in 1595 he became one of Essex's secretaries, but prudently was abroad at the time of the Earl's rebellion and arrest. Knighted in 1604, he went as ambassador to Venice, where he served, with two intervals, for twenty years. In 1624 he was made Provost of Eton, and three years later took deacon's orders. He was an intimate friend of Donne, and was to have written his life as preface to his collected sermons; but he died leaving the task to Walton, whom he had employed to collect material. Walton performed the same office for Wotton.

WILLIAM BUTLER YEATS (1865–1939), eldest son of John Butler Yeats, painter, came of Anglo-Irish Protestant stock. Commenting on 'The Tragic

Generation', his friends of the Rhymers' Club in the nineties, Yeats asked 'Why are these strange souls born everywhere today, with hearts that Christianity, as shaped by history, cannot satisfy?' From his student days he was attracted to esoteric and theosophical circles, and, after his marriage in 1917, he worked out the elaborate astrological-historical system set out in *A Vision* (1925). The extent of Yeats's commitment to his own system may be questioned. He himself said that the spirits who communicated with him by means of his wife's gift of automatic writing declared that they came to give him 'metaphors for poetry'. His commitment to belief in supernatural reality, apprehended in visionary experience and in images arising out of an *Anima Mundi*, 'which has a memory independent of embodied individual memories, though they constantly enrich it with their images and thoughts', cannot be questioned.

Collected Poems, second edition, Macmillan, London, 1950.

EDWARD YOUNG (1683–1765), educated at Winchester, New College and Corpus Christi College, Oxford, after a period as Law Fellow at All Souls, embarked on a literary and political career in London. In 1725 he began the series of satires on 'The Universal Passion', collected in 1728. The date of his taking Orders is uncertain; but in 1728 he was made chaplain to the King and in 1730 presented to the rectory of Welwyn in Hertfordshire. Ecclesiastical preferment, like political, eluded him; but his *Night Thoughts* were immensely popular, their mixture of religious sentimentalism and churchyard gloom being much to the taste of his age.

Poetical Works, Ward, Lock and Co., London, 1882.

INDEX OF FIRST LINES

Index of First Lines